W9-CRC-637

This Business Of ART

BY

DIANE COCHRANE

WATSON-GUPTILL PUBLICATIONS / NEW YORK

Copyright ©1978 by Watson-Guptill Publications

First published 1978 in New York by Watson-Guptill Publications,
a division of Billboard Publications, Inc.,
1515 Broadway, New York, N.Y. 10036

Library of Congress Cataloging in Publication Data
Cochrane, Diane.
  This business of art.
  Bibliography: p.
  Includes index.
  1. Art—Marketing. I. Title
N8600.C62   658'.91'7   77-26337
ISBN 0-8230-5360-1

All rights reserved. No part of this publication may be
reproduced or used in any form or by any means—graphic,
electronic, or mechanical, including photocopying, recording,
taping, or information storage and retrieval systems—without
written permission of the publisher.

Manufactured in U.S.A.

First Printing, 1978

6   7   8   9/86   85   84   83

To my loving husband, Bob

Special thanks for the expertise and assistance of
Howard Thorkelson, Esq.

Contents

1. First Things First: Contracts

· Elements of a contract
· Written vs. oral
· Offer and acceptance
· Getting it in writing
· Breach of contract
· Suing

How to start a how-to book? What subject should come first? What advice is of top priority? The day I sat down at the typewriter, *The New York Times* had coincidentally published in an editorial piece by Erica Jong—author of *Fear of Flying*—a call for new laws to guarantee artists the right to protect the quality of their creations and to profit fairly from their success.

To show the insufficiency of artists' rights, Jong cited three cases in which artists were unable to exercise artistic control after they had parted with their work: Ken Kesey's inability to exert any artistic control over the movie version of *One Flew Over the Cuckoo's Nest* or to claim a share of the movie's abundant profits (after having sold the movie rights years before for very little money); the Monty Python Troupe's initial failure to prevent network television from re-editing its shows (the Troupe sued ABC for editing its script without its permission and won the case); and the attempt of two sculptors participating in an exhibition at the Whitney Museum of American Art to withdraw their works because they objected to the manner of their display.

Jong wrote: "It is a fact little known by the public that the artist normally relinquishes all creative control at the time of sale of a work, that oral promises of excellence are completely unenforceable, and that cash percentages are received only by those with enough business clout to enforce them—which rarely includes the artist."

Jong has a point. But, like so much other artists' rights rhetoric, her statement tends to emasculate the artist. Artists are already too easily persuaded of their own powerlessness and that only new legislation can safeguard them against ripoffs and doublecrosses.

What she and others forget is that the law of contracts already on the books can protect artists to the same extent it protects everyone else. The contract, or whatever you want to call it—an agreement, a deal, an exchange of promises—is the foundation of all business relationships, and art is not exempt. The courts can make life unpleasant for someone who doesn't live up to his side of an enforceable bargain.

One major problem, of course, is that a contract can be either oral or written. When Ms. Jong says that oral "promises of excellence" are unenforceable, she's probably right in a practical sense. Excellence may be in the eye of the beholder, and letting a deal float on vague and relative language like that creates unnecessary risks. The essence of a contract, legally, is said to be a meeting of the minds. This means that it is not just a tête-à-tête about excellence, but it is also an explicit acknowledgement of the parties' terms in a provable fashion, preferably in writing. The transfer of a valuable work of art should be based on nothing less, and nothing prevents you from refusing to part with your work unless the buyer signs a written contract giving you the specific artistic controls you want.

Nor is Jong fair to the artist when she says that "cash percentages are received only by those with enough business clout to enforce them." You may feel that you lack sufficient bargaining power to demand and get the *exact* deal you want. But you probably *can* bring off a reasonable deal—even if your limited bargaining power means making some compromises—and you can get the promise of payment in a written agreement. And it *doesn't* take any business clout to enforce that written agreement. You may have to hire a lawyer and threaten to sue if the other party reneges. But that's what everybody else does—businessmen, doctors, lawyers—when a contract is breached.

The reason that artists seem to come off so badly in business dealings is not that they're more vulnerable, but that they rarely arm themselves and fight back with the same legal weapons that others use. So, instead of speculating on new laws, this book will show you how to defend yourself with the legal artillery available to you now. And the strongest weapon is the written contract. Hence, this opening chapter on the basics of contractual law. Specific contracts—commission agreements, gallery contracts, and so on—are discussed in later chapters.

What is a contract?

Before getting to a definition of the word *contract,* it may be useful to get rid of any preconceived ideas you may have about it. Many people think of a contract as a lengthy, formal document, drawn up by a battery of lawyers. A contract may be just that, but it can also be a verbal deal, an exchange of letters, or just one short letter signed by two or more people. If you're one of those people for whom the word *contract* triggers visions of a 20-page legal document, you might want to substitute the word *agreement,* and remember that a contract is any legally binding agreement. More about what's legally binding in a moment.

Now for a definition of a contract. A contract is a voluntary agreement between two or more persons. Both parties—either orally or in writing—promise to do something or *not* to do something, and both have the right to demand that the other carry out his side of the bargain.

When do artists make contracts?

You make oral contracts all the time. For instance, when you buy art supplies, you make an oral agreement to exchange money for canvas. But the contracts generally referred to in this book are agreements that are somewhat more complicated: contracts you make when you consign or sell work to a gallery; when you sell or rent work directly to a collector; when you accept a commission; when you sell reproduction rights to a publisher; when you exhibit your work; or when you lend work to a museum.

When is a contract enforceable by law?

Four conditions must be met before any contract can be enforced by law: (1) competence of the parties involved; (2) legality of purpose; (3) mutual agreement; and (4) consideration.

What does competence of parties mean? Competence of parties refers to mental competence. This means that you can forget about making binding contracts with people who are senile, under the influence of alcohol or drugs, or certified insane. Minors are not the greatest category of people to make contracts with either as they can rescind them at *their* option unless the contract is for a "necessary," meaning something necessary to their lives or livelihoods, such as food or clothing.

What does legality of purpose mean? There must be nothing illegal about the agreement, nor can anything in the agreement be interpreted as being against public policy.

For example, if you and a publisher agree to make an edition of reproductions produced by a photomechanical process and then to sell them as original prints, your purpose is to defraud the public. In the event that you sue the publisher for some reason—say nonpayment—his defense could be that the contract was invalid because its purpose was illegal.

You might also find yourself tied into a contract with an illegal purpose if your product can be construed as obscene or libelous. Suppose that a magazine asks you to draw a politician and emphasize his drinking habits. If the publication reneges on payment and you sue, the court might find the drawing libelous, rule the contract void, and you would not get paid.

Or you might accept a commission to paint a mural for a public place, realistically portraying nudes embracing. In your eyes, the figures express the joy of love; but looking through his glasses darkly, a judge might decide that your mural is obscene and void your contract if you were suing to recover an unpaid fee.

The problem with libel and obscenity in relation to art is that there aren't any legal definitions spelling out exactly what they are. Each case is interpreted on its own merits. So proceed carefully before making a contract that looks dubious to you on these grounds.

What does mutual agreement mean? In every contract, both parties must agree on the same set of terms. For example, if you offer to sell four paintings for $2,000 and a collector accepts, you've got a contract. But if he says he wants five paintings for $2,000, there's no contract because you and he haven't agreed to the same terms.

What does consideration mean? Whoever makes a contract must get something for it. Consideration is the money or object or whatever you must give to get what you want. And both parties must give consideration. In other words, if you offer to sell a painting for $500 and your client agrees, you've made a contract. Your contribution to the contract (your consideration) is the painting; your client's is the cash. But if you merely promise to *give* a painting to a friend and then change your mind, he can't force you to hand it over because he would be getting something for nothing.

Must consideration be explicitly stated? Yes, consideration must be clearly spelled out. A contract must state, "I will paint your portrait for $500," not "I will paint it if you will pay me," or "if you will pay me a reasonable sum." The last two examples don't qualify as valid statements of consideration.

Should a contract be in writing?

Not all contracts must be in writing. In the ordinary course of the day, you make dozens of oral agreements. You may order groceries or supplies over the phone, or you may hire a model. Naturally, these agreements needn't be confirmed in writing—if they did, you'd drown in paperwork. But as soon as a situation arises where it's important to prevent misunderstandings, put the deal in writing. Arrangements made with galleries, clients, publishers, museums, and so on, demand written agreements.

Sure, oral contracts are enforceable *in theory.* But when it comes down to your word against theirs as to the terms of a contract—or even whether one exists—you'd better have some mighty reliable witnesses to back you up. And money to finance a lawsuit! The failure to get a written contract has deflated many high hopes and inflated the wallets of those in the legal profession.

Why are artists reluctant to press for written contracts?

Many artists are afraid that prospective clients, galleries, and other business contacts will think of a written agreement as a hassle—and far be it from artists to create any unpleasantness! Instead, they're often willing to perpetuate their own weaknesses by not standing up for their rights.

But why? Most clients and dealers are businessmen. They wouldn't think of operating without contracts themselves. Why should an artist be any different? If you don't respect your work enough to hold out for the best deal you can get—and to get it in writing—you're doing yourself a disfavor.

When is a written contract required by law?

According to the Uniform Commercial Code (a set of laws for commercial dealings and for the sale of goods), you must have a written contract if: (1) the contract states that the agreement cannot be completed within one year from the date of the contract (called the one-year rule); or (2) the contract is for the sale of goods priced at $500 or more. In both cases, oral agreements won't stand up in court.

What exactly is the one-year rule? This is most easily explained by an example. If a publisher plans to buy one print from you each month for the next 18 months, this cannot be completed in one year. And even if you contract to sell him one print each month for the next 12 months beginning next month, this—again—cannot be completed within one year. Both of these contracts must be in writing to be enforceable in a court of law.

Would commissions fall under the Code rule? No, commissions to make artwork are considered services, not goods, and thus don't fall under this law. (They do not have to be in writing.)

What terms should always be stated in written agreements?

Although the Code provides that certain terms—even the price—can be left out of a contract, it is wise to put in the names and addresses of the parties who sign the agreement; the date the contract was made; delivery or completion dates; and the consideration—price and quantity. For instance, "I will sell two paintings for $1,000"; or "For $5,000 I will sell five paintings plus all reproduction rights"; or "I consign 20 works to you and in return you will pay me the price you receive for each work sold, less a 40% commission" will suffice.

After you read the rest of the chapters in this book that refer to contracts, you may find more possibilities of what should go into your own. The subsequent chapters deal with galleries, exhibitors, clients, people who commission your work, publishers, and museums. You won't be interested in each and every possibility, but you can pick and choose the clauses you want to include in a written contract.

Are any oral contracts enforceable?

Theoretically, if a contract involves the sale of goods worth less than $500 or the contract will be fulfilled within less than a year, an oral agreement is as valid as a written one and is enforceable by law. But *realistically,* an oral agreement is only as good as the witnesses who hear it, so why take the chance of jeopardizing yourself? Write it down. If you've already placed yourself in jeopardy by making an oral agreement, however, see below for what you can do when an oral agreement falls apart.

What is the simplest type of contract?

Someone makes an offer and someone else accepts the offer.

This can be as simple as a brief dialogue followed by a handshake, which people do all the time. One person says something like, "I'll sell you a painting for $500." The other says, "Agreed." And the next thing you know, they're shaking hands.

Exactly the same thing can be done by an exchange of letters, one person making an offer and the other accepting it. Or both parties can sign the letter that makes the offer—so just one letter will do.

Can I take back an offer once I've made it?

Yes, but only if the offer hasn't been accepted. If your offer is in writing, take it back in writing—and do it soon! If your offer has been accepted and you revoke it, you can be sued for breach of contract.

Are advertisements or catalogs considered offers?

Sometimes. For instance, if you send out a brochure showing

pictures of your work and listing prices, you can't raise the price when a buyer turns up. He's accepting the offer in the ad or catalog and you're stuck with the terms you've printed.

Is a gallery display of my work with a price tag an offer?

Yes. It's just like an advertisement or a catalog with printed prices. You can't raise the price.

What if the other party wants time to think an offer over?

You have two choices.

Suppose a client drops into your studio one afternoon, and you offer to sell him a piece. He says he'd like to sleep on the matter overnight. You'll probably agree to extend the time as a courtesy.

But suppose you're having a show, and a number of prospective buyers are present. Giving one client 24 hours to think about the purchase *may* mean that you'll have to turn down other offers. So you'd give the first prospect an *option* on his offer.

What is an option?

An option is a special agreement to keep an offer open for a certain period of time. The option is usually considered separate from the final contract, and consideration must be present to protect both parties to the agreement.

Suppose you put your studio up for sale for $15,000. A prospective buyer is interested, but wants a month to see if he can raise the money. In the meantime, you might have to turn down other offers—offers which may not come your way again for some time. Your wisest course of action would be to offer him an option on the studio in which you promise not to sell it for a month if he'll give you a percentage of your asking price for that waiting period. Then, if he rejects the offer, you've been compensated by the money paid for the privilege of delaying the decision. If he accepts the original offer when the option expires, you write up a purchase contract deducting the option fee from the purchase price.

If the offer has been made and accepted orally, what's next?

Offers are frequently made and accepted in conversation, but while you're talking, you should make one of the conditions of the deal be that it will be put into writing later. If the agreement is relatively simple, your next step would be to summarize its terms in a letter of agreement. You should do this no matter whether you made the offer or accepted it. Here's an example of a letter of agreement couched in plain, everyday, nonlegal terms:

Dear John Dealer:
This letter confirms the details of the agreement we made over the telephone this afternoon.

Between January 15 and February 2, 1978, you will mount a one-person exhibition of 20 of my paintings at your gallery at 2 South Broadway, New York City. Your commission on all sales will be 40% of the retail price, which we will mutually determine.

You will prepare and pay for one ad in *American Artist* and one ad in *The New York Times*. You will also have designed and printed and will pay for a postcard announcement showing my painting *New Dawn* on the front in color. You will mail the announcement to 2,000 people and pay all postage. You will insure the 20 paintings at 60% of retail price, and you will pay for wine and cheese for an opening on January 15 for 200 people.

I will arrange and pay for the framing of all 20 paintings and help with the installation of the show.

If you are in agreement with these terms, please sign at the bottom of both this letter and the attached copy, return this letter to me, and keep the copy for your records.

What if he doesn't return my letter, but replies with his own letter, outlining the terms? Providing that the terms are the same, a letter bearing his signature would be the equivalent of signing and returning your letter. Now make sure that you file both his letter and a copy of yours.

What if his own reply letter outlines different terms? If the terms are substantially the same as yours and/or you decide to agree to them, you don't have to do anything. If, however, you don't agree with his terms, simply reply in writing informing him that the deal is off and why. And remember, always keep a copy of all correspondence for your files.

What if he doesn't answer at all? Your oral agreement is theoretically valid, but before you carry out your end of the deal, it's best to insist that he sign and return your letter. His refusal to do so might indicate unwillingness to fulfill his side of the bargain.

How do I back out if I don't get a reply? Write another letter saying that he failed to fulfill one of the conditions of the oral agreement —that the contract was to be put in writing—and that therefore you consider the deal finished.

If we make an oral agreement and he confirms in writing, can I back out?

According to the Uniform Commercial Code, an oral agreement made between "merchants" and followed by a written confirmation can be rejected in writing within 10 days after it's received. Even though there aren't two signatures on the written confirmation the receiver's lack of response means that he accepts the offer. For example, suppose you agree to sell six etchings for $800 to a dealer, who confirms the terms of the sale by letter. If you change your mind, but don't respond in writing within 10 days, the etchings are his.

Am I considered a merchant?

The Code says, "A merchant means a person who deals in goods of the kind or otherwise by his occupation holds himself out as having knowledge or skill peculiar to the practices or goods involved in the transaction." Granted this is an ambiguous statement, so there's no way to be sure whether or not a court would decide that you are a "merchant." But why bother to take a chance? Play it safe—behave like a merchant, and reject the offer in writing. You may save yourself a lot of grief later on.

When should I get a lawyer to help draft a contract?

The only way to answer this question is to use your common sense. Anytime you hire a lawyer, you're going to run up a substantial legal bill—maybe $100 or $200 for a couple of hours' work. So you've got to figure out if you'll make enough money on the deal to justify the fee. If the deal is a $1,000 commission and it's a perfectly straightforward arrangement, a $100 or $200 legal bill might not be worth it.

On the other hand, if a lot of money is involved; if a number of steps are involved in the commission (sketches, models, and so on); if you have to please more than one person; or if you want to know what to do about selling a copyright or reproduction rights, then getting advice from an attorney may be worth it to prevent headaches later on. Besides, if the contract involves tough negotiation, a lawyer may be a better bargainer than you and will be able to secure a better agreement. Only after weighing all these factors can you decide if you need legal advice.

However, you may be eligible for some free legal advice. A number of art-conscious lawyers around the country have banded together to form groups of "Volunteer Lawyers for the Arts." They give free legal aid to artists unable to afford legal fees. For a list of these groups, see the appendix.

If I sign a contract, but later decide it isn't fair, what can I do?

Nothing, unless you can prove there's something illegal about it. But if you mean it's "unfair" because you think you're not getting a fair shake, you've had it. Suppose the rules of a juried exhibition state that reproduction rights for the winning work must be transferred to the sponsor in exchange for the prize money. When you entered the exhibit, you agreed; but later, when you won, you felt that you were being taken. Too bad. The time to make that decision was before—not after—signing the entry form, which *is* a contract.

What if the other party doesn't fulfill his part of the contract?

If the other person doesn't live up to his side of the agreement—or in legal terms, breaches the contract—you can *threaten* to sue. Sometimes a little "persuasion" can turn the trick and the other party might fulfill his obligations.

If this doesn't work, you'll have to bring in the heavy artillery: hire a lawyer and sue.

What can I sue for?

You can sue for specific performance, recision of the contract, an injunction, and/or money damages.

What is specific performance? Theoretically, this means that you can sue to force someone to perform or carry out the specific terms of the agreement. But in *reality,* it works only in a few special cases. The courts don't want the job of overseeing the fulfillment of contracts, so they limit this kind of legal action to the sale of land and certain personal property which is so unique, like a Rembrandt painting, that it can't be obtained readily in the market. So forget about specific performance and look to the other ways to satisfy your claim.

What is recision? Recision restores you and the other person to where you were *before* you made your bargain. In other words, recision undoes the contract. Suppose you discover that your dealer, with whom you have a written contract, hasn't been living up to his agreement to insure your work while it was on his premises, to furnish you with names of collectors, and so on. You can simply sue for recision, get out of the whole arrangement, and get your work back.

What is an injunction? An injunction is a court order preventing one party from doing something injurious to the other. Imagine that you have a contract with a publisher to make an edition of original lithographs, but you discover that he's been producing cheap reproductions of the same work on the side. An injunction will stop him because it isn't part of the contract.

Looking at a legal suit from another point of view, suppose you have a contract with a dealer, but refuse to consign any more work to him. Though it's impossible to force someone to do something —specific performance won't apply—he *could* ask the court for an injunction to prevent you from consigning work to anyone else.

What sort of money damages can I sue for? You can sue for either the amount actually due you or for compensatory damages. Compensatory damages are paid when you sustain a loss because someone breaches the agreement. Let's say that a corporation commissions you to create a large outdoor sculpture. Since you know that this will take six months, you turn down several other lucrative offers because you won't have the time for them. The corporation then reneges on the deal, and you're out of work for six months. Even though you haven't started the commission, you've sustained a loss, and you should be compensated for it. Of course, the court won't be sympathetic to demands for substantial damages if you do have the opportunity to substitute another commission for the one you lost (and the corporation will try to prove this).

If I don't have a written agreement and can't prove the terms of an oral one, must I suffer a total loss if the contract is breached?

Not necessarily. Fortunately, some help is available to legal innocents under the doctrine of "unjust enrichment," which holds that one person cannot enrich himself unjustly at the expense of another. So if you agree to paint a series of murals for a restaurant for $5,000 and the owner refuses to pay you on completion, you can take him to court. But now it's the court's job to put a price tag on the work, since there's no written agreement. That price might not be as high as yours, once more proving the value of a written contract.

2. Copyright and Other Rights

- · Publication
- · Copyright notice
- · Registration
- · Duration
- · International protection
- · Transfer
- · Fair use
- · Suing for infringement
- · Patents

Many years ago the Museum of Modern Art in New York bought *Christina's World* from Andrew Wyeth for a few hundred dollars. Since that time, the museum has earned over $1,000,000 from reproductions, while not a dime in royalties has found its way to Wyeth.

How could it happen that an artist wasn't compensated for the money his work generated? This is only surmise, but based on the copyright law then in existence, it could have come about in a number of ways. Naturally, Wyeth might have willingly given the museum the copyright. But he might also have unknowingly sold it along with the painting itself. Or he might have unwittingly "published" (an ill-defined term explained below) the painting without copyright notice, a fatal error which gives to anyone who wants it the right to copy the work.

Today, the Copyright Revision Act of 1976, effective January 1, 1978, goes a long way to protect artists against the accidental loss of copyright and furnishes them with a good defense in court against infringers. The best defense, however, is to secure copyright properly.

And it's so easy. Yet whether through ignorance or fear that copyright notice will deface their artwork, thousands upon thousands of artists omit it, only to see their works later reproduced on calendars, greeting cards, or prints, or transformed into T-shirts, needlepoint designs, or whatever. You name it—it's been done.

And money isn't the only issue. Royalties and other fees may be small compensation for a tarnished reputation. As a reputable fine artist, your name will hardly be enhanced by the appearance of one of your paintings on a sleazy greeting card or cheap liquor advertisement.

Control over who uses your work and in what way is what you want. And control can be exerted if you know your rights under copyright law. This knowledge, coupled with what you learned about contracts in Chapter 1, should arm you well in the world of business.

What is a copyright?

A copyright gives its owner the exclusive rights to reproduce, sell, distribute, display, and publish artwork and to make other types of work from it, such as reproductions from a painting or a sculpture from a drawing. Conversely, copyright prevents anyone else from doing these same things.

What can I copyright?

Anything that's artistic (two and three-dimensional works of fine, graphic, and applied art) and original. The law doesn't mean that a work has to measure up to any esthetic standard to be considered artistic; even a minimally artistic work, such as a child's drawing, can be copyrighted. The law also doesn't define originality in the way you do. You equate originality with imagination and creativity. But as far as the law is concerned, as long as you don't copyright someone else's work, it's original.

Can ideas be copyrighted?

People ask this question all the time, but the answer is no. Suppose you have an idea for a cartoon. If you want to hold on to it, don't mention the idea to a fellow-cartoonist. Or suppose you have a new idea for painting in egg tempera, and you approach a publisher about the possibility of writing a book on it. If you're afraid he'll steal your idea, you'll just have to take your chances. Ideas aren't copyrightable—only the product, which in these cases would be the cartoon or the completed book.

Can I copyright subject matter or themes?

No. Subject matter, themes, and ideas don't belong to anyone. So there's nothing you can do if another artist chooses to use the same source material.

For example, nearly every artist who goes to Rockport, Massachusetts, immediately sets up his easel in front of two picturesque fishing shacks at the end of a wharf. It's one of the most frequently painted scenes in the world; in fact, as a joke, it's called Motif No. 1. Thousands and thousands of paintings have been done of this view, and it wouldn't be surprising if many were similar, even almost identical. But the fact is that every painting is original because it was painted from a subject accessible to everyone. No one can claim that anyone stole anything from anybody else. The only way that you could be accused of copyright infringement would be if you copied someone's painting directly.

What kind of artwork can be copyrighted?

Almost anything you can think of: paintings, sculpture, drawings, photography, graphics, jewelry, models and maquettes, book illustrations, cartoons, reproductions, mixed media objects, and videotapes.

You can't, however, copyright solely utilitarian objects, even though they may be so attractively shaped as to be considered artwork by some.

What is a "solely utilitarian" object?

Furniture, flatware, dishes, and tools would be examples that fall into this category.

Can I copyright artwork that's also useful?

Yes, as long as it's not solely utilitarian. This subtle distinction allows you to copyright artwork that is also an article of utility—like stained glass windows—or that is embodied in useful articles. For example, you can't copyright a decorative shopping bag, but you can copyright the design painted on it.

Can I copyright crafts?

The same rules apply to crafts as to fine arts. Therefore, you can copyright wall hangings, ornamental pots, and so on. You can also copyright designs painted on utilitarian objects, like cups and bowls.

Can I copyright my handmade cups and bowls?

No. Despite the fact that they may be beautifully shaped, you can't copyright them, although it may be possible to obtain a design patent (see below) on them.

Can I copyright titles of artwork?

No. We may associate *Christina's World* with Andrew Wyeth, but he can't prevent anyone else from using the same title by getting a copyright.

Can I copyright material that might be considered obscene?

The courts have taken the stand that obscene material is not eligible for copyright. But the Copyright Office has publicly declared that it won't refuse registration (defined later) on these grounds for the simple reason that it isn't going to get into the business of defining obscenity. So you can copyright and register such a work with the Copyright Office. But look out when you try to bring legal action to stop someone from illegally reproducing it. The infringer may argue that the material is immoral, which, if proven, will render your copyright invalid. The issue then becomes what's obscene and, in some cases, how much is obscene. One scene in a videotape could, depending on how much footage it consumes, destroy the validity of the copyright of the whole tape. It's up to the court to decide the issue.

What happens if I don't copyright my work?

If you don't copyright your work as explained below, it falls into the public domain, which means that anyone is free to copy it.

How do I get copyright protection?

At first you don't have to do anything. According to the Copyright Revision Act, your work is automatically protected from the date of completion until the date of publication (see below). At the time of publication, you should protect your work by placing copyright notice (also described below) on the work. Before publication, you don't have to put a notice on your work or file papers or anything unless you want to, and, as explained below, there are some very good reasons why you may choose to do so.

What is publication?

Publication occurs when a work has been made public, or, to say it another way, when you have made it available to the public in some fashion. But, as yet, we are not sure what this means under the Copyright Revision Act, which defines publication as follows:

'Publication' is the distribution ... to the public by sale or other transfer of ownership, or by rental, lease, or lending. The offering to distribute ... to a group of persons for purposes of further distribution, public performance or public display, constitutes publication. A public performance or display of a work does not of itself constitute publication.

All of which makes the definition of publication as clear as mud. This law—as any law—must be transformed into reality through court cases. Once there are enough court cases to define a law, we have a better idea of what it means. As the Copyright Revision Act has just gone into effect and there are no cases decided under it, we have to make some educated guesses based on the old law about what certain things mean. So let's look at the possible ways in which you can publish work, ways to protect yourself against inadvertent publication, and what to do if you have already published by mistake.

Does publication occur if my work is offered for sale?

Maybe. If you offer a client a work in your own studio, publication doesn't occur because you're not making the work available to the public at large. But if your dealer offers it for sale in his gallery, the answer may be yes, although some Congressmen involved in the writing of the bill feel that in the future the courts won't interpret an offer for sale of a one-of-a-kind work (a painting, a drawing), as publication. These same legislators, on the other hand, believe that the offering for sale of work that is not one-of-a-kind (original graphics, multiples, or reproductions) does constitute publication.

What if a reproduction of my work appears in promotional material or in publications?

Under the old law you could be fairly certain that you had published if a work was shown on handbills, flyers, postcards, advertisements, mailings, annual reports, posters, calendars, or accompanying advertisements or feature stories in newspapers or magazines.

Under the new law this is probably still true, although there haven't been any court cases yet to prove it.

You can be certain your work won't be published if a reproduction which you don't authorize accompanies a critical review of your work, because this falls under the category of "fair use," which is described later. But all other reproductions that you authorize will probably publish your work. The smart thing to do, therefore, is to place copyright notice (explained on page 25) on the work as soon as it's completed.

Does publication occur when I exhibit in a gallery or museum?

Court cases interpreting the old law said that if photographing and copying were permitted in a gallery or museum, the work was published by exhibition in the gallery or museum whether or not it was actually photographed or copied.

Today, no such guidelines exist. Since there haven't been any court cases yet to interpret the new law's stand on this question, it's anyone's guess, although—once again—those same legislators mentioned above think that a display of one-of-a-kind works won't be interpreted as publication. Nevertheless, put your copyright notice on your completed work to be safe.

Does publication of a final work occur if a model of it has been published?

Yes. This was so under the old law, and there doesn't seem to be any reason why it should change. In the famous *Chicago Picasso* case, a company that wanted to make reproductions of the monumental sculpture Picasso donated to the city of Chicago argued that the copyright on the large-scale sculpture was invalid because the model it was made from had been published without a copyright. The company won. The court said that the maquette (a small three-dimensional model) was an original work which could have been copyrighted, and the sculpture was only a copy of the maquette.

If I publish an edition of reproductions, will this publish the original painting?

Probably, though under existing law, it isn't clear.

How can I protect myself against accidental publication?

This question and the one about what you can do if you've already published inadvertently should logically be answered here. But you need some more information before you can understand the answers, so hold on a bit.

What is proper copyright notice?

Copyright notice is something you put on the work of art. It is not something you send to the Copyright Office for purposes of registration (see below).

What does copyright notice include?

The word "Copyright," its abbreviation, "Copr.," or its symbol "©"; the name of the copyright owner; and the year of first publication (or year of completion).

Which form of copyright is best?

There isn't any best form, but since you'll want to keep visual clutter to a minimum, © will probably be your choice. Furthermore, it's wise to use the © because that's the accepted symbol both in the United States and abroad.

Can my name be abbreviated?

Yes, under American copyright law you can use your initials: © DCG 1977. Unfortunately, initials are not always sufficient to secure international copyright—so it's better to use your full name.

Should I include the year in the copyright notice on an artwork?

Under the law that expired December 31, 1977, it wasn't necessary to include a date with copyright notice. Under the law that went into effect January 1, 1978, it is. The only exception to this rule occurs where a pictorial, graphic, or sculptured work is reproduced in or on greeting cards, postcards, stationery, jewelry, dolls, toys, or any useful article.

Where is copyright notice placed?

The law demands that notice must be placed where the public can see it if the public looks for it, but the law doesn't spell out exactly where it should be put. At the time of this writing, the Copyright Office is working on new regulations that may clarify the issue. If they don't, the safest course dictates placement on the front of a two-dimensional object. Down in the left-hand corner, for example, is perfectly all right, providing the frame doesn't cover it up.

An equally obvious placement on a three-dimensional object would also be wise, as long as you don't put the notice on a base that isn't permanently attached to the object. In any case, check with the Copyright Office to see if its new regulations change this.

Can I put notice on the back or bottom of a work?

There have been court cases under the old law that said you can put the notice on the back of a painting or bottom of an object—providing it could be seen if someone were looking for it. In other words, you could put it on the back of a painting, photograph, lithograph, and so on, if it wasn't covered by a backing or a frame. The bottom of a three-dimensional work was also acceptable, providing it could be picked up easily. So, while you might have gotten away with putting a copyright notice on the bottom of a seven-pound sculpture, you wouldn't with one weighing 300 pounds. But once again, check this out with the Copyright Office —the new regulations may change this.

Is copyright notice on artwork reproduced in printed form sufficient notice?

It may be, but chances are the reproduction will reduce the size of the notice to the point where it can't be seen. So don't take a chance—ask in writing whoever is publishing the reproduction to insert another notice under the picture.

Must I register my work to secure copyright protection?

No. Your rights are protected by the law automatically, from completion until publication. After the publication date, all rights are secured by putting the copyright notice on the work.

The only time you *have to* register your copyright with the Register of Copyrights is if you're planning a legal action against an infringer of your copyright. In other words, if you open up a magazine one day and see an identical version of a painting of yours being offered for sale as a cheap reproduction, you can sue immediately if you have a Certificate of Registration. If you don't, you'll have to delay your suit until you get the certificate.

When can I register?

You can register artwork either before publication—as soon as it's completed, if you want—or anytime afterwards.

How do I register a copyright?

Write to the Copyright Office (Library of Congress, Washington, D.C. 20559) for the proper application forms. Before the new law there were a number of different classifications for works of art, and for each classification there was a different form. As of this writing, the Copyright Office has made a preliminary decision to simplify this—all works of art will fall into Class VA for visual arts.

After filling out the form, return it to the Copyright Office with a fee of $10 plus one photograph of an unpublished original work (paintings, sculpture, original graphics) or two photographs if it's published. If the work is a reproduction, you'll have to send one actual reproduction if the work is unpublished, and two if it is published. The Registrar then issues a Certificate of Registration.

Do I have to register every work separately?

Not always. You can register a group of related works under a single registration. Just what a group of related works constitutes hasn't been clarified at this time, but, hopefully, the regulations—which the Copyright Office is now in the process of writing—will define it. So far, a spokesman from the Copyright Office has said that examples of related works would be a "group of related jewelry designs, a group of photographs by one photographer, a series of greeting cards related to each other in some way."

Why should I register copyright before I discover infringement?

Under the old law, it wasn't really necessary to register prior to instituting a law suit. Now it's almost a must; indeed, the provisions regarding registration are among the most stringent in the new copyright law.

First, according to the Copyright Revision Act, a Certificate of Registration issued before publication or within five years of publication represents far superior evidence that your claim to copyright is valid than one dated after five years of publication. In fact, if you discover you're being ripped off six years after publication and you haven't either registered or placed copyright notice on the work, you'll probably have a difficult time proving your case.

Second, registration is essential if you expect to be awarded certain damages from a law suit—if your unpublished work is infringed before the date of registration (the date your application, deposit, and fee are received by the Copyright Office), you won't be entitled to attorneys' fees or statutory damages (see below). The same holds true if a published work is infringed before the date of registration, unless registration is made within three months after publication of the work.

So if you think your work is the kind of art that is susceptible to infringement—your landscapes make ideal calendar pictures, for example—register right away.

Must I re-register after publication if I've registered before publication?

No, not unlesss you've changed the work and aren't sure the original copyright will still apply to the altered work.

If I make an edition of reproductions from a copyrighted painting, must I copyright the reproductions?

Yes, you have to go through the whole procedure—copyright and registration—all over again for the reproductions.

If I forget to put copyright notice on my work and it's published, do I lose my copyright?

Under the old law, the answer would have been "yes" 99 times out of 100. The work would have passed out of your control and anyone could have reproduced it.

Now, thanks to what may be the most important provision in the Copyright Revision Act, you can omit the name or date, or omit the entire notice, without losing your copyright, if:

1. The notice has been omitted from no more than a relatively small number of works. Keep in mind that copyright law is primarily directed toward printed material and records. So what a "small number" of works means exactly to the artist is unfathomable at this time. Since most of you make one-of-a-kind objects or small editions of works, leaving copyright off an original work or a few graphics might be construed as a "relatively small number." But we'll have to wait for the courts to straighten out the semantics. Anyway, the next two circumstances have much greater impact for you.

2. Registration for the work is made before publication or within five years after publication without notice, and you make a reasonable effort (another phrase awaiting interpretation) to add notice to all copies.

3. You sign a contract with someone, and, in the contract, he agrees to attach copyright notice as a condition to your allowing him to publicly distribute the work, but he fails to do so. In other words, if you have a written contract with a publisher requiring him to place copyright notice on all copies of an edition of reproductions and he fails to fulfill this condition, your copyright is still valid.

What if I publish accidentally without copyright notice?

If it's within five years of publication, register it immediately and add the copyright notice to the work. If the work is out of your hands, ask the new owner to put copyright notice on it for you.

What if I make an error in the date?

If the wrong date is more than a year later than the actual date of publication, the same rule applies to the error that applies to the omission of copyright notice.

If the date is earlier than the publication date, the copyright is valid from that date even though it's in error.

Now let's get back to the question of protection.

What is the best way to protect my copyright?

As soon as the work is completed, place a copyright notice on it, using the year in which it's completed as the year of publication. Then register it with the Copyright Office. This way, even if you accidentally publish the work, you'll be completely covered.

What if the date of completion is different than the year of publication?

No problem. This is considered an error in the date, and, since it's earlier than the actual publication date, the copyright is still valid and the copyright term is computed from the earlier date.

How long does copyright protection last?

The copyright on any work created on or after January 1, 1978, lasts from its completion for the lifetime of its creator plus 50 years. If two or more people own the copyright, it endures for the life of the last survivor plus 50 years. For example, if you're commissioned to create a work of art and by special agreement you and your client jointly own the copyright, it will last until both of you die and then for another 50 years.

Under the old copyright law, protection lasted from date of publication for 28 years, and then—if you remembered to renew —for another 28 years.

What if I published and copyrighted a work before January 1, 1978, and plan to renew it after January 1, 1978? Because you copyrighted under the old law, your first term remains the same: 28 years from date of publication. But when you go to renew after the 28 years are up, you're entitled to a second term of 47 years if you register with the Copyright Office within one year prior to the expiration date of the original term.

What if I created a work before January 1, 1978, but do not publish before that date? The same rules apply that would if you created the work after January 1, 1978. In other words, the copyright will last for your life plus 50 years. But since this might create a hardship for the heirs of deceased artists, the law says that no copyright on unpublished work created before January 1, 1978, can expire before December 31, 2002. It also says that if the work is published on or before December 31, 2002, the copyright can't expire before December 31, 2027.

Does my U.S. copyright give me international protection?

There are three major copyright organizations in the world governing international copyright: the Universal Copyright Convention (UCC), whose members include most industrialized countries; the Buenos Aires Convention, comprised of most South American nations; and the Berne Convention. The United States belongs to the UCC and the Buenos Aires Convention. Therefore, your U.S. copyright protects you in all the countries that belong to these two conventions.

How do I get copyright protection from the Berne Convention?

It's difficult, so first figure out if you need it by deciding in which countries you want a copyright. It could be that the same countries you're interested in that belong to the Berne Convention also belong to the UCC, so there would be no need to subject yourself to the procedure. To find these facts out, write to the Copyright Office.

If you find you do want protection in a country governed only by the Berne Convention, you must publish your work in a country which is a party to the Berne Convention at the same time it's published in the U.S.

What if I want copyright protection in a country that doesn't belong to any of these conventions?

The United States has individual copyright treaties with other countries. Check with a lawyer or the Copyright Office to see what deals we have with the countries you're considering.

Is copyright notice the same all over the world?

No. The UCC demands that you use the symbol ©, your full name, and the year of first publication. Other conventions and individual arrangements may have different regulations, so ask the Copyright Office.

If I'm not a U.S. citizen, can I obtain copyright protection here?

You'll acquire copyright protection for a work published in the United States if: you lived in the United States at the time of first publication; you're a national of a country participating in the Universal Copyright Convention; or you're a citizen or national of other countries with which the United States has a reciprocal agreement or treaty.

Unpublished works are protected no matter what your national status is.

How long does international protection last?

Protection of a lifetime plus 50 years is common throughout the world, and one of the reasons why the Copyright Revision Act extended the maximum term beyond the old term of 56 years (two terms of 28) was to conform with this international standard.

Am I entitled to the copyright on works created for an employer?

No. The copyright on works made for hire belongs to your employer unless you have a written agreement that specifically allows you to own the copyright.

Can I copyright work I create for a commission?

Yes, unless you agree in writing to give up your rights.

Does this mean I can copyright illustrations commissioned by books or magazines?

Yes, unless you agree in writing that the work was made for hire. The agreement should be signed by both you and a representative of the publication.

Do I retain copyright after a work is sold?

Yes. When the work is sold, the new owner acquires the rights to sell, give, rent, loan, and display the work. But—and this is very important—sale of the work doesn't bestow on the new owner the rights to reproduce the work or to make other types of work from it unless the original owner specifically transfers these rights by a written document, such as a sales contract, memo, or letter, to the new owner. However, if you retain copyright, make sure it states in the sales contract that you'll have "reasonable access to the work" so you'll have the opportunity to reproduce it. If the owner refuses to allow you to come in his house to photograph the work after you have written in advance and offered a choice of dates, the courts will probably uphold your demand.

What happens to my copyright after I die?

It's passed on to your heirs through your will (or if you don't have a will, to whomever the law considers your legal heirs), and it's their job to renew copyright on a work created and published before January 1, 1978, if they wish to benefit from it. If it's published after January 1, 1978, the term is automatic and not renewable.

Can I sell my copyright, but not the original artwork?

Certainly, it's done all the time. You can sell your copyright to a greeting card company, keep the painting for yourself, and then sell it to someone else.

You can even sell parts of your copyright. For example, you can sell the exclusive rights to an illustration to a magazine and then turn around and sell exclusive rights for its reproduction as a greeting card to another company. Both types of sales are called transfers of copyright.

What is a transfer of copyright?

A transfer of copyright occurs when you sell or give or trade your copyright or grant someone an exclusive license.

What's an exclusive license? An exclusive license is a transfer usually limited to time or place or form of reproduction. For example, if you're an illustrator, you might sell a magazine first serial rights (serial refers to the fact that periodicals are published in a serial, or continuing, manner). First serial rights entitle the magazine to publish your illustrations for the first time. Or you might grant one license to a magazine stating no other magazine could ever reproduce a certain work and another to a greeting card publisher giving him the right to be the only greeting card company to reproduce that work. Another possibility is to limit a license to a geographical area as you would do if you sold First U.S. Serial Rights or First U.S. Rights (if it's a book).

A nonexclusive license means you're letting a number of people do the same thing. For example, you could sell rights to a number of greeting card companies to reproduce the same painting.

If a magazine or book reproduces an unpublished work, am I protected by the publication's copyright?

Yes. This wasn't always the case, but it is now under the Copyright Revision Act.

Does such a reproduction constitute publication? Probably, so you should place copyright notice on the work and register it.

If a publication prints a published and copyrighted work lacking copyright notice, am I protected by the copyright?

Yes. You're protected either way—by your own copyright or the publication's.

Should I ask that copyright notice accompany the reproduction of my work in a publication?

Yes. The reason for this is that placement of copyright notice will probably limit the publisher to the right to reproduce the work only once. Otherwise, unless you have a written agreement specifying the specific rights you're granting him, he may be able to use it again in a revised edition of the publication without paying you. This is all right, if this is what you want. But if it isn't, the copyright notice will protect you. In any case, the best course of action would be to put in writing exactly what rights you're transferring to him.

What should I do when I transfer my copyright?

You don't have to do anything, but the new owner should file a written document, or a notarized copy of it, with the Copyright Office, along with $10, within one month of transfer (or two months, if executed outside the United States). Once this has been accomplished, the Copyright Office will furnish him with a Certificate of Recordation.

The transfer document doesn't have to have any particular form, except that it must be signed by you. For example, suppose you sell the copyright on an oil painting to a friend who's in the greeting card business. He might ask you to write a letter saying something like this:

"I, Henry Artist, sell to John Hallmark, for a fee of $1,000, all rights of reproduction to my oil painting *Winter Storm,* which bears copyright registration number 240951." (Registration must precede the filing of a transfer.)

Must the new owner record the transfer?

He doesn't have to but he'd be very foolish not to. The reason the new owner should record the transfer is to prove that he really owns the copyright in case someone else should also claim that he bought it.

The new owner also needs a Certificate of Recordation before he can start any legal action against an infringer.

Can my work ever be used without my permission?

Yes, under the doctrine of fair use.

What is fair use?

Fair use gives others the right to use without permission of the copyright owner copyrighted material for such purposes as criticism, comment, news reporting, teaching, scholarship, or research. It also allows the copying of a certain amount of the copyrighted material. But as you might expect, the law doesn't spell out exactly how much or what percentage of the whole work can be legally copied.

What is an example of fair use? The reproduction of an artwork accompanying a newspaper review or an article describing an art competition.

If I make some drawings based directly on parts of copyrighted material, can I claim fair use?

As I said, no formula or guidelines spell out the specific amount of work that can be safely duplicated without permission. If you plan to use only a small portion of the material, the fair use doctrine may cover you. If you're uncertain whether the portion represents a substantial or unsubstantial amount of copying, ask a lawyer. Use of a substantial part of it demands that you seek permission from the copyright holder.

How can I locate the copyright owner?

Tracing the owner and determining whether a copyright is still in effect may not be easy, but the Copyright Office will do it for you for a fee. Write the Copyright Office, giving it as much information as you can, and it will send you an estimate of the cost of the search.

Can I incorporate photographs and other copyrighted material in my collages without infringing?

Technically speaking, you may be infringing. But in reality, this kind of case is unlikely to come to court.

Will reproduction of my work under the fair use doctrine publish my unpublished work?

No, unauthorized use of unpublished work under the fair use doctrine does not constitute publication.

Can anyone else use my work without authorization?

Yes, a special provision in the Copyright Revision Act allows non-commercial broadcasting systems (i.e., public TV) to use pictorial and graphic work without permission of the owner. These systems will have to pay royalties for such use, however, and a brand new organization called the Copyright Royalty Tribunal has been created by the Copyright Revision Act to determine what the rates will be.

Will these public broadcasting systems automatically send me my royalties?

The Copyright Royalty Tribunal is supposed to establish requirements by which copyright owners will receive notice of the use of their works and to organize the records the public broadcasting systems must keep regarding this use. However, this system hasn't been worked out yet, so for the time being, the answer is no.

If infringement occurs, what can I sue for?

First, you can sue for an injunction. This means you can stop the infringers from any further reproduction.

Second, money. You can sue for actual damages and/or the infringer's profits, or you can sue for statutory damages. Actual damages are often hard to determine. You would have to prove, for example, how much money you really lost because of the competition between an infringer's reproductions of one of your works and your own reproductions. So people frequently sue for statutory damages, which are amounts arbitrarily determined by the courts according to certain limits set down by the Copyright Revsion Act. That's why it's so important to register early—if you register after an infringement occurs, you won't be able to sue for statutory damages (unless you register within three months of publication).

Third, you can sue to prevent the infringing material from being distributed for the duration of the legal action and to destroy the infringing copies and plates, if you win.

Fourth, the court may force the defendant to pay your court costs and attorney fees (although you won't be able to sue for attorney's fees if you register after infringement).

Last, the courts may fine the infringer and/or put him in jail.

If the infringement occurs because I didn't put copyright notice on the work, can I sue?

Yes, you can sue to stop the infringer from infringing. But in such a case, if the person *innocently* infringed your copyright because notice wasn't there, the court won't give you either actual or statutory damages, although it may force the infringer to pay you the profits he made.

Do I have the right to demand that my work be credited to me?

No. This right is usually called a moral right. Many European countries recognize the doctrine of moral rights (the rights to maintain the integrity of a work against deformation, to claim authorship, and to deny exhibition without proper accreditation among others), but it has never been accepted in the United States. Apparently, American lawmakers don't value the contributions of artists as highly as their counterparts across the Atlantic, a lesson learned the hard way by a number of artists who have engaged in legal battles on this issue.

Do I have the right to a royalty on the profit made from reselling my work?

The right to profits from resale, known in France as *droit de suite,* is available only in California at the time of this writing. If you live in California, you're entitled by a state law to 5% of the gross resale price (before commissions are subtracted), if the price exceeds $1,000 and this money represents a profit. The sale must take place either in California or be made by a California resident elsewhere.

In the rest of the United States, where no such laws exist, some artists have begun inserting this or similar provisions into their sales contracts. Others, with the backing of a few interested congressmen, are pushing to make such resale royalties required by a federal law. The pros and cons of royalties are discussed in the next chapter.

What is a patent?

A patent protects the invention of machines, devices, processes, substances, and designs of articles of manufacture. The big difference between a copyright and a patent is that a potentially patentable invention must be totally new and novel, while copyrightable material need be original only to you. This means that the Copyright Office doesn't check to see if you're duplicating someone else's idea. The Patent Office, on the other hand, sets rigid standards for meeting the test of newness and searches its records prior to issuing a patent to make sure the process, design, or whatever is indeed unique.

How long do patents last?

Patents protect devices, machines, processes, and substances for 17 years. Design patents last for 3½, 7, or 14 years, as the applicant elects.

How do I get a patent?

Filing for a patent is a complicated and expensive process. While you're permitted to prepare and file your own patent application by law, only the foolhardy would do so. And patent attorneys aren't inexpensive. The simplest procedure could run at least $1,000.

Why would I want a patent?

You probably wouldn't. Because of the utilitarian nature of patentable objects, visual artists aren't commonly potential applicants. Occasionally, however, the two areas overlap. The designer of a novelty watch bearing a caricature of Spiro Agnew applied for and received both a copyright for the caricature and a design patent for the watch some years ago.

3. The Artist as Seller and Exhibitor

· Pricing
· Cataloging
· Discounts
· Sales invoices
· Reserved rights
· Rentals
· Exhibitions

Most artists reading this book are probably reading it because they're exhibiting and making money from their work or are planning to do so. So, right off the bat, let's get into the questions about the two ways to make money—selling and renting—and exhibiting.

How do I decide what is a fair price for my work?

The strategy of pricing is really a *marketing* problem and therefore outside the scope of this book, but there are two excellent books dealing with the question—Calvin Goodman's *Marketing Art* and Betty Chamberlain's *The Artist's Guide to His Market* (see the bibliography).

Suffice it to say here that prices should cover all costs—both direct and indirect (see below)—and provide some profit. At the same time, your prices must be competitive in the market place. To evaluate whether they are or not, check what others, working in the same style or similar subject matter, with similar experience, education, and talent, are getting at dealers in your area.

How do I calculate direct costs?

Begin by getting a set of file cards. Assign a number to each work of art when you start to work on it, and write the number on one of the cards. Keep the card where it can be seen while the work is in progress (perhaps on a bulletin board) to remind you to record details on it.

What details do I record? Record your start and completion dates, plus the number of hours you work on the piece each day, including time spent *thinking* about it. Also jot down all materials you use—both amounts and costs—and record any other directly related expenses. If you hire assistants, mark down names, addresses, wages, and the hours they work. Figure out *your own* labor costs by multiplying the number of hours you work by what your labor is worth.

How do I decide what my labor is worth? If you have another job—as an art teacher, an illustrator, a framemaker—you can simply divide your weekly salary by the number of hours you normally work at that job. Even if you don't work at anything art-related—say you drive a cab—you can still make the same computation.

If you don't have another job, you can figure out what your labor is worth by determining what you need to survive. Suppose you're just out of art school, you've rented a cheap living-work space, and your needs are small. Take into consideration your rent, food bills, and other basics. If you decide, for example, that you can't get along on less than $125 a week, which is an amount you could earn by working on a job 35 hours a week, divide $125 by 35. You'd estimate your hourly wage, then, at about $4.

Later, as your market grows, you'll want to give yourself a raise to reflect a higher value for your labor. Obviously, your estimate has to be reasonable.

What are indirect costs?

Indirect costs can be lumped into three groups—material costs that you can't allocate to any one work (for example, you may only use a fraction of a tube of paint in a painting); overhead like rent, utilities, insurance, and so on; and selling costs, such as advertising, postage, framing, crating, shipping, entertainment, travel, and printing.

How do I figure out indirect costs? If you keep a yearly record of all expenses—as you must for tax purposes (see Chapter 12)—all you have to do is total these costs and divide by the number of hours you work per year, according to your file cards. So, if you spent $2,000 a year on selling expenses and work 1,000 hours, your selling costs are $2 an hour. Similarly, if your overhead is $2,000, your overhead costs are $2 per hour. And if incidental materials are costing you $1,000, this becomes another $1 per hour.

How do I put these cost figures together?

Simply add up your direct costs and indirect costs. Let's say that it takes you 20 hours to complete one canvas. You've decided that your labor is worth $5 an hour. You spent $30 for canvas and stretchers. Your direct costs, therefore, are $130. Now, using the figures determined above, let's say your hourly selling cost is $2, your overhead is $2, and your incidental materials are $1. Just multiply them by the number of hours spent creating the work. This is another $5 an hour, which you multiply by 20 hours for a total of $100. Your total costs (direct and indirect) would be $230.

Is this total the price I charge?

No. This amount doesn't take into consideration the fact that you, like most artists, probably won't sell all of your work. If you have a history of sales—even two or three years will give you an idea—you know about how many works you do sell each year.

Suppose, therefore, that you paint 20 oils each year and manage to sell about 10 of them. Just to break even on costs, you'll have to double the amount you charge for each work. While the total cost involved in *each* piece is $230, you'll have to get back at least $460 for each piece you sell, just to recover the cost of all 20 pieces.

Once I make this price adjustment, is this what I charge?

You could charge this amount, but you're still not making a profit. What you've done is cover costs and pay yourself for your labor. But this won't put any money in a savings account or help you take that trip to Europe which you think is necessary for the development of your art. You've got to think of yourself as a business—and businesses are in operation to make a profit.

How much should I charge then?

Most small businessmen try to make a minimum profit of 20%. At the very least, if it costs you $400 to make and sell a painting, you would add on 20% of $400 and charge about $500.

Must I always figure costs this way?

The calculations I've just outlined represent the ideal situation. Practically speaking, of course, they don't always work. Suppose, for example, that you're fresh out of school; you figure your labor is worth $5 an hour; and you do large, meticulous egg tempera paintings. Every painting takes you 200 hours. In this case, as a beginning artist, you can't expect to charge and get $1,000 for each painting in the market place just yet.

Nor will you feel that it's *always* necessary to price paintings this way. If you have another job and you don't depend on income from your art for support, you may feel that you can afford to be more flexible in your pricing policies.

But the fact remains that too many people ignore cost factors altogether. They price their work too low, and end up using income from other sources to support their art. In the beginning of your career, you might expect this to happen. However, you should begin to recover costs very quickly, and you won't be able to recover costs unless you figure out exactly what they *are*.

Are file cards the only records I should keep of my work?

A more elaborate system is needed if you want not only to calculate costs, but also to keep track of where your work goes, to protect yourself for insurance purposes, and to prove that the work has been copyrighted.

What sort of record-keeping system should I use?

One of the best cataloguing systems has been proposed by the Artists Equity Association. It includes the file cards described above, a record book, and photographs. The file cards record day-to-day details while work is in progress. The record book contains more long-range sales and exhibition data. And the photographs have a variety of uses, discussed below.

How do I organize this system? When you begin a work, assign a number to it. Write the number both in the record book and on the file card. Later, when the work is complete, photograph it and put the same number on the back of the picture.

What information do I put in the record book? Record your start and completion dates, and the price you hope to get. When the work is sold, add the name and address of the purchaser, the *actual* sales price (in case you give a discount, a subject discussed below), and the date of sale. Leave room for other information about when and where the work is exhibited and prizes it wins. And you'll also want to record changes in the purchaser's address and any data about new purchasers—if the work is resold and this information is available to you.

What is the significance of the photograph? A photograph provides a record for insurance purposes in case of loss or damage, proof of its original state in case alterations are made by purchasers, and, if you have placed a copyright notice on it, a record for copyright protection. In addition, you'll want the photograph for publicity purposes.

When do I give discounts?

Museums and other educational institutions sometimes expect discounts. So does the collector who buys more than one or two expensive works.

How much should the discount be?

Museums frequently ask for 10%, as do collectors, but that isn't to say that they won't ask for more—perhaps as much as 20%.

Do I have to give discounts?

If it's a museum, chances are you'll find it worthwhile to discount a work in exchange for the boost to your reputation. But with collectors, every case differs. Naturally, if they buy five or ten works, they're entitled to a discount because they're buying in quantity. But if it's just two or three works, you'll have to decide how much you value them as collectors.

Should I ever give a discount to a collector on just one work?

It's done all the time, because many collectors automatically ask for a 10% discount. But it's a lousy idea, because pretty soon the word will get around that your work can always be had for less.

When I make a sale, what written forms must I fill out?

A sales invoice (also known as a bill of sale) and possibly a separate contract reserving certain rights (see below).

Where do I get sales invoices?

Most stationery stores carry standard invoice forms. Or you could design one to fit your needs and have it printed (see Figure 1).

What is included on a sales invoice?

Some or all of the following items:

1. Date of sale.

2. Name and address of client.

3. Your name and address.

4. Description of the work sold (title, dimensions, medium, and date of completion).

5. Price.

Figure 1. This particular invoice was designed by Calvin Goodman for his book, Marketing Art. *You can design one to fit your own specific needs based on this form and have it printed. Or you can select one of the many standard invoice forms carried by most stationery stores.*

JOHN DOE, ARTIST   **SALES INVOICE**
1234 W. FIRST STREET
MIDDLETOWN, OHIO 23456
Telephone: (312) 435-9222

Terms   ☐ Visa #
Net   ☐ Cash Sale
                                         ☐ Master Charge #

Ship to: _____ Bill to: _____ Date: _____
         _____   _____ Via: _____

Item No.	Description: Medium, Title, Dimensions (HT X Width)	Price

All sales subject to terms and conditions on reverse of this invoice.

Received in good condition: Net | $
                                                    Sales Tax | $
_____
Client's Signature   Date   Total | $

TERMS AND CONDITIONS OF SALE

Payment for all works herein shall be in United States currency, net, on presentation of this invoice. Works may also be charged on valid Visa/Mastercharge credit accounts.

The buyer may return any work acquired herein for full credit against the purchase of any other works available at that time, provided only that said work shall be returned in good condition and within 30 days from the date herein.

Unless otherwise specifically indicated, all works herein are originals, executed by the artist and are certified to be free from all defects due to faulty craftsmanship or faulty materials for a period of twelve months from the date of sale. If flaws should appear during this period and be due to such causes, said works shall be subject to repair or replacement, at the option of the seller. Buyer is cautioned, however, that the seller cannot be responsible for fading, cracking, and other damage to these works caused by improvident exposure to sunlight and weather.

All shipments are fully insured by the shipper against damage or loss. If works are not received in good condition, please notify the seller within ten days of receipt.

All shipments are F.O.B. the seller's place of business and will be transferred via freight collect, unless prepaid by the buyer. Crating methods and charges are per art object freight company standard procedures and rates.

The original works described herein are copyrighted by the artist. The sale of such copyrighted work does not include the sale of rights to reproduction in any form unless specifically granted in writing by the artist.

6. Discount, if any.

7. Sales tax, if any (see Chapter 14).

8. Down payment and balance due, if any.

9. Payment dates.

10. Delivery date.

11. Provision regarding insurance and risk of loss.

12. Warranty.

13. Statement about ownership of reproduction rights.

14. Signature of the client indicating that the work was received in good condition.

What do you mean by the payment date?

The date—usually the first of the month—when payment is due if payments extend over a period of time. For example, it is not uncommon to allow a client up to 12 months to pay for work.

What do you mean by delivery date?

The date when the client can take possession of the work, meaning the date when he can either come to your studio to pick the work up or have you deliver it to him.

What if a sold work is stolen before being picked up?

If the work is stolen from your studio before the delivery date, that's your problem. You'll either have to replace it with another work or refund the client's money. If it's stolen after the delivery date but before the client picks it up, the law in many states says you're no longer responsible for it.

What happens if a work is stolen after an attempted delivery?

If you try to make delivery on the *arranged* delivery date and fail because the buyer wasn't there to take possession, you've fulfilled your end of the bargain legally in many states, and it's the buyer's loss. That's why it's important to have the delivery date as well as the payment date on the invoice, particularly if they aren't the same.

What should the invoice say about insurance and risk of loss?

It should state who has to pay for a work that is lost or damaged during shipping. If you're responsible and it gets lost or damaged before it gets to the client, you're the person who has to replace it or give him his money back. So terms of sale might read: "Shipment is fully insured by the shipper against damage or loss. If work is not received in good condition, notify us within 10 days."

Who pays for shipping?

This is a tossup. In these days of rising prices, more and more artists and galleries try to pass these costs on to the buyer, particularly if he has received a discount. Therefore, the invoice might read: "Purchaser pays for shipping."

What is a warranty?

Many collectors, usually those buying art for investment, want documentation stating that the work they buy is authentic, i.e., that it was really created by the artist who says he made it. (Documentation of prints is another matter and is taken up in Chapter 7.) Obviously, this sort of documentation has more relevance for works of dead or very famous artists, but it should not be overlooked by those of you who are alive and well and working at being famous.

Furthermore, it's good business to offer clients a limited guarantee that the work will last. By this I mean a promise that materials won't fade or crack under normal conditions. Your warranty should guarantee both authenticity and durability.

What would a typical warranty say? Typical isn't an operative word in the art world, but an example is given in Figure 1.

What about reproduction rights in a sales invoice?

If you plan to sell them along with the work, the sale must be spelled out in the invoice. Otherwise, according to the law, you retain the copyright, which means you have the opportunity to sell the reproduction rights to someone else, if you like.

Despite the fact that the law says that you retain copyright in the absence of a written agreement to the contrary, it is still a good idea to emphasize your ownership on the invoice to avoid confusion later on. So you might state on the invoice, "All reproduction rights to the work are reserved to the artist." This provision might also be included in a separate contract for reserved rights, also known as moral rights, if you plan to use one.

*Figure 2. This is an example of the enlightened contract
used by the City of Seattle when it purchases art from artists.*

PURCHASE CONTRACT

THIS AGREEMENT, dated *November 27, 1974,* between the City of Seattle, acting by and through the Seattle Arts Commission, hereinafter referred to as "City," and *Tony Smith,* hereinafter referred to as "Artist."

WHEREAS, the City is now implementing a public art program as set forth by Ordinance 102210 allocating certain funds for the establishment of artworks in public places and authorizing the Seattle Arts Commission to make payments for design, execution and placement of works; and

WHEREAS, the Artist has created the following work of art:
Title: *Moses*
Dimensions: *Height:* 11'4 1/4"; *Length:* 150"; *Depth:* 7'4"
Media: *Painted Steel Sculpture*
Hereinafter the above described work of art should be referred to as the "Work": and WHEREAS, the Work was selected for purchase by the City through procedures duly adopted by the City, and the Artist is willing to sell the Work, and both parties wish the integrity and clarity of the Artist's ideas and statements in the Work to be maintained;

NOW THEREFORE, the parties mutually agree as follows:

1. The Artist shall sell the Work to the City, subject to the conditions herein, for the price of *Forty-Two Thousand Dollars,* receipt of which is hereby acknowledged.

2. A public notice including the Artist's name and mention of the City's ownership shall be publicly displayed and identified with the Work, and shall be paid for by the City.

3. The Work shall be properly installed and displayed by the City at the Seattle Center, which is a facility frequented by and open to the general public.

4. The City agrees that it will not intentionally destroy, damage, alter, modify or change the Work in any way whatsoever. If any alteration of any kind occurs to the Work after it has been finally

---

completed and installed, whether such change is intentional or accidental and whether done by the City or others, then the Work will no longer be represented to be the Work of the Artist without his written consent. The City agrees to see that the Work is properly maintained and protected.

5. All repairs and restorations which are made during the lifetime of the Artist shall have his approval. To the extent practical, the Artist shall be given the opportunity to accomplish said repairs and restorations at a reasonable fee.

6. While recognizing that the City does not currently have the legal mechanism permitting the sale of works of art, the City agrees that if in the future the City does sell the Work, the City shall pay the Artist a sum equal of Fifteen Percent (15%) of the appreciated value of the Work.

7. The Artist agrees to notify the City of changes in his address and failure to do so shall be deemed a waiver to the Artist's rights in Paragraphs five and six above.

8. The City agrees to maintain on permanent file a record of this Agreement and of the location, condition and disposition of the Work.

9. The Artist hereby reserves all rights to copy or reproduce the Work, but shall not unreasonably refuse the City permission to reproduce the Work. The Artist also reserves all rights under any copyright laws to which the Work may be subject.

10. All Changes in this Agreement shall require written agreement signed by both parties.

SIGNED THIS *27th* Day of *November, 1974.*

For Seattle Arts Commission
John W Blaine
John Blaine

Tony Smith
Tony Smith

Dec. 4, 1974
Date

What are reserved rights?

A number of terms (see Figure 2) that you could impose as conditions of sale, which allow you to exert some control over the work after sale. Most commonly they are:

1. Reproduction rights.

2. The right to restore and repair the work yourself, or the right to approve any restoration or repairs.

3. The right to display the work at reasonable intervals (two months every five years would be considered reasonable).

4. The right to be properly credited as the creator of the work.

5. The right to prevent the work from being altered.

What other reserved rights could I ask for?

A more detailed list of rights is found in *The Artists Reserved Rights Transfer and Sales Agreement* by Robert Projansky, which was written to correct the artist's lack of control over use of his work and lack of participation in its profits after he no longer owns it (see Figure 3). But, basically, in this contract the artist is given the right to:

1. 15% of the gross profit each time a work is sold in the future.

2. Demand that each seller sign a contract with each new buyer and send a copy of it back to the artist.

3. Be notified before the owner commits the work to a show, giving him the details of the show.

4. Be consulted if repairs become necessary and be given first opportunity to restore it, if practical.

5. Half of any rental income.

6. All reproduction rights in the work.

7. Exhibit the work at a nonprofit institution for 60 days once every five years if the artist notifies the purchaser in writing 120 days in advance of the opening and promises to take care of all expenses and insurance.

8. Demand that the purchaser will not intentionally modify the work in any way.

Figure 3. This contract was written by Robert Projansky, a pioneer in the area of reserving rights to artists. Adopting it verbatim may not be useful to many artists, but it can be easily modified by picking out the rights you wish to reserve and putting them into your own sales contract.

PROJANSKY CONTRACT

fill in names, addresses of parties

Artist:_____ Address:_____

Purchaser:_____Address:_____

WHEREAS Artist has created that certain Work of Art ("the Work"):

fill in data identifying the Work

Title: _____dimensions: _____

media:_____ year:_____

WHEREAS the parties want the Artist to have certain rights in the future economics and integrity of the Work, the parties mutually agree as follows:

fill in agreed value.

1. **Sale**: Artist hereby sells the Work to Purchaser at the Agreed value of $_____.

2. **Retransfer**: If Purchaser in any way whatsoever sells, gives or trades the Work, or if it is inherited from Purchaser, or if a third party pays compensation for its destruction, Purchaser (or the representative of his estate) must within 30 days

    (a) Pay Artist 15% of the "gross art profit," if any, on the transfer; and

    (b) Get the new owner to ratify this contract by signing a properly filled out "Transfer Agreement and Record" (TAR); and

    (c) Deliver the signed TAR to the Artist.

    (d) "Gross art profit" for this contract means only: "Agreed value" on a TAR less the "agreed value" on the last prior TAR, or (if there hasn't been a prior resale) less the agreed value in Paragraph 1 of this contract.

(e) "Agreed value" to be filled in on each TAR shall be the actual sale price if the Work is sold for money or the fair market value at the time if transferred any other way.

3. **Non-Delivery**: If the TAR isn't delivered in 30 days, Artist may compute "gross art profit" and Artist's 15% as if it had, using the fair market value at the time of the transfer or at the time Artist discovers the transfer.

4. **Notice of Exhibition**: Before committing the Work to a show, Purchaser must give Artist notice of intent to do so, telling Artist all the details of the show that Purchaser then knows.

5. **Provenance**: Upon request Artist will furnish Purchaser and his successors a written history and provenance of the Work, based on TAR's and Artist's best information as to shows.

6. **Artists Exhibition**: Artist may show the Work for up to 60 days once every 5 years at a non-profit institution at no expense to Purchaser, upon written notice no later than 120 days before opening and upon satisfactory proof of insurance and prepaid transportation.

7. **Non-Destruction**: Purchaser will not permit any intentional destruction, damage or modification of the Work.

8. **Restoration**: If the Work is damaged, Purchaser will consult Artist before any restoration and must give Artist first opportunity to restore it, if practicable.

9. **Rents**: If the Work is rented, Purchaser must pay Artist 50% of the rents within 30 days of receipt.

10. **Reproduction**: Artist reserves all rights to reproduce the Work.

11. **Notice**: A Notice, in the form below, must be permanently affixed to the Work, warning that ownership, etc., are subject to this contract. If, however, a document represents the Work or is part of the Work, the Notice must instead be a permanent part of that document.

12. **Transferees Bound**: If anyone becomes the owner of the Work with notice of this contract, that person shall be bound to all its terms as if he had signed a TAR when he acquired the Work.

13. **Expiration**: This contract binds the parties, their heirs and all their successors in interest, and all Purchaser's obligations are attached to the Work and go with ownership of the Work, all for the life of the Artist and Artist's surviving spouse plus 21 years, except the obligations of Paragraphs 4, 6 and 8 shall last only for Artist's lifetime.

14. **Attorneys' Fees**: In any proceeding to enforce any part of this contract, the aggrieved party shall be entitled to reasonable attorneys' fees in addition to any available remedy.

fill in date
both sign

Date: _____

_____
Artist

_____
Purchaser

* * *

TRANSFER AGREEMENT AND RECORD

fill in data
identifying the
Work

Title: _____ dimensions: _____

media: _____ year: _____

Ownership of the above Work of Art has been transferred between the undersigned persons, and the new owner hereby expressly ratifies, assumes and agrees to be bound by the terms of

fill in date

the Contract dated _____ between:

fill in names,
addresses of
parties

Artist: _____ Address: _____

Purchaser: _____ Address: _____

Agreed value (as defined in said contract) at the time of this transfer: $ _____

do not fill in anything between these lines

Old owner: _____ address: _____

New owner: _____ address: _____

Date of this transfer: _____

* * *

SPECIMEN NOTICE

Ownership, transfer, exhibition and reproduction of this Work of Art are subject to a certain Contract

fill in date

dated _____ between:

fill in names of parties and Artist's address on both Notices

Artist: _____

Address: _____and

Purchaser: _____
Artist has a copy.

---

cut out, affix to Work

NOTICE

Ownership, transfer, exhibition and reproduction of this Work of Art are subject to a certain Contract

dated _____ between:

Artist: _____

Address: _____and

Purchaser: _____
Artist has a copy.

How long would these rights last? Numbers 1, 2, 5, and 8 would endure for the artist's and his spouse's lifetimes plus 21 years to help the artist's children while they are growing up. Numbers 3, 4, and 7 last only for the artist's life. Number 6, of course, would be governed by the copyright law.

Is the first provision what is called a droit de suite? Well, it's a variation of it. *Droit de suite,* a term loosely translated as "art proceeds rights" refers to certain European laws that provide the artist with a royalty whenever his work is sold. Its operation varies from country to country. In France, an artist or his heirs receive a fee regardless of whether the price of the work increases, whereas in Italy an artist is eligible only for *droit de suite* if the value increases. In France, an artist is entitled to 3% of the resale price; in Germany 1%. Minimum prices which the object must bring before an artist can collect and the lengths of time for which he can expect to collect also vary, as do the methods of sale. In France, for example, *droit de suite* applies only to artworks sold at auction.

What are the criticisms of the Projansky contract? There's no end to the faults critics can find, but here are some of the more obvious ones. First, it's hard enough to sell art without complicating the procedure. After all, if a buyer has to search out a second person willing to accept the same conditions, thus severely limiting his selling power, he may think twice about purchasing in the first place. Second, there is no feasible way to enforce *droit de suite*; sales can easily be made that will escape the artist's attention. Third, since most artwork never changes hands, and, when it does, it rarely resells at great increases, the contract may be an exercise in futility.

Don't some states guarantee a royalty on resale?

Yes, in 1976 California passed a law guaranteeing artists a royalty. Artists and their lawyers hope other states will pass similar legislation, or, better still, that the federal government will enact a royalty law.

What does the California law say?

The act provides that whenever a work of fine art is resold and the seller resides in California or the sale takes place in California, the seller must pay the artist 5% of the amount of sale within 90 days. It applies, however, only when the gross resale price (gross resale price includes the commission a dealer will charge the seller to sell it for him) exceeds $1,000 and represents a profit to the seller.

If the artist can't be located within 90 days, the money is deposited in a special fund while the California Arts Council tries to find him. If the attempt fails after seven years, the money is transferred to the California Arts Council.

If the seller doesn't comply with the law, the artist may sue for damages within three years of sale or within one year of discovery of the sale, whichever is longer.

Are there any criticisms of this law?

Yes, and some of them justified. Its attackers rightly point out that, at the moment, there is no way to police the law and that it applies only to a few superstars, not the average artist who could genuinely benefit from a financial shot in the arm. The critics also emphasize that the royalty is based on gross sales price, not on profit, a considerable difference that might make a prospective buyer hesitate to purchase. The constitutionality of the law has also been questioned: can a state law govern transactions that take place outside the state simply because one of the parties is a California resident?

How do the law's proponents answer these charges?

Philosophically, they feel that while it may not be the best of all laws, it's better than nothing, particularly if it will lead to national legislation. Moreover, they think that they will be able to establish some sort of enforcement agency to police the law. Hamish Sandison, executive director of the Bay Area Lawyers for the Arts, and one of the leading supporters of the legislation, maintained:

I still believe that it is important that the bill was enacted by the legislature. I think that you must make artists aware that there is a piece of property out there that can and should be theirs. You have to create the property, in this case the right to a 5% royalty, before artists will feel motivated to insure its enforcement.

What kind of contract will I need to rent artwork?

Most probably, you'll rent through an art rental outlet—usually a museum shop, but possibly a gallery—which gives its borrowers the option to buy. So you'll sign a contract with the outlet, and it in turn will make a deal with the person who plans to rent. Or you might want to rent directly. Either way, the terms of the contract will be pretty much the same.

What kinds of terms should be in the contract?

Most museums have standard rental contracts. But before signing, check to see if the following points are included. Or, if you're planning to rent directly to a client, make sure the following provisions are in your contract:

1. Selling price. This is the price on which rent will be based, and you should set it.

2. Rental fee. This usually hovers around 5% of the sales price per month.

3. Rental period. There is no set time on this, but many museums prefer a two-month period with a one-month renewal.

4. Percentage of the rental going back to you. Bear in mind that you may actually not get any of the rent. Some museums operate on the theory that most rental works are eventually purchased, and the rent they charge just covers handling and shipping. Other museums may deduct handling and shipping fees and remit the balance, leaving you very little.

5. Museum's commission. If the museum sells the rented work, its commission should be about 30%, from which it deducts the rental, because when the customer buys he pays the purchase price minus rental fees.

6. Shipping and insurance. You'll probably be responsible for arranging for these, and you'll probably have to pay the costs to and from your studio to the museum. Be sure, though, that this is spelled out. And if you're renting directly to a client, either one of you can make the arrangements, but the client should pay for the costs.

7. Loss or damage. If the work is lost or damaged in the museum or on the borrower's property, the museum or client should pay. Again, spell it out or you might get stuck.

8. Termination of the agreement. Rental agreements are usually terminated by written notice from either the artist or the museum, which ends the agreement within a short period of time, such as five days from the date of the notice. Should the borrower decide to buy within that period, he may do so.

9. Cleaning and repairing. Your contract should stipulate that your approval on whether a work is to be cleaned or repaired if damaged must be in writing.

10. Copyright protection. Your contract with the museum should have a clause requiring a provision in the museum's agreement with the borrower forbidding any reproduction of your work without your consent. You might also forbid the use of the work for any commercial purposes, such as exhibition in a restaurant.

Can corporations deduct art rentals from their tax?

I've frequently heard artists and dealers try to interest corporate collectors by tempting them with tax deductions on rentals. They claim that the corporation can pay off the purchase price through monthly rental payments that are tax deductible. Unfortunately, this isn't quite so. Rentals are tax deductible only for as long as they remain rentals. If the corporation buys the work, the I.R.S. will reject the previous deductions.

Should I sell work through charitable sales or auctions?

That depends on what sort of commission they plan to take. Prices at charitable auctions or sales rarely equal prices made from studio or gallery sales, so a 50-50 split would probably not make your entry worthwhile. Only when the charity sponsors plan a commission of say 20% to 25% would such a sale make sense.

Should I deal with charities at all?

Everywhere I go, artists complain to me about the constant pressure they are under from charitable organizations to donate artwork for sales or auctions. It's about time artists began to say no to this practice instead of submitting as soon as the sponsor says, "Well, everybody else is giving us something." Remember, you can't deduct the price of an artwork from your income tax—only the cost of the materials that went into it. So while you're giving up income, it's illegal for you, unlike the collector, to compensate for this loss with a substantial tax deduction. If you can afford to be charitable, fine; otherwise, you're losing valuable income.

Before I enter a juried show, what should I look for in a contract?

Since contracts vary, all the terms you might come across which must be checked out before you sign can't be anticipated. But in general, when you read the description of a show and the contract, look for the answers to these questions:

Who is sponsoring the show? An art organization? A museum? An art school? A group of professional fund raisers? Or someone you've never heard of before? Check the credentials of the organization to see if it has sponsored other exhibits and find out about them.

Who are the jurors? Don't accept the promise of a "jury composed of eminent art specialists." This may indicate a tacky, if not downright dishonest, fly-by-night entrepreneur. And if the flyer does name names, check on them in *Who's Who in American Art* (available in most sizable libraries) to see if they are indeed eminent.

How much are the prizes? Make sure a description of the prizes includes a breakdown in amounts for 1st, 2nd, and 3rd prizes in the various mediums. "Many valuable prizes" or "$25,000 in prizes" is too vague and again may suggest the show is less than what it seems.

If purchase prizes are awarded, how much are they? Purchase prizes should correspond to your own sales prices and, at the very least, should not be less than two-thirds of the price you sell for on the retail market.

Is there to be a catalog? Sponsors sometimes charge higher entry fees because they say they plan to publish a catalog. Find out what they mean by a catalog. Not infrequently, catalogs turn out to be nothing more than price lists, hardly justifying a high entry fee.

Will the sponsor charge a commission, and, if so, how much? If the sponsor does charge, a 30% commission is not unreasonable.

What is the entry fee? When deciding whether the entry fee is reasonable, remember that a stiff fee plus a high shipping charge may outweigh the chancey possibilities for sales or prizes.

Who will assume responsibility for the safety of work while at the show and for its return? This is an important consideration. The sponsor *should*—if he won't, don't send your work.

Who will own the reproduction rights on a work that wins a prize? Some sponsors may require that you assign them the copyright on award-winning works. And the time to decide if you want to give up these rights is *before,* not after, you sign the contract.

Is there a prospectus? The larger, well known institutions that sponsor competitions put out prospectuses that detail all the above information—jurors, prizes, and so on. When such information is not forthcoming in the form of a prospectus, check the exhibition yourself if you can, and think carefully before entering.

How many entrants will be chosen? The fewer people chosen, the smaller your chance of being picked and the more likely you'll lose the entry fee and shipping charges. So find out in advance how many entries will be selected for exhibition, and figure out for yourself whether it's going to be worthwhile to enter.

Do some art groups think entry fees for juried shows are morally wrong?

Yes, Artists Equity Association and many other groups argue that entry fees are unreasonable, particularly when the rejection rate is high. And they're right. If 3,000 people enter a big annual or a highly promoted festival, each paying a $10 entry fee, the organizers will gross $30,000. Now suppose they accept only 100 applicants. They just made a profit of $29,000 (minus their expenses, of course).

What should I look for in a contract before I enter a nonjuried outdoor festival?

Many of the same things mentioned above for juried shows. In addition, ask if the grounds are secured at night; how you'll be protected from rain; and how you'll get your location—is it on a first come, first served basis or by assignment. If there is a rental fee involved, weigh the advantages of the possibilities for publicity and sales opportunities against the size of the fee.

4. Commission Agreements

- Proposal
- Budget
- Commissions
- Terms of commission agreements

Back in the fifteenth century, when most art was custom-made, a client and the artist entered into a legal agreement in which the latter committed himself to deliver exactly what the former had requested. The client tolerated no deviation from the drawing he chose for his altarpiece or whatever, and demanded in writing that only certain colors be used to insure the finest quality. Not for him any inferior grades of gold or ultramarine, the most difficult colors to get and apply at that time. These patrons left very little to chance even though they were dealing with the likes of Botticelli and Fra Angelico.

Today, a great deal of art is still made to order. There's a lot of opportunity and money out there for artists to do monumental pieces for public spaces, portraits of public and private citizens, collections of works depicting industry or some other human endeavors, and paintings and drawings for record and book jackets, among other types of regularly commissioned works.

There is also a chance for a lot of satisfaction, too, since sometimes the best part about a commission is that many times it gives you the chance to do something you don't ordinarily have the funds or facilities to do.

Yet, despite both the volume of work and the amounts of money involved, artist/client relationships are generally characterized by looser arrangements than those between such teams as Filippo Lippi and Giovanni di Cosimo de'Medici.

Many modern day contracts consist of a single paragraph that leaves out more about a project than it puts in. As a result, the client has one idea of what's going to happen while the artist has a different idea. And when commissions go sour, it's usually because there wasn't a real meeting of the minds. Once such a meeting of the minds takes place and is written into a contract to the best of everyone's ability, most problems will vanish.

How do I find out what the client needs?

This can be done by some judicious probing during the initial interview. However, analyzing what a client wants a piece of artwork to accomplish isn't always so easy. Even if you've been chosen on the basis of past work, he may have something very definite in mind which he has difficulty communicating to you. Or maybe he has only the foggiest idea of what he needs. In either case, you might ask him a series of questions such as:

What does he need? The client may only know that he needs something large to hang on his lobby walls. You can help him decide whether he wants a large canvas, a mural, a series of smaller paintings, or whatever.

What kind of mood and colors does he need? A bank president may want something warm to take the chill off the coldness and sterility of an impersonal interior. In this case, he probably needs some red or earth tones, not blues or greens. So if you're showing slides of your work, pick two slides that express different moods through varying colors, and ask which he prefers.

Where will the work hang or be installed? If your client wants a portrait of himself, for instance, find out what kind of space he plans to hang it in, since this will affect size and shape. Also ask what other art it will compete with.

What does he want the art to communicate? A bank president may want the artwork to project a feeling of strength, security, progress, or even serenity, but he may not be able to articulate these concepts. Again, you can help him crystalize his thinking through the use of slides that describe these feelings.

Does he want a regional flavor? If it's a company in New Jersey, for example, perhaps an industrial scene would be appropriate.

How do I find out if he will be receptive to my ideas?

You can determine this by tossing out some ideas of your own. For example, "Instead, Mr. President, of a large impersonal abstract design, how about a series of paintings depicting the workings of your industry or a history of the town?" Whether or not he finally accepts the ideas doesn't matter. Just find out at this stage whether or not he's willing to consider them.

What if I don't like his ideas?

Now's the time to back out graciously. I recently heard about a talented abstract artist who was recommended to a record company executive looking for someone to paint a scene for the cover of a recording of Caribbean music. The executive said he wanted a realistic Caribbean cityscape. The artist replied that if that's what he wanted, that's what he would get.

But the painter couldn't deliver. His style was abstract; he wasn't happy working any other way. The preliminary sketches revealed this. Dissatisfied with the results, the executive paid him for his efforts and terminated the relationship, making a mental note never to consider his work again. Had the painter said right away that it wasn't the job for him, the executive might have kept him in mind for future, more appropriate work.

So if you can't perform, say so. If a potential portrait subject wants you to trim 30 pounds off his beefy frame, decide if this is going to go against your esthetic grain before you waste any time on the project.

What else should I ask in the initial interview?

Be sure to ask how much money will be allocated for a commission. If the work is to be included in an overall design budget, the architect or designer usually knows what percentage he wants to spend on artwork. This is particularly true if it's a public building in a geographical area which has passed legislation that demands a certain percentage (usually 1%) of the construction costs be spent on art.

If no such exact information is forthcoming, at least get a rough estimate so you can operate within the right price range. No point slaving over a design for a $15,000 masterpiece when only $10,-000 is available. Give them a design for a $10,000 masterpiece instead.

After the interview, what is the next step?

The first step is submitting a proposal, which usually consists of a visual aid or aids, a written description of the work detailing sizes, shapes, materials, and so on, and a budget. It may also include a résumé of your career, any pertinent publicity, and examples of your work. In other words, it's a package showing what you have done, and, more importantly, what you'd like to do for this project.

What kind of visual aids should I include?

The visual aid might be as simple as a rough sketch for a painting. Or it might be a maquette for a piece of sculpture. If the client wants something more elaborate to give him a more precise idea of what he's getting, a series of drawings showing the relative scale superimposed on photographs of the actual site or a mockup of the site complete with miniature people and trees may be in order.

Do all clients demand a proposal?

Most clients will ask for a proposal, but should this not be the case, it's up to you to take this step to clarify the project. Here's an example that illustrates why this step is so important. Several years ago, I received a letter from a painter who had been commissioned by a midwest company on the basis of previous work to paint 100 watercolors for its executive offices. After agreeing on a fee and signing a contract, he found himself in a head-on confrontation with a number of fussy executives, some rejecting work outright, others demanding revisions, and all driving the poor guy mad. His letter was a cry of help, but it was a little late.

First, he should have offered a proposal based on, perhaps, 10 paintings. Had he tested out his audience's reaction before taking the plunge into a full-scale project, he might have considered one or more of the following alternatives: revising his overall fee upwards to account for the additional time he would have to spend satisfying his group of clients; charging for each and every revision; asking that the number of decision-makers be reduced; or bowing out before an ulcer attack.

A proposal is a must no matter what the project. Even a portrait painter benefits from preliminary sketches. A rough charcoal sketch of a company president might reveal the absence of his beloved pipe, which he feels is part and parcel of his self-image. Better to find that out now, than when the portrait is complete.

How do I estimate the budget for the project?

It all depends on what expenses you plan to pay for (a partial list can be found in the contract in Figure 4). Let's suppose that you opt to pay for the major ones—materials and outside labor. You'd total these costs, add in the costs of your own labor, operating expenses, and selling costs, and then mark the fee up to make a profit.

How do I figure out the cost of materials?

If it's a relatively simple project, like the commission awarded to the watercolorist, you would simply add up the cost of the paper and paint. A more complicated project will demand that you figure out just how many yards of concrete you need, how much scaffolding, how many forms for pouring concrete or whatever are necessary, and multiply by their unit costs. Previous similar projects recorded on the file cards mentioned in Chapter 3 will give you an estimate of prices—but in these inflationary times, recheck them or you may underestimate. And after you have totaled these items, add in an additional 10% of the total for wastage.

How do I figure outside labor expenses?

Again, your file cards will enable you to estimate the approximate number of man-hours necessary to complete the project. But check hourly rates of outside labor, especially if you're dealing with unions, which may have negotiated wage increases for their members.

How do I figure my own labor?

How much your time is worth depends on what you make, or could make, on another job, plus your reputation as an artist (see Chapter 3).

How long it will take you to complete the job will be based on your records and on some preliminary work, which may reveal all sorts of unexpected, time-consuming problems. The watercolorist I mentioned above ordinarily spent three hours on a half-sheet. Had he taken the time to make a preliminary study of the working conditions prior to submitting a proposal, he would have revised his hourly estimate considerably.

How do I calculate overhead and selling costs?

Just as you did in Chapter 3. At this point, however, you might want to give your client a break. If you're selling many works instead of one, you might want to trim your selling costs. Taking the example of the watercolorist once again, he sustained fewer selling costs by making one sale of 100 works than he would have if he had had to sell 100 works individually. Therefore, he would give his client a discount of 5% to 10% of the total fee.

What would my total fee be?

After costs have been covered, to make a minimum 20% profit (see Chapter 3), you would have to raise your fee by at least 25%. So if the project costs $10,000, charge $12,500.

Figure 4. This commission agreement for the design of work was created by northwestern Minnesota artists P. Richard Szeitz and Patricia McGowan Szeitz. They've found it very helpful in clarifying their relations with clients.

COMMISSION AGREEMENT FOR DESIGN OF ARTWORK

The Collector_____ residing at

_____, acknowledges sufficient familiarity

with the style and quality of the work of the Artist_____

residing at _____.
The parties have made and entered into this agreement on this

_____ day of_____,   19 _____.

1. **Description.** The Artist in consideration of the covenants and agreements herein contained, agrees to design _____

_____
(hereinafter "Work") as preparation for its creation by the Artist for an approximate production budget of between $____ and $____

    a. Approximate size of finished Work:

    b. Material & construction:

    c. Scope of the Artist's work:

    d. Collector is responsible for:

2. **Design Agreement.** The receipt of good and valuable consideration of $_____ on this day for the design work to be provided by Artist after signing of this agreement is hereby mutually acknowledged.

    a. Artist agrees to provide reasonable study, sketch or mockette of the Work to the Collector on or about _____ (date). Upon receipt of design, the Collector shall notify Artist within ten (10) days of any proposed changes in design.

b. Artist will provide a maximum of _____ designs or revisions for this Work. Additional designs or revisions shall cost an additional design fee of $_____ per hour.

c. If Collector decides not to proceed with creation of the Work, all designs must be returned to Artist, Artist shall retain the design fee, and this agreement shall be terminated.

d. If Collector determines to proceed with creation of the Work pursuant to a selected design, the WORK OF ART COMMISSION AGREEMENT must be completed and signed by both parties, and the first one-third progress payment will be paid at that time.

3. **Copyright.** It is agreed that all designs are instruments of service and shall remain in the possession of and the property of the Artist, and thereby Artist retains the exclusive right to use and create Works according to the designs. Collector agrees to make no public display or commercial use of the designs, or any copy or facsimile thereof, without the Artist's consent. It is agreed that if consent is granted for commercial use, the Artist shall be entitled to a minimum of ten percent (10%) of any and all consideration paid or exchanged for such commercial use.

IN WITNESS WHEREOF the parties have hereunto set their hands.

By_____
                    Artist

By_____
                    Collector

If I am a portrait painter, isn't there an easier way to arrive at my fee?

Sure. In advance of any commission, you would simply make up a table of prices based on content and size. For example:

	9″ × 12″	18″ × 24″	2′ × 3′	4′ × 6′
Head and shoulders				
Full bust				
Half figure				
Full figure				

And you could make several tables for oils, charcoal, or pastel. But you'll still have to do some preliminary work to make sure problems aren't going to arise that might double or triple your time on the project.

Will I get paid for the proposal?

Sometimes you do get paid, and sometimes you don't. If it's a competition for a commissioned work, you'll know right away. Announcements appear periodically in art magazines and newspapers saying that some organization wants to commission a work. The organization invites artists to enter the competition and states at the outset whether a fee will be included.

If it's not a competition, your client may tell you immediately if he's prepared to pay a fee. But when payment isn't mentioned, it's up to you to decide whether or not to ask for one.

How should I decide to ask for a fee?

A rule of thumb used by Calvin Goodman—West Lost Angeles consultant to artists—in advising his clients on the appropriateness of charging a fee may help you decide. He says that where direct costs for materials and labor for the preliminary work represent over 5% of the total fee, an initial fee is justified; when they run less than 5%, it is not.

Therefore, if your preliminary costs run over $100 on a relatively modest project of about $2,000, ask for payment. On the other hand, the $500 or $600 spent trying to secure a $20,000 commission would not be unreasonable for you to absorb yourself.

How do I charge for preliminary work?

The answer depends on what you're selling—a work of art itself, part of the final commission, or a design that is without value unless the commission is executed—for example, a crude maquette made of impermanent material or rough drawings which you can't sell later.

How do I charge for a separate artwork? Price it as if you were selling an already complete work. For example, suppose you made a maquette of a large-scale sculpture that cost $500 for fabrication costs and the cost of your time. If the piece is a finished work of art which you would sell for $1,000 elsewhere (after you added in overhead and selling costs plus a markup), by all means charge $1,000.

What if it's part of the final commission? If the preliminary work is actually part of the commission, you might charge a percentage of the total fee. In the case of the watercolorist, for example, had he done 10 paintings preliminary to the 100-work commission, he would have been justified in charging 10% of the commission fee.

What if it's only a rough model or drawing? When the design work is not artwork or part of the project, your fee should be based on the cost of your time spent researching the project, thinking about it, and executing the model or design.

Will this initial fee be included in the total project fee?

Most likely the preliminary fee will be included in the total cost of the project if you are awarded the commission unless it is a separate piece of artwork. But, and this is an important but, make sure that your agreement states that if the client decides not to go ahead with the project, you keep the preliminary fee.

Can the client use my preliminary work as the basis for future work?

If the client does not give you the commission, he cannot use your preliminary work as a basis for future work even if he pays for it. By law, the creator retains the reproduction rights and the right to make derivative works (works based on the original work) from it. But don't expect your client to know the terms of the Copyright Law. Get the issue clarified right away. Then, when you sell the design, place a copyright notice on the piece and mark on the sales invoice that all rights are reserved to you, the copyright owner.

Should a contract accompany the proposal?

Yes. A simple letter will suffice, stating what's being sold (the design, model or whatever), for how much, that you will copyright the work, and that you will retain the fee in the event that you don't get the commission. Or you could use a more formal document such as the design contract shown in Figure 5.

Will my dealer expect a commission when I am asked to create a work of art?

He certainly will if he did the work to get it for you. And even if you got the commission yourself, he may still ask for his fee, reasoning that the work he put into developing your reputation and visability enabled you to get the job. Many dealers, however, don't require the same fee they collect for work sold on consignment (see Chapter 5).

In any case, sort out with your dealer in advance of any such projects what he is to get or not get when you're commissioned to do artwork. Of course, when you work with several casual dealers where you leave art on consignment from time to time, you won't owe any of them anything except the one who actually helps you to get the commission. And if your gallery or anyone else charges a commission, make sure you adjust your fee to accommodate it and not let it bite into your profit.

Who else might expect a commission?

If you're awarded a contract to create a work of art, interior designers and art consultants may expect a commission. If an interior designer comes to your studio or gallery, and, after looking at your work, recommends you to his client, he will expect one.

The same holds true of art consultants. Art consultants are individuals who make a living by searching for works of art for corporations. These people also recommend artists for special projects.

How much will interior designers and art consultants expect? Some expect nothing if their clients are paying them a fee for the project. Others, not being paid by their clients but earning a living by working on commmssions, may charge from 10% to 40% of the total project fee, depending on the selling effort made on your behalf and whether or not they have to split their fee with your gallery. If the latter is true, 10% to 20% of the total commission project fee will probably go to the designer or consultant. So if your dealer's usual commission is 50%, the designer might receive 15% and the dealer 35%.

Of course, there are always designers and consultants who take from both ends, charging a commission while on the client's payroll. This is considered somewhat unethical, but it's a rather common practice.

Do galleries always split the commission with designers and consultants?

No, occasionally you'll run into a dealer who expects you to pay him his full fee plus that of the designer or consultant, leaving you with very little.

Do architects charge commissions?

Although architects frequently perform the same role as interior designers or art consultants, they shouldn't charge a fee if they recommend your work to their clients. The leaders of the architectural profession consider this an unethical practice.

What should go into an agreement for a commissioned work of art?

Clauses describing the following should go into such an agreement: the scope of work; obligations and duties of artist and client; fee and schedule of payments; cancellation, cancellation fee, and a release if work is rejected; ownership of copyright; reserved rights; starting and completion dates; delivery of work; death and disability; and arbitration.

All of these are mentioned in Howard Thorkelson's, "Commission Agreement between Artist and Client" (see Figure 5). Many of them should be included in any standard contract; your project, however, may entail other situations that should be covered in an agreement, and some of these will be mentioned below.

What is the scope of work?

The approximate dimensions of the piece and the mediums and materials used. The physical, as opposed to the creative, aspects of the work come into play here.

What will a clause about duties and obligations say?

It will spell out who's responsible for what, particularly with respect to who is to arrange and pay for certain materials and services. A number of these obligations are listed in Clause 3 of Figure 5. You should supplement this list with others that are pertinent to your project or eliminate those that are unnecessary.

Figure 5. This contract was drafted by Howard Thorkelson, former editor of Art and The Law, *the publication of the Volunteer Lawyers for the Arts. It isn't meant as the end-all in commission contracts; it's merely a guide to help you think out what you should put in your contract.*

COMMISSION AGREEMENT BETWEEN ARTIST AND CLIENT

1. **Agreement.** This is an agreement between

Name_____ Address_____
(hereinafter referred to as the "client") and

Name_____ Address_____
(hereinafter referred to as the "artist") for the creation and transfer of the work. All rights and liabilities of either party in the work shall be governed by this agreement.

2. **Description of the work.** The work, to be created by the artist, shall be (a portrait, a mural, or whatever . . .) (. . . of the approximate dimensions of . . .) (. . . in medium or materials).

3. **Obligations of the artist and client.**
   a) The artist/client shall designate and purchase materials necessary for the creation of the work.
   b) The client shall bear the expense of any transportation or living costs incurred by the artist away from his home or studio, long-distance telephone calls or telegrams, sales taxes, or customs duties, insofar as such expenses are reasonably incident to, or entailed by, the artist's creation, delivery or installation of the work (or supervision thereof).
   c) The artist shall create the work.
   d) The artist/client shall provide for the framing and installation of the work, at the artist/client's expense, subject to the artist's right to supervise any such work.
   e) Artist/client shall hire and compensate any additional labor services necessary for the creation and installation of the work.
   f) The artist/client shall secure any building permits necessary for the lawful creation and execution of the work.
   g) The artist/client shall hire and compensate any consulting engineering services necessary to the creation and installation of the work.
   h) The artist/client shall obtain (fire, casualty, and personal injury liability) insurance on the work to be in effect until the (delivery) (completion of installation).

i) The artist/client shall provide for the workmen's compensation coverage for any employees of the artist during the creation or installation of the work.

j) The client shall bear the rental expense of any new and additional work space necessary for the artist's creation or installation of the work.

4. **Start and completion dates.** The artist shall undertake the creation of the work on approximately _____ and shall complete the work by _____.

5. **Fees and schedule of payment.** The client shall pay to the artist the sum of $_____ in total payment for the work. This amount shall be paid in equal one-fourth installments as follows: $_____ upon the execution of this agreement (or the start-up date, if later); $_____ on _____; $_____ on _____; and $_____ on _____ (completion date).

6. **Cancellation and cancellation fee.** The client shall not unreasonably withhold acceptance of or payment for the work. If prior to the work's completion, the client observes or otherwise becomes aware of any fault or defect in the work or noncomformance with the design plan, he shall notify the artist promptly. However, the client's objection to any feature of the work (not specifically indicated by the design plan but) attributable to the exercise of the artist's esthetic judgment in the creation of the work on the basis of the design plan shall not justify the client's withholding acceptance of or payment for the work. In the event that the client (unreasonably) rejects the work after having made one or two installment payments, the artist shall be entitled to keep any monies so paid. In the event that the client rejects the work after three installment payments and before the completion date, the artist shall be entitled to be paid such additional sums as will raise the total amount of payments for the work to 85% of the amount of the entire fee. Notwithstanding the rejection of the work and the payment of any cancellation fee, all rights in the work shall vest in the artist, who shall be entitled to complete it, without regard to the design plan, and to make appropriate identification of the subject matter in connection with any display or exhibition of the work. In the

event that the client fails to pay the fee or any portion thereof for thirty days following the relevant date specified in the schedule of payments, the artist may terminate this agreement and, thereby, have the right to keep all amounts theretofore paid and to collect any amounts then due.

7. **Copyright.** The artist shall copyright the work in his own name (and such rights shall not be affected by the transfer of the work itself) (but the artist shall assign all such rights to the client effective with the transfer of the work itself).

8. **Exploitation of the work.** Notwithstanding the assignment of any copyrights to the client, the artist shall retain certain rights relating to the use and maintenance of the work. The artist shall be entitled to reasonable advance notice of any temporary public exhibition or display of the work so that he may advise on the physical circumstances and esthetic manner of its exhibition or display. In connection with any proposed commercial exploitation of the work, the artist shall be entitled to advance notification so that he may authorize or deny identification of himself as the artist and, in the case of proposed photographic reproduction, may veto it. In the case of any noncommercial or authorized commercial use or published writing or publicity featuring the work, the artist shall be entitled to customary and appropriate identification as the creator of the work. Upon giving reasonable advance notice to the client, and at his own expense, the artist shall be entitled to borrow the work, for (a) period(s) not to exceed _____ weeks cumulatively in any continuous _____-year period, for the purpose of public exhibition; and the client shall be entitled to customary and appropriate identification as the owner.

9. **Maintenance of the work.** The client shall notify the artist promptly in the event of the need for any maintenance or restoration services so that the artist may have a reasonable opportunity either to perform such work himself or to supervise or consult in its performance. The artist shall be reasonably compensated by the client for all such maintenance or restoration services. In the absence of any need for restoration or maintenance, the work shall remain free of alteration by the client, who shall take reasonable precautions to protect it against damage or destruction by external forces. (In the event of possible alteration or destruction of the work due to proposed renovation or demolition of a structure to which the work is affixed, the artist shall be entitled to notification, by the client, affording the artist a reasonable opportunity to reclaim the work by removing it whole at his own expense).

10. **Warranty.** The artist warrants that the completed work will be fit and suitable for use and exploitation in the manner (and to the extent/and for the duration) for which it is to be created, but this warranty is conditioned upon the client's compliance with the provisions hereof relating to installation, maintenance and exploitation.

11. **Delivery.** The artist shall prepare the work to be ready for delivery to the client on _____. Delivery and physical transfer of the work shall be accomplished (by the artist's notification to the client that the work is ready for pick-up at the artist's studio) (by the artist's causing the work to be sent, insured and shipping charges prepaid, to the client).

12. **Title of ownership.** Title of ownership in the work shall pass from the artist to the client upon the client's payment of the fourth installment of the artist's fee for the work.

13. **Death and disability.** In the event of an incapacitating illness or injury of the artist and a delay arising therefrom in the execution of the work, the artist shall notify the client of such delay and the client's obligation to make payments shall cease until such time as the artist notifies the client he has recovered and is ready to thereupon resume. The death of the artist shall terminate this agreement, and the artist's estate shall be entitled to retain any payments already made by the client and to be reimbursed for which the client would have been obliged to pay the artist; the client shall be entitled to claim the work and any unused materials acquired for its execution (and to have the work completed by another artist without regard to the original design).

14. **Other delay.** If the execution of the work is delayed by the act or neglect of the client, by labor disputes, fire, unusual transportation delays, or by other external forces or natural calamities outside the artist's control, the artist shall be entitled to extend the completion date, by notification to the client, by the time equivalent to the period of such delay.

15. **Arbitration.** Any dispute hereunder between the parties (not involving money claims by either party in excess of $_____) shall be resolved by resort to arbitration (in accordance with the standards and procedures of the American Arbitration Association).

16. **Construction.** Construction of this agreement shall be governed by the laws of the state of _____.

Who pays for materials and labor?

In many cases, it might seem more advantageous for the client to assume the responsibility. Otherwise, you might find yourself staying up nights paying bills and keeping accounts. On the other hand, to avoid any disputes over the quality of labor and materials, it might be wise to arrange and pay for them yourself.

Can I protect myself against inflation if I pay for materials and labor?

When the project looks as though it will take a long time, you can protect yourself in three ways—first, by carefully assessing the costs of each and every possible expense so your initial estimate will be accurate. Second, by including the 10% allowance for wastage mentioned above in the budget. And third, by making the contract good only for a certain length of time—perhaps 90 to 120 days—after which the contract would have to be renegotiated.

Who pays for expenses other than materials and labor?

Again, that's up to you and your client. The client will probably pay for such items as public liability insurance (see Chapter 11), for example, but you may decide to pay for travel expenses. The point is that to avoid misunderstandings each and every expense should be spelled out. Both you and the client must know not only what he's paying for, but what he's not paying for.

And finally, if your client picks up the tab for expenses you've incurred, he'll expect you to keep accurate, accessible records.

If I don't pay for the framing or installation, can I control them?

The effectiveness of any artwork can be destroyed by shoddy installation or a cheap framing job. So make sure your contract contains a clause stating that you are to be consulted on or supervise installation or framing.

How do I provide for the size of the project changing?

With a price revision clause. This is a clause in your contract dealing with compensation for increases and decreases in the scope of work on a square foot or hourly basis. To take an example, suppose before signing a $7,500 contract for the execution of a 75-foot mural, you were wise enough to insert a clause saying that payment was to be based on a $100 per square foot charge and total payment would depend on final size. Then, if the 75-foot mural grows to 85 feet, you can raise your fee by $1,000.

What do you mean by a schedule of payments?

A schedule of payments is a clause in your contract indicating when a series of payments are to be made. In other words, as soon as the agreement is signed, you should receive your first payment (which might also include the fee for your preliminary work). If you plan to pay for labor and materials, this payment should be sufficient to enable you to start buying materials and hiring labor. Thereafter, your fee might be paid in periodic installments or at various stages in the creative process (perhaps as every third is complete).

Proof of the work's progress can be ascertained by a visit by your client to your studio or wherever the work is being made. If this is impossible, however, you could take photographs to show its status.

Your client, if he's smart, will withhold 10% of the total fee until installation is finished and he's totally satisfied. So if you are awarded a $10,000 commission, you might ask for $1,000 to begin, two interim payments of $3,000, and a third of $2,000 with your client holding back $1,000 until the project is cleaned up.

Why is a schedule of payments important?

Each payment indicates approval or satisfaction and gives the go-ahead to the next phase. More important is its negative aspect—since each payment is an advance payment for the next work period, your agreement should state that if the client withdraws at any stage, you'll retain all payments received up to that point.

A schedule of payments is warranted even for a small commission, such as a portrait. You might ask for a payment when the preliminary sketch is approved, when the preliminary blocking-in is finished, and then when the portrait is complete.

What if my client won't agree to a schedule of payments?

If for some reason—usually because you're just not in a strong enough bargaining position—you can't force progressive payments out of the client, the contract should stipulate that he approve the work at various stages by initialing it (for example, "approved 9/1/77, B.D."). These okays are evidence that the client was happy up to a certain point in case he reneges on payment. In other words, suppose your client rejects your finished portrait of him, claiming it doesn't satisfy him, and he refuses to pay your agreed upon $1,000 fee. If you take him to court, these initialed and dated approvals indicating that he was satisfied for a while would probably persuade the court to award you a percentage of the fee.

Can I prevent a client from cancelling a commission?

No, if the client is dissatisfied, you can only hope to cut your losses. Commissions for artwork are one instance of the customer being just about always right. Case after court case has ruled that when a contract states that payment depends on the client's satisfaction—no matter how many artists, curators, or critics would testify to the satisfactoriness of a work—it is up to the client alone to decide this.

Of course, you could try to prove that his dissatisfaction is fake —that the real reason why he rejected the portrait you painted of his wife was that he was getting ready to divorce her. But convincing the court of his state of mind would be very tricky.

But don't let this discourage you. You can do a pretty good job of protecting yourself with a schedule of payments, a cancellation penalty, and a clause reserving the right to sell the rejected work, all described below.

Can a client cancel a project because I deviate from the original design?

Yes, but only if this is a term in the contract. Some clients won't allow any deviation from an initial concept, but others will. If your client agrees that you need a certain amount of latitude in your creative activity, get this agreement in the contract. You might word the clause in the terms Thorkelson used in Clause 6 of his commission agreement. He says that "the client's objection to any feature of the work (not specifically indicated by the design plan, but) attributable to the exercise of the artist's esthetic judgment on the basis of the design plan shall not be a basis for withholding acceptance of or payment for the work."

Spelling out artistic freedom or defining the fine line between an acceptable and unacceptable deviation, however, isn't as easy as outlining the scope of work or duties and obligations in a contract. So use your common sense. Major changes will be rejected by all but the most lenient of clients.

What if a client refuses to pay for work permanently attached to his property?

If he does nothing to remove it after rejection, you can sue him under the doctrine of unjust enrichment (see Chapter 1)—no one can enrich himself unjustly at someone else's expense.

But if he attempts to get rid of the offending piece, he not only won't have to pay your full fee, but you may end up paying him. Suppose, for example, you painted a mural on his wall. If he doesn't like it and gets a housepainter to paint it out, he can sue you for damages and perhaps force you to pay the fee.

Can I protect myself against the client suing me for damages?

Yes. Any time you create a work that will be permanently attached to property, such as a mural on a wall or a large-scale sculpture in a permanent installation, ask that your contract include a clause saying that you won't have to pay damages to have the piece removed if the client is dissatisfied.

What is a cancellation penalty?

A cancellation penalty insures you a percentage of the total fee even if the client rejects the completed work. Such a clause should state that if the work is rejected, the client will still have to pay you a substantial amount, say 85% of the total fee. Going back to the example of the $10,000 commission, suppose you receive the initial payment and the two interim payments for a total of $7,000. Then, on completion, the client rejects the work. If your contract contained a cancellation penalty of 85% of the total fee, you'd still be entitled to another $1,500.

Why should I have a clause that allows me to sell a rejected work?

If a commissioned work is rejected, you'll naturally want to sell it to someone else if you can. And usually this won't be a problem— if your client doesn't want the work, he's not going to object to your selling it to someone else.

But the portrait artist should take note—selling or exhibiting the rejected work might invade the subject's right to privacy, particularly if he's someone famous. So get a release in writing before —not after—rejection, when chances are he's not going to feel too kindly toward you. The release should be included in the contract and would read something like this: "If the client is dissatisfied and rejects the final work, the client waives all rights in the work and consents to its sale or exhibition by the artist."

Is there anything else I should do to protect myself?

Yes, make sure you have a title of ownership clause stating that the client can't become the owner of the work until all payments have been made. A contract with a title of ownership clause will also serve notice on creditors if the client goes bankrupt that you —not he—are the owner if the work isn't completely paid for.

What reserved rights can I ask for?

Any of the reserved rights discussed in Chapter 3. The most important of these is the right to maintain the integrity of a work. Alterations, for example, can be prevented by a clause like this: "The client may not alter the work in any way without permission of the artist." Or to prevent total destruction, which could occur if the building containing the work was to be torn down or renovated, you might insert a clause reserving the right to remove the work at your own expense. See how other rights are handled by Thorkelson in Clause 9 of his contract.

Can I insist on the right to exhibit my work? You can't *insist* on anything, but you *can* bargain for it. Ask your client for the right to exhibit the work for certain periods of time. Two months out of five years is considered a reasonable amount of time to borrow a work for exhibition.

How do I arrange for ongoing maintenance? You can do this by inserting a clause requiring continued maintenance, and, if possible, designating you as supervisor of it.

You might also withhold your warranty guaranteeing the durability of the piece if it's not properly maintained. In other words, it isn't reasonable to guarantee a piece if your client isn't going to take proper care of it—if he, for instance, places a fragile piece of sculpture meant to be displayed indoors outdoors, exposing it to the elements.

At the same time, you might suggest a yearly maintenance contract, offering for a fee to take care of necessary repairs or whatever to keep the work from deteriorating.

Is it important to demand proper credit in publicity material? Certainly. If an article appeared in the media about your work but failed to credit you as the artist, you'd probably be very upset. But what can you do if a credit clause isn't in your contract. Ask for a clause saying that any publicity material dispensed by the client must give you proper credit. Bear in mind, however, that when the media gets hold of the material, that's the end of any control the client has over it. So you might still open up the newspaper and see a picture of your work without your name attached.

Should starting and completion dates be in the contract?

Yes, approximate dates are essential to the well-made contract.

What happens if I am late meeting the deadline?

A few clients may demand a penalty clause for lateness; most won't. In fact, if you bring the project in more or less on time, chances are nothing will happen. Nevertheless, you should protect yourself in the contract with provisions covering sickness or injury and other events over which you have no control.

What should I say about sickness or injury in a contract? Read Clause 13 in Figure 5. Thorkelson advises bargaining for a clause stating that once the client has been notified of your disability, he'll extend the deadline by the amount of time it takes you to recover. He, of course, will be given the right to suspend payments until you resume work.

What should I say about an event that is out of my control that holds the project up? Once again, you should ask for a time extension equivalent to the delay. A clause like this might read:

If the artist is delayed at any time in the progress of the work by the act or neglect of the client or by changes ordered in the work or by labor disputes, fire, unusual transportation delays, strikes, unavoidable catastrophes or casualties, the client will extend to the artist the time equivalent to the time lost by reason of any of these circumstances.

What if I don't complete the work at all?

Most likely the client will insist on a clause stating that after a certain length of time—say 60 days after the promised completion date—if the project has not been finished, you'll have to return all payments you received. However, you might try to modify the harshness of this clause to read that, if failure to complete the project is caused by permanent disability, you won't have to return payments received up until the time of disability.

What if I die before the project is completed?

Although death terminates the contract, your efforts up until that time should be compensated. So a provision should be included in the contract similar to the one in Clause 13 of Figure 5. It provides for your estate to retain all payments paid to you and to be entitled to any repayment of any expenses incurred that the client would have been obliged to pay.

What if the client dies before the project is completed?

The contract should provide for this eventuality as well by stating that you're to keep all fees already received and collect from his estate any others due you for expenses.

What if the client doesn't pay me on time?

If he's a few days overdue in making payments according to the schedule, it will be to your advantage to bear with him. But if he's very late, you may want to terminate the contract. In this case the agreement might say:

If the client does not pay the artist within 30 days of the dates described in the schedule of payments, the artist shall have the right to terminate the contract, in which case, the artist shall be entitled to retain all amounts received prior to termination and collect any sums still due.

What is arbitration?

If any dispute over the project should arise, such as if the client does not repay you for expenses, you can settle it in one of two ways: either by taking him to court or by arbitration. Arbitration means that a neutral third party imposes a decision that is binding on both parties.

Where do I find arbitrators?

Neutral third parties are available from the American Arbitration Association in over 1,300 cities in the United States. To locate one in your area, write the association at 140 West 51 Street, New York, New York 10020.

What are the advantages and disadvantages of arbitration?

Arbitration is less expensive and quicker than formal litigation. But it's binding on the parties, so if you think you received an unfair decision from the arbitrator, you cannot appeal it in any court of law.

How is arbitration written into a contract?

Clause 15 of Thorkelson's contract in Figure 5 illustrates how arbitration is written into a contract. But consider this clause carefully—if you think you'd rather sue than arbitrate a controversy or claim arising from your commission agreement, don't put this clause in. If you do and then try to sue, your dealer will claim you're breaching the contract.

5. The Artist and His Dealer

· Definition of dealer
· Vanity galleries
· Advances and stipends
· Outright purchases
· Consignment sales
· Terms of consignment agreements

Stories about the terrible deals artists get from their dealers get a lot of press. No one hears much about the honest, fair-minded, even generous, business arrangements that unite the majority of artists and their dealers. But there's no denying that some artists do get skinned: a dealer goes bankrupt and disappears, leaving the artist holding neither his work nor the money for it; a gallery cancels a promised exhibition an artist has invested time and money in while turning down other offers.

Less dramatic but certainly equally frustrating are the following examples.

A painter in Utah told me how he had been locked into a three-year exclusive contract with no termination clause with a gallery in Salt Lake City. The dealer refused requests from out-of-state galleries interested in showing the painter's work, effectively stunting the growth of his reputation throughout the West during this period.

And a painter from Ohio, after sending a number of paintings to a New York gallery he knew very little about, heard nothing from them for two years until a check arrived for the sale of two works. Neither the check nor subsequent inquiries revealed how much the individual works sold for, who bought them, or the status of the other paintings.

These situations and others of a similar nature could have been avoided if the artist had known at the outset what he was getting into. Parties to the best artist-dealer relationships, like those in the best marriages, suffer no delusions about what to expect from each other.

The object of this chapter is to alert you to the terms you should clarify with a dealer before entering into a deal with him. Of course, a number of them won't be relevant to your particular situation—who's responsible for shipping costs won't mean much if your gallery is within easy reach by car; insurance will be less important if you use a private dealer who doesn't have a gallery in which to show and store work. But you can pick and choose those terms that are most important to you, and then try to hammer out the most favorable agreement you can in relation to these terms.

Obviously, the bigger your star, the better your bargaining power. And it's important to assess just how much clout you do have, a step many artists fail to take. All too often I hear of totally unknown artists—with no selling or critical records—making outrageous demands, or, conversely, recognized artists failing to negotiate the kinds of deals they could easily demand.

How do you define the term "dealer"?

Anyone who sells fine art, except auctioneers. Included in the definition are people who run both large galleries and small frame shops, as well as those who operate without public sales facilities but rather sell from their houses or apartments. The latter are sometimes referred to as private dealers, artists' agents, or art consultants. Whatever title they go by, if they take work on consignment from you or buy it, they're dealers, though there is a distinction between retail and wholesale dealers.

What's the difference between a retail and a wholesale dealer?

Ten years ago, almost all dealers were retailers. In other words, they sold to the collector, the person who bought artwork for display in his own home or office. The increasing demand for art, however, has changed the nature of the art market, resulting in a proliferation of wholesalers: businesses that buy art outright to sell to the trade—retail galleries, interior designers, architects, department stores, and so on.

How can I check on the reliability of a dealer?

The Better Business Bureau, the Chamber of Commerce, curators of local museums, and art groups—such as local chapters of Artists Equity Association—are possible sources of information. Another way is to ask the dealer in question for a list of the artists he handles and contact some of them. Find out if they're pleased with the financial arrangements, if they're supplied with details of each sale, and if they receive prompt payment.

If you're unable to get any information on a dealer who approaches you about the possibility of representing your work, don't take the chance on trusting work to him. And if it's a vanity gallery, think long and hard before agreeing to a show.

What are vanity galleries?

Galleries that invite you to mount a one-person show in return for which you pay all or almost all expenses. In other words, you rent the gallery to put on the show.

Would I want to show at a vanity gallery?

Occasionally, vanity galleries perform useful functions in nonmetropolitan areas. But exhibiting in a gallery in a major city that every knowledgeable person in the art world knows is a vanity gallery is not going to bring you fame or glory. In fact, if you have any reputation at all, it will be rendered somewhat suspect by an exhibition at a vanity gallery.

Are vanity galleries reputable?

Many are perfectly honorable in their dealings, but others are not. In fact, you might get royally taken. A not untypical case goes like this:

A gallery in New York City calls or writes, inviting you to show at its prestigious address on Madison Avenue. It promises to handle the details—placing ads, sending out invitations, providing the champagne and hors d'oeuvres, and so on—in return for a 10% commission on sales. All you have to do is put up $300. And these galleries don't ask just anyone—if they've done their homework properly, you're probably the wife of a successful doctor or lawyer on Long Island or Westchester County.

And then comes the kicker. Sometime after the invitations have been mailed and all your friends and your husband's business associates have announced plans to attend the opening comes another call or letter from the gallery, this time asking for the other $2,700 they need to pay expenses.

So you're left with the choice of recalling the invitations and retreating in embarrassment, or paying up.

Does a dealer ever support struggling artists?

Yes, but with decreasing frequency. It's a risky business, and these days few dealers can afford to gamble on the future success of a favorite artist. Nevertheless, some dealers will support artists during their early years either by paying them an annual stipend or by giving them money advances against the time when they can generate more sales. Stipends and advances sound highly desirable from an artist's point of view, but they should be carefully considered before acceptance—they can destroy a good business relationship.

What's wrong with advances and stipends?

There's nothing wrong with advances or stipends themselves; it's how they are to be repaid that can be a problem. Will the dealer want cash or will he want some of your work? If you're not selling well and he wants cash, how will you be able to repay him? If sales are strong and he opts for work, will he demand the cream of the crop? And if so, how many will he think are justified? These prickly problems can sour an otherwise successful relationship.

In addition, repayment may not be the only thorn in your side. Your dealer may try to influence your stylistic and esthetic development. If, for example, your lyrical landscapes are starting to sell well, he might not be pleased to see you change directions and embark on something that may not be as salable.

What sort of business arrangements do dealers offer?

Two general types, and combinations of them. You can sell work outright to a dealer who acts as a retailer or a wholesaler, or you can consign work to a retail dealer. Wholesalers almost never get involved in consignment sales. In a consignment arrangement, described in more detail below, you retain ownership of the work until the dealer sells it for you.

If he buys work, how much will he pay?

It's impossible to generalize. A retailer buying one or two works might pay you the same amount you would get from a consignment sale—the retail selling price minus the dealers' commission. For example, suppose your work sells through retail galleries for $500 and dealers in the area usually take a 40% commission, leaving $300. A dealer buying one work might also offer you the $300. But if he buys a number of pieces, an additional 10% to 15% on top of the 40% would not be out of order.

A wholesaler's discount will be far greater and with good reason. Look at the economics of it. He must buy cheaply so he can resell at a profit, and, at the same time, allow the retailer to do the same. This means that he will probably buy your work for half (or a little more or less) of what he plans to sell it to the retailer for so the retailer can buy the work at half (or a little more or less) of what he plans to sell it for in his gallery. So if you sell a work to a wholesaler at $100, he may sell it to the retailer for $200, and the retailer may charge his customer $400. In other words, each person who buys the work just about doubles his price.

This may seem outrageous to you, but it's a perfectly acceptable fact of life in any merchandising business.

What are the benefits of direct purchase?

Immediate cash is the greatest benefit. Emotional gratification isn't too far behind.

What are the disadvantages of outright sales?

If you sell a work cheaply and the dealer can sell it for more than you anticipated, you won't benefit from the increase in value.

What would I include in an outright purchase arrangement?

You and the dealer would spell out how much work he is to purchase. For example, he may want: (1) to buy all of your work, in which case—if you agree—you must sell him everything you produce; (2) to purchase a specific portion; (3) to have first refusal rights (in this instance the agreement should state that you may sell work he rejects to anyone you like); or (4) to buy only occasional works.

Other terms would be similar to those included in the sales agreement explained in Chapter 3 concerning, for instance, copyright, delivery dates, and payments.

When I consign work, how is the dealer compensated?

He is compensated in one of two ways: either profit earned over the net price or a percentage of the sales price, which is the more common method.

What is a net price?

An agreed upon amount which you'll be paid no matter what the work sells for. For example, you might say to your dealer, "I want $700 for this work. You can sell it at whatever price you want as long as I get my $700." Under this method, you would probably determine what you think is a fair net price by first figuring what your work should retail for and then deducting the going commission in your area from the retail sales price. For instance, if you think certain works of similar size will sell for $1,000 and that most dealers in your area are charging a 40% commission, you would ask for a net price of $600.

What are the risks involved in the net price system?

Obviously, if your dealer is able to charge more than you expected, he—not you—will make more profit. Less obviously, if your dealer thinks he might have to lower prices to sell your work, he'll be less interested in selling them at all.

If I have several dealers, should I use the net price system?

No. Since the dealer, not you, sets the prices, chances are prices will vary—and they'll vary a lot. (The same thing will occur if you make outright sales to a number of dealers.) It isn't difficult to imagine the ensuing chaos. Dissatisfied clients will soon demand to know why work sells for more in one gallery than in another in a different city. They'll also wonder what its real value is.

What exactly does the term "consignment" mean?

When you consign work to a dealer, you set up an agency relationship with him. Under the law, as an agent, he must take care of your work and pay for any loss or damage suffered while work is in his possession if he hasn't exercised reasonable care to protect it. In other words, if work is stolen from an unattended, unlocked gallery, the dealer would have to repay you for the work.

Consignment also means that while your dealer has the power to sell your work, you own it until you have been paid in full for it.

Now this sounds good, but in actuality, a dealer-agency relationship is fraught with a certain amount of danger. If the dealer goes bankrupt, consigned work may be seized to satisfy the claims of his creditors.

How can I prevent my work from being seized by creditors?

It's difficult unless you live in New York or California (see below for what happens in these two states). About the only recourse you have is to fill out UCC Form No. 1 (see Figure 6), which guarantees your rights to your work under the Code.

What does a UCC Form No. 1 do?

It prevents consigned work from being subject to the claims of creditors. In essence, it allows you to place a lien against the work. This means you have first claim on it and will get it back if and when creditors descend on the dealer.

What's wrong with filing this form?

It's a cumbersome procedure, and one which most dealers are reluctant to agree to. When you file a UCC Form No. 1, your dealer cannot sell the work until the lien is removed by you. This means he's got to contact you and you have to remove the lien on the work in writing, a process not designed to expedite sales. Nevertheless, if you consign a number of works each worth hundreds of dollars, you can't risk not asking your dealer to allow you to file a UCC form on the work.

*Figure 6. The Uniform Commercial Code form shown
below should be filled out if you're consigning work of
considerable value to a gallery. If you don't and the gallery
goes bankrupt, your work may be seized by creditors unless
you live in New York or California. Legislation in these
two states prevents seizure of artwork by creditors.*

```
STANDARD FORM - FORM UCC-1.
UNIFORM COMMERCIAL CODE – FINANCING STATEMENT – FORM UCC-1
                     JULIUS BLUMBERG, INC., 80 EXCHANGE PL., NYC. 10004  212-431-5000
              IMPORTANT — Read instructions on back before filling out form

This FINANCING STATEMENT is presented to a filing office for filing pursuant to the Uniform Commercial Code:  3. Maturity date (if any):
1. Debtor(s) (Last Name First) and address(es)   2. Secured Party(ies) and address(es)   For Filing Officer (Date, Time, Number,
                                                                                         and Filing Office)

4. This financing statement covers the following types (or items) of property:

                                                                                         5. Assignee(s) of Secured Party and
                                                                                            Address(es)

This statement is filed without the debtor's signature to perfect a security interest in collateral.   (check [X] if so)
   ☐ already subject to a security interest in another jurisdiction when it was brought into this state.
   ☐ which is proceeds of the original collateral described above in which a security interest was perfected:
Check [X] if covered: ☐ Proceeds of Collateral are also covered. ☐ Products of Collateral are also covered. No. of additional Sheets presented:
Filed with:


By: _____        By: _____
        Signature(s) of Debtor(s)                    Signature(s) of Secured Party(ies)
(1) Filing Officer Copy – Alphabetical    STANDARD FORM - FORM UCC-1.    (FOR USE IN MOST STATES)
```

Where do I get and file this form?

Most legal stationery stores carry them or can get them for you.
To file the form, check with either your County Clerk's office or
the Secretary of State for the proper procedure; they'll tell you
where to file the form and how much it will cost to file—usually a
few dollars.

Why is it unnecessary to file this in New York or California?

These two states have enacted laws automatically guaranteeing
the rights the filed form provides, so you don't have to worry
about work being claimed by creditors. The California law goes
even further in protecting the artist in artist-dealer relationships.

How does the California law protect artists?

The law provides that: (1) when work is purchased from a dealer, the artist must receive his share of the purchase price *before* the dealer, in case it is not paid for all at once; (2) if the dealer misappropriates either the work or the money from its sale, he may be prosecuted for embezzlement; and (3) the dealer is responsible for loss or damage of work in his possession whether he is negligent or not, meaning that even if he locked all the doors and took all possible precautions against theft, he must pay you for any work that is stolen.

What other legal rights do I have when I consign work?

Under contractual law, you have the right to be paid. Your offer of the work and the dealer's acceptance represents a valid oral contract. When the work sells, it is implicitly understood that he must pay you the purchase price, minus his commission, and you can sue him if he doesn't. But that's all you can expect under this minimal type of contract.

What sort of contract should I have with my dealer?

You should have a clearly worded written document that spells out all the terms, such as insurance and exhibitions, that are relevant to your arrangement with him.

Do I need a contract to consign only a few works?

Yes, but if you occasionally consign a few works to a dealer or dealers, none of whom promises you an exhibition or any long-term arrangements, you could use the simple form of consignment contract shown in Figure 7.

What would be the format of a more complicated agreement?

In most cases, this will depend on your status. A big reputation demands protection from a good lawyer, who, to earn his fee, will probably set forth the terms in a multitude of clauses starting with "herewiths" and "wherefors."

If you're less established or unknown and don't have a lawyer, you can use one of the model contracts shown in this chapter (see Figures 8 and 9). Rather than adopt one of these verbatim, however, a wiser choice would be to adapt one to your particular needs by eliminating some clauses and modifying others.

For example, Clause 11 of the Bay Area Lawyers for the Arts (BALA) "Artist-Gallery Agreement" (Figure 9) states that, "The division of financial responsibility for the costs of exhibitions and other promotion efforts shall be mutually agreed in advance." This could be changed to state your exact arrangements, such as, "Dealer agrees to pay for two half-page national magazine advertisements. Any further magazine advertising must be paid for by the Artist."

Can't I just write a letter?

Yes, you can protect yourself by writing a letter in your own language stating what you think the terms of your agreement are and asking the dealer to initial and return it to you.

Figure 7. This is an example of the simplest form of a consignment agreement. It might be used when you consign only one or two works to a gallery.

SIMPLE CONSIGNMENT AGREEMENT

Smith Galleries, Inc.   (date)
2404 State Street
New City, New York

You hereby acknowledge receipt of the following painting created by me:

"Sea Storm," an oil painting, 40" x 60".

I am consigning to you this painting at the retail price of $1,000.

You shall deliver to me within ten (10) days after the date on which you make delivery under a sale or contract of sale the purchase price of the painting less your commission of _____%. Title to the painting is reserved in me until sale of the painting.

Any time prior to the sale of the painting, you will deliver the painting to me immediately upon receipt of instructions from my asking for its return.

_____
Artist

The foregoing is confirmed and agreed to by _____
Smith Galleries, Inc.

Figure 8. A number of organizations have prepared artist-dealer agreements. Artists Equity Association drew this one up.

ARTISTS EQUITY ASSOCIATION, INC.
MINIMUM ARTIST-DEALER AGREEMENT

Prepare this agreement in duplicate. N.B. This agreement should not be considered the last word in artist-dealer contracts. Artist Equity's National Board holds that the best agreements are carefully tailored to meet the specific needs and interests of the artist and dealer involved. Therefore please feel free to adapt and modify the terms set down here to meet your own needs, interests and opportunities. You may also find it wise to enlist the assistance of an attorney skilled in drafting contracts.

Artist Equity's National Office receives many requests for advice regarding appropriate trade discounts to dealers. Such discounts vary widely, depending entirely upon the services performed by the dealer for the artist and no general rules can be established. For example, a dealer who absorbs the entire cost of an exhibition may well be entitled to a better discount than one who shares such costs with the artist. Obviously, a dealer who purchases works outright is entitled to a better discount than one who sells consigned works.

It is hereby agreed between _____, the artist, address:

_____

and _____, the dealer, address:_____

that the dealer shall exhibit the artist's work at the dealer's premises under the following conditions:

1. The works hereby consigned for exhibition and sale by the dealer as agent for the artist are enumerated, described, and priced at retail on the attached list. Such works are warranted by the artist: to be free of inherent vice, to be his/her own original creations, and to be the unencumbered property of the artist. They shall remain the property of the artist unless and until they are purchased by collectors or by the dealer.

2. The works here listed shall be exhibited by the dealer from _____(date) to and including _____ (date). These works shall constitute a solo/part of a group (*choose either term*) exhibition. Such exhibitions shall be held approximately every _____ months.

3. Approximately _____ works on the attached list shall be hung during the exhibition period. The remainder shall be available for inspection by prospective purchasers. After the exhibition period, the artist's consigned works may be retained by the dealer for sale for a term of _____ months. At the end of that period, they may be individually removed by the artist providing five days prior written notice has been given. Other works may be supplied as additions or replacements for works sold or removed from time to time by mutual written agreement of artist and dealer. The term for retention of works may be thereafter extended annually by mutual written agreement.

4. The artist will assist the dealer by: (*select appropriate responsibilities/eliminate inappropriate items*)
   a) crating and shipping works to the dealer,
   b) framing the works for exhibition,
   c) furnishing advice, cooperation, and assistance in advertising and publicizing the artist's work,
   d) furnishing data regarding prospective and existing collectors.

5. The dealer will pay the artist _____% of the retail sales price on any works sold. Notice of all sales, including the name and address of purchaser will be given to the artist at the conclusion of each month and payment of all monies due shall be made not more than thirty days after the receipt of payment by the dealer. The dealer assumes full risk of non-payment by the purchaser. However, if a work is returned in good condition by a client for credit, the dealer will make appropriate pro rata adjustments in future payments to the artist.

6. During the term of this agreement or any extension thereof and during the shipment to the artist of works from the dealer, the dealer shall cause all of the artist's works consigned to the dealer to be insured to the benefit of the artist against any and all loss in an amount equal to the artist's portion of the retail sales price.

7. No unsold works shall be removed from the dealer's premises and no discounts shall be permitted except by specific permission of the artist.

8. The artist shall have the right to inventory all consigned works at reasonable times and to obtain a full accounting for any works not present at the dealer's premises at such time.

9. The artist reserves all rights to the reproduction of works in any manner. This restriction shall be indicated by the dealer in writing on all sales invoices and memoranda. However the artist will not withhold permission for the reproduction of such works for promotional purposes.

10. During the term of this agreement, the dealer will exclusively represent the artist in the following geographical area:

_____

_____

However, the artist takes the following exceptions to such exclusive representation* (e.g.: *The artist reserves the right to sell works from his/her own studio. In this case, the artist will remit* _____ % *of the proceeds of such sales to the dealer*)

_____

_____

_____

11. Costs of crating and shipping shall be absorbed as follows: (*Indicate responsibility of artist and/or dealer*)_____

_____

12. Promotion and advertising costs shall be absorbed as follows: (*Indicate responsibility of artist and/or dealer*)

_____

_____

13. Costs of an exhibition opening in conjunction with the exhibition provided above shall be absorbed as follows: (*Indicate responsibility of artist and/or dealer*) _____

_____

14. In the event that a dispute arises under this agreement involving the interpretation of any of the provisions herein which cannot be resolved by discussion between the artist and the dealer, both parties will submit such dispute to an arbitrator appointed by the American Arbitration Association, who shall decide the issue in accordance with the terms of the agreement and the laws of the State of _____. Costs in such cases shall be borne equally by both parties.

_____   _____
Artist   **Dealer**

_____   _____
Date   **Date**

*Eliminate if not appropriate

What should my contract with a dealer contain?

Many of the following points are issues which crop up in relation to consignment sales, the most common arrangement between artists and dealers in the United States: exclusivity; scope of work; title and receipt; sales prices; discounts; commissions; payments; approval sales; accounting; sales contract; rentals; copyright; delivery and return costs; loss or damage and insurance; exhibitions; duration of agreement; assignability; termination; and arbitration. And attached to your agreement should be a "Consignment Sheet" (see Figure 9), listing all work consigned to the dealer.

The list is not meant to be definitive; only you can supply the full list of issues relevant to your situation. Nor would you want to include all of these issues in a contract. But many of them are musts and are explained below in detail, including the problems involved with each, along with how you might resolve them in a contract.

Each point or issue has almost limitless negotiating possibilities. In most instances, the most favorable arrangement to the artist is given, but compromise will usually be the name of the game. And, if you discover you cannot agree on enough points, it's far better to find that out before you consign any work. This way you can look for a better deal elsewhere.

Will a dealer want exclusive geographical rights to my work?

He may. Many dealers will want geographical exclusivity. For example, if you have a New York City dealer, he will probably not allow you to sell through other dealers in many parts of New York State, New Jersey, and Connecticut—areas where he would compete with local dealers.

How will this be put into a contract?

A clause might read: "Artist appoints Dealer his sole and exclusive agent for the sale and exhibition of his works of art in (city, state, or region)."

This clause also establishes your agency relationship, so, at the very least, your dealer must exert reasonable care to protect your work and act in your interests. It does not, however, insure that your work will be protected from creditors (if you live outside California or New York) in case of bankruptcy.

Figure 9. Another version of an artist-dealer agreement was drawn up by the Bay Area Lawyers for the Arts (BALA) in California. Note that Clause 15 refers to copyright protection as it was provided for under the old copyright law. Under the 1976 Copyright Revision Act, it's only necessary to say that "The Artist reserves copyright, including all reproduction rights."

Clauses 8 and 12 refer to certain protections guaranteed under California law. You can guarantee yourself the same rights by including these two clauses in your contract.

Clause 16 refers to another protection provided by California law. Unfortunately, the only way you can guarantee yourself the same protection is by filing UCC Form No. 1.

BAY AREA LAWYERS FOR THE ARTS
ARTIST-GALLERY AGREEMENT

This Agreement is made the _____ day of _____ 197__ between:

NAME: _____
ADDRESS: _____
PHONE: _____ ("the Artist")

and

NAME: _____
ADDRESS: _____
PHONE: _____ ("the Gallery")
which is organized as a _____

The parties agree as follows:

1. Agency. The Artist appoints the Gallery his/her agent for the purpose of exhibition and sale of the consigned works of art in the following geographical area: _____

2. Consignment. The Artist shall consign to the Gallery and the Gallery shall accept consignment of the following works of art during the term of this Agreement:

☐ All new works created by the Artist (in the following media: ____
_____)

☐ All works which the Gallery shall select. The Gallery shall have the first choice of all new works created by the Artist (in the following media: _____)

☐ Not less than ____ new works per year (in the following media:
_____)

☐ All new works created by the Artist excluding works reserved by the Artist for studio sales and commission sales made directly by the Artist

☐ The works described in the Consignment Sheet (Schedule A of this Agreement) and such additional works as shall be mutually agreed and described in a similar Consignment Sheet

The Artist shall not exhibit or sell any consigned work outside the Gallery without the prior written approval of the Gallery. The Artist shall be free to exhibit and sell any work not consigned to the Gallery under this Agreement.

3. Delivery. _____ shall be responsible for delivery of the consigned works to the Gallery. All costs of delivery (including transportation and insurance) shall be paid as follows:

    (a) _____% by the Artist
    (b) _____% by the Gallery.

4. Title & Receipt. The Artist warrants that he/she created and possesses unencumbered title to all works of art consigned to the Gallery under this Agreement. Title to the consigned work shall remain in the Artist until he/she is paid in full. The Gallery acknowledges receipt of the works described in the Consignment Sheet (Schedule A of this Agreement) and shall give the Artist a similar Consignment Sheet to acknowledge receipt of all additional works consigned to the Gallery under this Agreement.

5. Promotion. The Gallery shall make reasonable and good faith efforts to promote the Artist and to sell the consigned works as follows: _____

_____ .

6. Sales price. The Gallery shall sell the consigned works at the retail price mutually agreed by both parties and specified in writing in the Consignment Sheet. The Gallery shall have discretion to vary the agreed retail price by ____% in the case of discount sales.

7. Sales commission. The Gallery shall receive the following sales commission:

    (a) _____% of the agreed retail price for selling works in the following medium:

_____ .

(b) _____% of the agreed retail price for selling works in the following medium:

_____ .

(c) _____% of the amount paid for studio sales or commission sales made directly by the Artist.

The remainder shall be paid to the Artist. In the case of discount sales, the amount of the discount shall be deducted from the Gallery's sales commission.

8. Payment.

(a) *On outright sales,* the Gallery shall pay the Artist's share within 30 days after the date of sale.

(b) *On deferred payment sales,* the Gallery shall pay the Artist's share within 90 days after the date of sale.

(c) *On installment sales,* the Gallery shall first apply the proceeds from sale of the work to pay the Artist's share. Payment shall be made within 30 days after the Gallery's receipt of each installment.

As provided by California law, the Gallery shall hold the proceeds from sale of the consigned works in trust for the benefit of the Artist. The Gallery agrees to guarantee the credit of its customers, and to bear all losses due to the failure of the customer's credit.

9. Approval sales. The Gallery shall not permit any consigned work to remain in the possession of a customer for the purpose of sale on approval for a period exceeding 14 days.

10. Rentals. The Gallery may not rent any consigned work without the prior written consent of the Artist. The rental period may not exceed _____ weeks unless a longer period is approved by the Artist. The Gallery shall receive _____% of the rental fees, and the remainder shall be paid to the Artist within 30 days after the Gallery's receipt of each rental fee.

11. Exhibitions. The Gallery shall arrange, install, and publicize at least _____ solo exhibitions of the Artist's work of not less than ___ ___ weeks duration each, and shall make reasonable efforts to arrange other solo and group exhibitions thereafter. The Artist's work may not be included in any group exhibition without his/her prior written approval. The division of financial responsibility for the costs of exhibitions and other promotional efforts shall be mutually agreed in advance, and neither party may obtain reimbursement for such costs without the prior written approval of the other party.

12. Loss or damage. As provided by California law, the Gallery shall be responsible for loss of or damage to the consigned work from the date of delivery to the Gallery until the date of delivery to the purchaser or repossession by the Artist. The Gallery shall insure the consigned works for the benefit of the Artist up to ____% of the agreed retail price.

13. Statements of account. The Gallery shall give the Artist a Statement of Account (similar to Schedule B of this Agreement) within 15 days after the end of each calendar quarter beginning with _____ 197__. The Statement shall include the following information:
    (1) the works sold or rented
    (2) the date, price, and terms of sale or rental
    (3) the commission due to the Gallery
    (4) the name and address of each purchaser or renter
    (5) the amount due to the Artist
    (6) the location of all unsold works (if not on the Gallery's premises).
The Gallery warrants that the Statement shall be accurate and complete in all respects. The Artist and the Gallery (or their authorized representatives) shall have the mutual right to inspect the financial records of the other party pertaining to any transaction involving the Artist's work.

14. Contract for sale. The Gallery shall use the Artist's own contract for sale (a copy of which is appended to this Agreement) in any sale of the consigned works.

15. Copyright. The Artist reserves the common law copyright including all reproduction rights and the right to claim statutory copyright in all works consigned to the Gallery. No work may be reproduced by the Gallery without the prior written approval of the Artist. All approved reproductions in catalogues, brochures, advertisements, and other promotional literature shall carry the following notice: © by (name of the Artist) 197__ (year of publication).

16. Security. As provided by California law, the consigned works shall be held in trust for the benefit of the Artist, and shall not be subject to claim by a creditor of the Gallery. In the event of any default by the Gallery, the Artist shall have all the rights of a secured party under the Uniform Commercial Code.

17. Duration of Agreement. This Agreement shall commence upon the date of signing and shall continue in effect until the ____ _____ day of _____ 197__. Either party may terminate the Agreement by giving 30 days prior written notice, except that the Agreement may not be terminated for 90 days following a solo exhibition of the Artist's work in the Gallery.

18. Return of works. _____ shall be responsible for return of all works not sold upon termination of the Agreement. All costs of return (including transportation and insurance) shall be paid as follows:

(a) ____% by the Artist
(b) ____% by the Gallery

If the Artist fails to accept return of the works within ____ days after written request by the Gallery, the Artist shall pay reasonable storage costs.

19. Non-assignability. This Agreement may not be assigned by the Gallery to another person without the prior written approval of the Artist. The Gallery shall notify the Artist in advance of any change in personnel in charge of the Gallery or of any change in ownership of the Gallery.

20. Arbitration. All disputes arising out of this Agreement shall be submitted to binding arbitration. The arbitrator shall be selected in the sole discretion of the Executive Director of Bay Area Lawyers for the Arts, Inc. If such arbitrator is not available the dispute shall be submitted to arbitration in accordance with the rules of the American Arbitration Association. The arbitrator's award shall be final, and judgment may be entered upon it in any court having jurisdiction thereof.

21. Entire agreement. This Agreement represents the entire agreement between the Artist and the Gallery and supercedes all prior negotiations, representations and agreements whether oral or written. This Agreement may only be amended by written instrument signed by both parties.

22. Governing law. This Agreement shall be governed by the laws of the State of California.

IN WITNESS WHEREOF the parties hereto have executed this Agreement on the day and year first above written.

| _____ | _____ |
| The Artist | For the Gallery |

This Consignment Sheet must accompany the BALA contract. Furthermore, each time new works are consigned to a dealer, an additional sheet must be filled out and attached to the agreement.

CONSIGNMENT SHEET (SCHEDULE A)

RECEIVED FROM: _____ DATE: _____

THE FOLLOWING WORKS OF ART:

TITLE:	MEDIUM:	SIZE:	RETAIL PRICE:	MAY BE RENTED:
1.				
2.				
3.				

SIGNED BY:

_____   _____
The Artist   For the Gallery

BALA also recommends that this Statement of Accounts be used in conjunction with its contract so the artist is assured an accurate accounting.

STATEMENT OF ACCOUNT (SCHEDULE B)

ARTIST: _____ DATE: _____

ADDRESS: _____ QUARTER: _____

TITLE:	RETAIL PRICE:	SALES COMMISSION:	DUE TO ARTIST:
1.			
2.			
3.			

NET AMOUNT DUE TO ARTIST: $_____

_____
For the Gallery

What do you mean by scope of work?

When referring to consignment sales, scope of work means the amount and kind of works you want the dealer to sell for you. For example, you might want to consign to one dealer your paintings and sculpture and to another your graphics. To make sure there is no misunderstanding about who gets what, specify the scope of work each one can handle in your contract (see Clause 2 in Figure 9). Ask yourself the following questions:

Do you want him to represent all your work even if you create in different mediums and styles? If not, say so specifically.

Do you want him to represent the work produced prior to your agreement? This, of course, depends a lot on what the dealer wants, too.

Do you want to give him your entire output or a specific number each year? If it's the latter, your dealer will probably want to reserve the right to choose what he wants.

Will you want to reserve certain works for gifts, bartering, bequests, or studio sales? Unless you're in a strong bargaining position, most dealers won't let you hold back work for these purposes, particularly if it's some of your best.

What do you mean by title?

The dealer has the right to expect that the work you consign is owned by you or, put in legalese, that you "possess unencumbered title" to it. In other words, he expects that you aren't trying to pass off works of others as your own and that you haven't already sold the work to someone else or given it as collateral on a loan or whatever. And he'll want this in the contract. To protect your interests, you'll want the agreement to state that you retain title until the work is sold and paid for in full.

What do you mean by receipt?

You should make sure that you get a receipt for all work consigned to the gallery both initially and every time you bring in more. The way to do this is by writing this condition into the contract and attaching a consignment sheet (see Figure 9) to it. A consignment sheet lists every work turned over to your dealer along with sizes, mediums, and retail prices, and a separate consignment sheet should be filled out and attached to the contract with every new delivery. Each sheet should be signed by both artist and dealer.

How do I write a title and receipt clause into a contract?

A good example can be found in Clause 4 of the BALA contract in Figure 9.

Who establishes the sale prices on my work?

The best price policy is one mutually determined by you and your dealer. And prices should be periodically reviewed once or twice a year to bring them into line with your growing reputation and what the market will bear.

Will I be expected to discount my work for anyone?

Yes, museums usually ask for and get a 10% discount or sometimes more, as do clients who buy in quantity. Some galleries also discount work for valued clients—although this is by no means standard practice—and for architects and interior designers. The latter groups usually receive a 15% discount, although architects and sometimes designers pass the discount on to their clients.

What kind of discount does a dealer give other dealers?

Dealers frequently give other dealers, such as out-of-town galleries and private dealers (those people who operate without galleries) a discount that amounts to half of their own commission. In other words, if your dealer charges a commission of 40%, he may give the other dealer a 20% discount and charge you only a 20% commission.

Some dealers, however, expect their full commission after discounting the work, forcing the artist, in essence, to pay two commissions. This sort of deal can be prevented if you can negotiate a clause stating that discounts must be deducted from sales commissions.

Can a dealer discount my work without my permission?

Not if you don't want him to, but this must be made clear in the agreement. As a rule, you'll want to give him some leeway in discounting work, so you and he should decide whom he can discount work for and how much he can reduce prices without consulting you. Ten percent would be reasonable. Any time he wants to increase this discount, he must consult you.

How do I write sales prices and discounts into my consignment agreement?

You might say something like this:

Sales shall be made at a price no less than the sale price agreed to in writing on the consignment sheet. The Artist authorizes the Dealer to give a customary trade discount (which shall not exceed X% of sale price, except with the artist's prior written consent) on sales to museums, other dealers, decorators, and architects. In the case of discount sales, the discount shall be deducted from the dealer's sales commission. Dealer and artist agree to review sale prices every _____ months.

How are commission fees established?

By the kind of services offered. A dealer who absorbs the costs of an exhibition, for example, may be entitled to a larger commission than one who shares the costs with you.

A private dealer or artists' agent (if your sole dealer) may sometimes take a smaller commission because he doesn't have to pay rent or other expenses for a gallery. On the other hand, an aggressive private dealer or agent stumping the countryside for you or otherwise doing a bang-up selling job should earn as big a commission as a dealer with a fancy gallery.

Does a dealer charge all artists the same commission?

Not necessarily. The more successful you are, the better financial deal you can bargain for. I know superstars in New York giving up only 33⅓% to dealers who charge other artists 50% and 60%.

Lower commissions are also charged sometimes if an artist makes a large investment in his work. Suppose you're a sculptor whose costs represent a significant portion of the selling price. Suppose further that costs run as high as 40%, leaving only 60% profit to be split by you and the dealer. A dealer ordinarily charging 50% might reduce his commission to 30% (or 50% of 60%).

Will a dealer charge the same commission in all situations?

Not always. A dealer may have a policy to charge different commissions for different media: 40% on paintings, for example, and 50% for graphics.

His commission policy may also depend on whether a sale is made by him or by you from your studio.

Why do I have to pay the gallery any commission on studio sales?

Collectors often try to buy directly from artists—figuring they can get a bargain by avoiding dealer commissions—if the artist is willing to lower the retail selling price. Artists sometimes go along with these sales because they get a bigger share of the profits.

Dealers resent this practice both because it places them in competition with the artist and because they feel they are not being fairly compensated. After all, they reason, an artist's selling prices and popularity may be primarily due to their selling ability. Therefore, a dealer may insist that he be paid his regular commission on all sales no matter where they are made. Or if he's willing to compromise, he may ask for a commission, but reduce it for studio sales. Of course, if you have real clout you can exempt studio sales altogether in the Scope of Work clause.

How do I write commissions into an agreement?

A sales commission clause might state:

The gallery shall receive the following sales commission:
  (a) ____% *of the agreed sales price for works in the following medium:*
_____;
  (b) ____% *of the agreed sales price for works in the following medium:*
_____:
  (c) ____% *of the amount paid for studio sales made directly by the* artist.

Will the dealer expect a percentage of commissioned projects?

That depends on whether you secure the commission or he gets it for you, and on his attitude toward commissions in general. If he takes the approach that only through his efforts at enhancing your name and reputation could you have been awarded the commission, he'll ask for his full commission no matter who actually obtains it. Many dealers, however, will have two different rates.

How would fees for commissioned projects be stated in an agreement?

If the commission award represents a fee for your services only, a contract might read:

The Dealer shall receive (a) ____% of the price of any commissioned projects awarded to the Artist when such commissions are obtained for him by the Dealer, and (b) ____% of any such commissions the Artist obtains directly during the term of this agreement.

Or if you have enough bargaining power, "The Dealer shall receive no commission if the Artist obtains the commission himself."

If you are responsible for paying for materials and/or labor costs for the project, you would want to word the agreement differently. For example:

The Dealer shall receive ____% of the net balance of the Artist's commission after deducting expenses for materials and/or labor actually used in executing the project when such commissions are obtained for him by the Dealer.

How soon after sale of work should I be paid?

The most businesslike arrangement is to insist on payment within 30 days of the purchaser's payment to the dealer.

When should I receive my share if the client pays in installments?

The same principle should hold true. You should receive your share of each installment payment within 30 days of the receipt of payment by the dealer.

How do I protect myself against a client's failure to pay?

It should be the dealer's responsibility to find out how financially stable his clients are. Therefore, your consignment agreement should read that the dealer assumes the full risk of default of payment by a client.

How do I put terms of payment and default into a contract?

The BALA contract handles this very nicely in Clause 8.

How should approval sales be handled?

There are several ways of approaching the issue of approval sales, i.e., the practice of allowing a client to take work home to see if he can live with it. Actually the crux of the issue is whether or not the client pays for the work before taking it home for a certain time period. If he does not pay first and then fails to either return the work or pay for it, the dealer is confronted with the tricky job of getting the work back.

How is this handled in an agreement?

Dealers confident of their clients' reliability may insist on a clause similar to Clause 9 in the BALA contract (see Figure 9).

On the other hand, both you and he might feel somewhat reluctant to pursue this lenient policy. In this case, your agreement might state:

No unsold works shall be removed from the dealer's premises. However, if a work is returned in good condition within 30 days by the client, it may be exchanged for cash or work. If returned in good condition after 30 days, the work may be exchanged for other work.

What if the client wants his money back?

If your dealer has already paid you, he shouldn't ask you to return your share of the sales price. Instead, he should deduct the amount of the credit from payments he makes to you in the future. So your contract might read something like this: "If a work is returned within 30 days in good condition for a cash credit, the dealer will make appropriate pro rata adjustments in future payments to the Artist."

Can I inspect my dealer's financial records?

Yes, it should be your privilege to inspect those records that pertain to transactions involving your work—and if you sell a lot of works from your studio, he may demand equal rights and want to inspect your records. You should also ask for an accounting from your dealer at regular intervals, usually once every three months, in the form of a statement of account. A typical Statement of Account is shown in Figure 9, and Clause 13 of the BALA contract demonstrates how to write this demand into a contract.

Will my dealer tell me whom he sold my work to?

Many dealers prefer not to, believing that you'll be tempted to sell to customers directly. Therefore, you should state in your contract that he must either list names and addresses of clients on your quarterly Statement of Account or attach to the Statement copies of sales receipts showing this information.

Can I ask my dealer to use my own sales contract?

Yes. As mentioned in Chapter 3, you may want to reserve certain rights in your work after it is sold, such as the right to borrow work back for exhibition, the right to approve or supervise repairs, or even the right to a royalty on resale. The place to reserve these rights is in a sales contract. Thus, one of the terms of your consignment agreement should require your dealer to insist that all purchasers of your work sign a contract reserving these rights to you. This contract could be the Projansky agreement (see Figure 3), a variation of it, or one of your own making. And to write this into the agreement use Clause 14 of the BALA contract.

Do dealers ever rent work?

Not very often. Unless there's a good chance that the rentor will become a buyer, rentals offer few advantages for the dealer—they take work out of circulation for little gain to either them or the artist.

If he wants to rent work, how should I proceed?

First, look over the rental agreement your dealer plans to use for clients. Check to see if it basically conforms to the terms discussed in Chapter 3 on rentals, making sure that his commission fee corresponds to what was suggested there. Then bargain with your dealer for the right to refuse the rental of any particular work and to limit rentals to a period of about a month. The resultant clause should resemble No. 10 of the BALA contract (see Figure 9).

How do I protect my copyright in a consignment agreement?

Let's assume that you have already copyrighted by placing proper copyright notice on your work (see Chapter 2). In this case, you don't actually have to do anything further since you automatically retain copyright. Nevertheless, to make sure no misunderstandings arise between you and either your dealer or a client, your consignment agreement should discuss copyright.

What would the consignment agreement say about copyright?

Something like this:

The Artist reserves copyright in all works consigned to the Dealer.

The dealer will not permit any of these works of art to be reproduced except for the purpose of appearing in a catalogue or advertisement of the Artist's work or with the prior written consent of the Artist. All approved reproductions shall carry the following notice: © by (name of artist) 19____ (year of publication).

The Dealer shall print on each bill of sale in a prominent place the following notice: All rights to reproduction are reserved to the Artist.

What will my dealers get for arranging the sale of reproduction rights?

Dealers usually take a 10% or 20% commission on the royalty payments or flat fees you receive when they arrange for or sell reproduction rights. So your contract might read: "If the Dealer sells or arranges for the sale of reproduction rights with the Artist's prior written approval, Dealer's commission will be ____%."

Who arranges and pays for the delivery of work to and from the dealer?

The most common arrangement between artists and their dealers is for the artist to arrange and pay for costs of delivery (including transportation and insurance) and for the dealer to be responsible for arranging and paying for costs of return. Clauses 3 and 18 of the BALA contract illustrate how this can be written into your consignment agreement (see Figure 9).

Who's responsible for loss or damage?

Unless you live in California—where work is protected by state law—you might suffer a complete loss if work in possession of the dealer is lost or damaged and the dealer can prove he wasn't negligent. So ask your dealer to promise in the agreement that he'll be responsible for loss or damage to consigned work from the date of delivery to the gallery until the date of delivery to the purchaser or repossession by you. This means he must either insure the work or pay for it if it's lost or must be repaired.

What kind of insurance should he carry?

An all-risk policy that insures against fire, flood, theft, or other damage to work while in his possession. It should cover work not only while in his place of business but also while traveling to shows.

How much are works insured for?

Most dealers insure works up to an amount equal to the artist's share of the retail sales price. In other words, if the dealer takes a 40% commission, he'll most likely insure the work for 60% of the retail price.

Who does the insurance company reimburse for work?

This is a point to bargain for. Ideally, your name should appear on the insurance policy as the "loss payee," or person to be paid, in case of a claim. But this may not always be practical from the dealer's standpoint.

How is loss or damage written into a contract?

You could say something like this:

For the benefit of the Artist, the Dealer will provide at his expense all-risk insurance on all of the Artist's work of art listed on the Consignment Sheets up to _____% of the agreed sale price from date of delivery to the Dealer until date of delivery to the purchaser or repossession by the Artist.

What information on exhibitions should be in a consignment agreement?

Before listing the provisions that should be considered for inclusion into an exhibition clause, let me point out that they could form the basis of a separate contract if your sole contact with a dealer is to be a one-time, one-person show. The following points should be covered:

1. Location and frequency. Spell out where the exhibitions are to take place, how many rooms will be allotted to your work, and how often you can expect solo exhibitions. A show every one and a half or two years is average.

2. Choice of work. Determine in advance who will choose the work for the exhibition—the best choice is usually mutual.

3. Hanging and installing. Arrange who will pay for this and who will be in charge.

4. Framing or bases (for sculpture). Again, decide who will arrange for this and who will pay for it.

5. Partitions and painting. Decide the same as above.

6. Advertising. Determine where the show will be advertised, and who will bear the expense.

7. Invitations and postage. Spell out how many invitations will be mailed and who will pay for the printing and postage.

8. Brochure or catalog. Will there be one, and, if so, who will pay for it; who will decide on its format; and who will have control over its quality?

9. Refreshments. Will there be any, and, if so, who will pay?

Obviously, the stronger your bargaining power, the more favorable your arrangements will be, and the more likely you'll be able to persuade the dealer to absorb most or all of the expenses connected with the show.

What should I bargain for concerning group exhibitions?

Some artistic control, such as a clause that permits you to withdraw works from group exhibitions which you don't feel are appropriate for the display of your works. But if your dealer agrees, don't use this power thoughtlessly. Remember, he's got a stake in your career too, and he probably has good reason for wanting to enter your work in certain group shows.

What will an exhibition clause look like?

Clause 11 of the BALA contract is a good example of an exhibition clause (see Figure 9), but, since it's a part of a model contract, it can't spell out all the points raised above. It's up to you to do this based on your particular situation.

What is an arbitration clause in an artist-dealer agreement like?

It is similar to one in a commission agreement, and Clause 20 of the BALA contract illustrates just how arbitration is written into an artist-dealer contract (see Figure 9).

How long should a consignment agreement last?

Time limits, like other terms, are usually set by the stronger party in negotiations. A dealer signing on a relatively unknown artist may dictate a one-year contract with an option to renew for two one-year periods. An artist of considerable renown may want the renewal option to be his rather than the dealer's. Indeed, getting the option to renew is a show of power.

Power plays aside, a few practical guidelines should be considered when negotiating the length of a contract. If you're young, tying yourself to a dealer for an extended period may not be a good idea. On the other hand, a dealer will want to know that he can count on your being around for a reasonable length of time before he'll invest any time and money promoting your work. Most dealers, for example, will want you to remain with them through at least two exhibitions of your work. Therefore, you might consider the advice Calvin Goodman gives. He suggests his clients negotiate five-year contracts with an option open to both parties to cancel every year after the second year.

Can I terminate the agreement before the end of the contract?

Yes, if your contract permits such a release from the agreement. And there are many reasons why both you and your dealer might want such a clause: if the dealer fails to hold exhibitions as scheduled; if the dealer goes bankrupt; if the dealer doesn't sell a certain number of works within a given time; if you fail to create and deliver works as promised; or if gallery personnel changes. You might have a tough time writing the last possibility into a contract. But you should try, especially if you joined the gallery specifically because of a close relationship with an employee or with the director and you have great confidence in his selling ability. In this case, you may want to terminate the contract if he leaves the gallery.

How is termination accomplished?

Termination usually takes place a given number of days (normally 30 to 60 days) after you notify your dealer (or vice versa) in writing that you plan to terminate. However, this may not be easy if an exhibition has just taken place. To protect his interests, a dealer may insist in the contract that no termination take place for a given number of months after a one-person show or that you reimburse him for his expenses in mounting the show.

How should duration and termination be written into a contract?

A general example is found in Clause 17 of the BALA contract (see Figure 9). But in your own contract, you may wish to specify the situations that will result in termination, such as "Failure of the Dealer to hold at least ____ one-person exhibitions of the Artist's work every ____ months shall entitle the Artist to terminate the agreement."

Can a dealer assign or "sell" me to another dealer?

Yes, but you should try to prevent this in your contract. For one thing, if you joined a dealer because of your confidence in him, you won't want your contract to be transferred to anyone else. The dealer, on the other hand, may see you as an asset he can "sell" to another dealer if he wants to get out of the business. Resist this, and hold out for a clause that reads: "This Agreement may not be assigned by the dealer without the Artist's prior written consent."

Does death terminate the consignment agreement?

Yes, and this is fine for artists who want their agreement terminated with death. Other artists, however, prefer that their dealers sell work on hand and pay the proceeds to the estate. Still others want an on-going relationship between their heirs and dealers. But unless some provision is made in both your last will and in the consignment agreement concerning a continuing relationship, a dealer cannot automatically go on representing an estate, which could result in some annoying problems. Therefore, you should seek legal advice not only on writing a will, but also on the phrasing of the death clause in your consignment agreement, since they must dovetail.

6. Cooperative Galleries

- · Organization
- · Dues and fees
- · Commissions
- · Forming a co-op
- · Costs
- · Nonprofit co-ops

With art schools and colleges continuing to churn out more and more fine artists, the demand for exhibition and selling space has far outstripped commercial gallery facilities. To cope with these needs, many artists around the country have taken matters into their own hands. The result is that the number of cooperative galleries has mushroomed in the 70s. By running their own galleries, artists give themselves a place to show and sell on their own terms.

What exactly is a cooperative gallery?

While the structure and activities of co-ops vary a lot, generally they consist of a group of artists who have joined together to share the costs of running a gallery in which they can show their work in both one-person and group exhibitions. Occasionally, they put on guest shows, introducing the work of artists from other regions or sponsoring performances by dancers and musicians. But the underlying motivation is the artist's need for exposure to the public in a permanent gallery facility.

How many members belong to a co-op in general?

The average co-op is the size of most commercial galleries—20 to 25 members. This allows each member to exhibit his work, if he chooses, at least once every two years or 18 months. But describing what's average isn't particularly helpful. Depending on the priorities of the members, co-ops may include as few as three or four artists or as many as 36 or more if exhibition space is available.

Is there any structure to a co-op?

There should be. Some artists take the word cooperative literally, believing that everyone will willingly chip in to do his share of the work at exactly the right time and that to impose any kind of structure or organization on the group defeats the cooperative philosophy. That's nice in theory, but in practice it rarely works— particularly if there are more than three or four people involved. Someone must be in charge. To make things run smoothly, a co-op should elect a president, vice-president, secretary, and treasurer. Committees should also be set up to handle such responsibilities as installing shows, recruitment of new members, maintenance of the gallery, publicity, and so on. Members with particular expertise in certain areas should be appointed to the appropriate committee. For example, the painter with a flair for writing might be put in charge of publicity.

Who runs the gallery on a daily basis?

The members of a co-op may elect to hire a director to handle sales and promotion, or they can do it themselves. If the latter is the case, members usually rotate the task of "sitting" for the gallery; in other words, each member staffs the gallery one day a week or however often it's necessary. During this time they answer customers' questions and either make sales or refer the customer to the artist in whose work he's interested. The latter is a most inefficient way of promoting sales, for while it is true that an artist is usually able to talk about his work more effectively than anyone else, if the customer has to contact him or wait for the artist to get in touch, he may lose interest.

How are co-ops funded?

To cover expenses, members commonly pay an initial fee to join the cooperative and yearly or monthly dues. Both initiation fees and dues are determined both by costs discussed below and by the number of members available to share these costs.

How much are initiation fees and dues in general?

Because of the variables, such as rent and the number of services offered, there is no way to estimate an average initiation fee or amount for dues. Some cooperatives, for example, require their members to pay for all costs for a one-person show, including printing, mailing, advertising, and reception expenses. Dues in such a co-op will be less than those charged by co-ops which pay these costs out of the collective pot. When all services are paid for, annual dues can rise as high as $850 or $900 if the co-op is located in a high-rent district, such as New York City. In general, they'll be much less elsewhere.

How much does a co-op charge in commissions?

Some co-ops charge no commission at all. Others take from 5% to 30% on each sale. Those co-ops that establish commissions on the high side represent, in most cases, galleries with a paid director who receives a percentage of the commission plus a salary.

Cooperatives almost never charge as high a commission as commercial galleries in the same area do, a fact that should be pointed out to potential customers. The reason for this, of course, is that the artist is not looking to make a profit on the gallery itself, but on the individual sales of his work.

What is the director's percentage of the commission?

No hard and fast rules govern commissions. A commission of 25% might be divided up, with 20% going to the director and 5% to the gallery to help defray expenses, or vice versa. Or the co-op may have a policy to give the entire commission to the director, rejecting any part of it for itself.

Why would a co-op charge no commission?

It goes without saying that in most galleries certain artists will sell better than others. Therefore, if commissions are used to defray expenses, the better selling artists would, in effect, be supporting the gallery and subsidizing those who don't sell as well. To avoid this, co-op members may feel that it is more equitable for everyone to support the gallery solely by dues and initiation fees.

On the other hand, if everyone in the co-op sells relatively well, it would be a good idea not only to charge a commission but a relatively high one at that. Then with commissions offsetting costs, dues could be reduced.

Can I expect to sell well through a co-op?

The odds on selling well through a cooperative gallery depend to a great extent on how many commercial galleries operate in your area and how strong they are. If a number exist, but they're all new and haven't done a good marketing job, a co-op stands as good a chance of achieving a respectable sales record as they do, and an even better one if it can mount an imaginative and aggressive sales campaign.

But a co-op can rarely expect to make it in an area where commercial galleries are all-powerful. In New York, for example, where commercial dealers maintain a stranglehold on the art market, many artists have ceased to think of the co-op as a profit-making vehicle for its members.

Then what's the point of joining a co-op?

These New York artists insist that the function of a co-operative gallery in New York is to show—not sell—and to give members an opportunity for uncensored exposure. In other words, they feel it's worth paying the price for an artistic freedom that allows them to exhibit as they please and not as dictated by dealers.

How do I decide if a co-op is the place for me?

First, decide what it is that you want a co-op to do for you. Is your first priority sales? Or will you be satisfied with the right to show? If sales are your goal, perhaps you should hold out for commercial representation. Or spend the money saved by not paying dues to increase sales from your studio.

Also consider the demands a co-op will make on your time and decide whether this time could be spent more productively working on your art. Are you willing, for example, to give up a day every now and then to "sit" for the gallery or to keep the books? I know of a co-op in the Southwest made up of five women who operate without a hired director. Each sells well, but each must contribute one out of every five days to minding the store, as well as putting in some extra time delivering work, hanging shows, bookkeeping, and so on. These particular women rate their gallery a success. They believe they've learned a great deal from each other and have benefited from their association in terms of creative efforts and financial reward.

And it may well be. Still, one or all of these members—if they devoted the time spent working in the gallery to painting—might conceivably do better financially in a commercial gallery. With someone else handling all the details, they might be able to produce enough to more than compensate for higher commissions. On the other hand, not every one can work seven days a week, and talking to clients might be downright stimulating. So you have to weigh the advantages and disadvantages.

To form a co-op, what are the first steps?

If sales are your objective, assess the sales potential in your area. The first order of business would be to check out the existing commercial galleries and see if you can compete with them. If there aren't many other galleries, the next step is to evaluate the potential market for work. Are there many known collectors in your area or other people who could be counted on as possible clients? Is your area receptive to the arts? Do you have a museum or arts center through which you might be able to promote work? Do your local newspapers and radio and TV stations cover exhibitions? Can you get publicity in these media? After you've made these assessments, you might discover that you'd be better off opening a co-op 30 miles away in a more receptive area.

What's next before actually forming a co-op?

Decide on the approximate number of members you ultimately want in your gallery. Then ask yourself whether you can get certain types of people to join. For instance, you'll need members capable of acting as bookkeepers, publicists, and administrators. If you plan to run the gallery without a hired professional director, you'll also want members who are personable and articulate.

Once you've resolved all those problems, start looking for gallery space.

Where should we look for gallery space?

The best place to set up a co-op is alongside your competitors and other businesses that cater to the sort of clientele you want to attract. If you're looking for well-heeled clients, settle down near the posher antique stores and art galleries. If you see the novice collector in the suburbs as your ideal customer, craft shops or boutiques make good neighbors.

Is a second floor location as good as one on the ground floor?

No. Most co-ops depend heavily on pedestrians brought into an area by surrounding businesses. So being as visible as possible should be one of your top priorities. After the co-op establishes itself firmly in an area, you might be able to move above street level or on to a side street. But keeping a low profile when you're starting out could signal an early demise for your operation.

What if we can't afford both the ground floor and the best street?

Compromise, but only after a careful investigation of pedestrian traffic patterns. A second floor location on a heavily trafficked street advertised by a colorful banner might be preferable to a ground floor gallery around the corner on an often empty street. However, street level galleries are a must in areas where businesses are more spread out.

What other traffic patterns should we look for?

Make sure pedestrian traffic is heavy during afternoons and Saturdays and watch out for traffic lights that halt the flow of people before they get to you. Also avoid buildings which are satisfactory traffic-wise but have consistently been rented to businesses that go out of business in a hurry. Even if you can't figure out the reason for this history of failure, don't tempt fate by trying to break the cycle.

What should we look for in physical facilities?

There are many specific things you'll need, but, in general, be sure to consider the following:

1. Sufficient space. You'll need two show rooms at least—one for solo shows and one for private viewings—and storage space for a sample of each member's work.

2. Watertight building. See if the roof leaks. If you're on the ground floor of a multiple-storied building which has a single-story extension in the roof, check this, too. Give the walls a good going over for dampness and examine windows to make sure they're watertight and not filled with dry rot.

3. Walls made of the right material for hanging paintings. Walls faced with metal are not good—in fact, they're useless, unless you're opening a sculpture gallery.

4. Ample-sized doors. If you plan to show large-scale works, make sure the doors are large enough to accommodate them.

5. Plumbing in good order.

6. Adequate toilet facilities for the public.

7. Floors that are in good condition and able to bear the stress of heavy sculpture.

8. Adequate heating.

9. Adequate ventilation.

10. Air conditioning. Will you need it? Does the building provide it or is it wired for it?

11. Humidity. Will you need a dehumidifier to control the atmosphere to avoid deterioration of work?

12. Electrical wiring. Consider whether there is enough wiring to handle your lighting requirements or whether you'll have to re-wire?

13. Quiet rooms. Check for excessive street noise and other tenants who might be noisy during gallery hours.

14. Cleanliness. Will outside conditions or other tenants subject you to dirt and other pollutants?

15. Good security. Will you need some sort of alarm system?

16. Zoning. Is the property zoned for commercial use? If it isn't, look elsewhere.

17. Safe access to the gallery. Check out hallways, stairs, and elevators to make sure they're safe and well-lit.

Do we need insurance?

This is a must, so make sure you can get it in the building you're considering. Ask a local property insurance agent if the building is insurable against fire and theft and at what rates. You might also consider plate glass insurance if you have a large storefront window.

How can we tell if the building is structurally sound?

If you're considering an old loft building or something similarly decrepit, look in the *Yellow Pages* for a real estate appraiser. These people will come to inspect the building and give you a written report of its condition.

What's next after we locate a possible space?

Now is the time to estimate costs. An accurate cost analysis will demonstrate how much you'll need to start up the gallery and maintain it. It could be that you'll find it's too expensive for the individual members. Or you might discover you can cover costs only by cutting corners. In this case, you'll have to decide whether you can compete with commercial galleries with something less than a first-class operation.

How do we estimate costs?

By making a list of all your expenses. Many are listed on the projected costs worksheet in Figure 10. Add to it any others you can think of, and think hard. This isn't the time to leave out an important item.

How do we estimate utilities? Call the local utility company, and ask the monthly cost for a similar facility in your neighborhood.

How do we calculate lighting costs? Unless you know precisely what fixtures you want and can take this list to a commercial lighting dealer, ask him to send someone over to discuss your needs and give you an estimate.

Figure 10. Before sinking any money into a cooperative gallery, an accurate assessment of costs is a must. So list all possible starting and on-going expenses on a worksheet like the one shown (taken from American Artist Business Letter*).*

PROJECTED COSTS WORKSHEET		
ESTIMATED MONTHLY EXPENSES		
	Your estimate of monthly expenses	Your estimate of how much cash you need to start your business (monthly expenses multiplied by six)
Salary of Director		
Rent		
Advertising and promotion		
Telephone		
Legal fees		
Insurance (liability, property, fine arts)		
Accounting fees		
Utilities		
Taxes		
Maintenance		
One-man shows (promotion, refreshments, etc.)		
Miscellaneous		
STARTING COSTS YOU ONLY PAY ONCE		
Renovations (new floor, paint, roof, wiring, partitions, labor)		
Rental equipment (sanders, paint sprayers)		
Rent deposit		
Telephone deposit		
Utilities deposit		
Legal fees		
Advertising and promotion for opening		
Fixtures (lighting and tracks)		
Installation of fixtures		
Furnishings and equipment (desks, chairs, filing cabinets, typewriter, fire extinguisher, storage bins)		
TOTAL ESTIMATED CASH YOU NEED TO START WITH		

How do we calculate costs for renovations we can't do ourselves? Once again ask the experts—electricians, plumbers, general contractors —for estimates. An honest contractor will furnish you with financial references and the names of previous customers you can check with to see if his work has been satisfactory. A reliable contractor will also agree in writing to a firm estimate of the total cost and a definite completion date. And don't stop at one. On any major repairs you should get at least three estimates.

What costs are usually borne by the members?

Costs of shipping, framing, photography, and insurance of the work itself are costs nearly always paid for out of each members' pockets. And your group may also decide to require members to pay for their own shows.

Once expenses are calculated, what do we do?

Estimate dues to see if you can afford them by dividing expenses by the planned number of members. Since you'll need enough cash to handle starting costs and monthly expenses for at least six months to give you a financial cushion in case of unanticipated expenses, you might want to collect one year's dues or six months plus an initiation fee in advance. In the beginning, sales will probably be negligible, so don't count on income from commissions to help defray expenses. Now, if these figures don't give you a heart attack, turn your attention to the lease.

What should we look for in a lease?

Before going any further, let me stress that this is now the time for you to consult a lawyer. Let him check the lease out. But if you're going to be stubborn and do it yourself, make sure to do the following four things:

1. Get an option clause which will extend the lease at your discretion. Once you've sunk a lot of money and time into renovations and established your location in the minds of clientele, you don't want the landlord to be able to kick you out when the lease expires.

2. If the landlord plans to charge you a monthly rent based on square footage of usable interior space, check the dimensions and figure out your own estimate. Don't rely on his figures.

3. Read the fine print in the lease, looking out for escalation clauses. The landlord will try to pass on to you increases in real

estate taxes and fuel costs. If you can't get them written out of the lease, they should be calculated in *your* estimated costs.

4. Find out exactly what your rent will include.

What should our rent include?

Your rent should entitle you to expect the landlord to be responsible for proper operation of heating, plumbing, and air conditioning (if there is any) systems, plus repair of the roof. You should also expect him to repair the parking lot and pavement in front of the building, when necessary. These are basic needs that should definitely be included in your lease. If they aren't, hesitate before you sign it, unless you don't mind paying the expenses involved in repairing them yourself.

Also check to see if the landlord is responsible for keeping the building clean, removing snow from the sidewalk out front, and supplying heat and electricity at all times. Ask questions about each individual item. Will he, for example, provide electricity in hallways and stairs? Will he heat the building when you require it? I know of one co-op that discovered that the heat was turned on only on weekdays, not on Saturday, and—you guessed it—they didn't find out until after they signed the lease.

The point is that you must sit down and think through all the possibilities that might affect the way you plan to use the space. Most landlords won't automatically provide each and every service you think you need, so bargain for them. If they refuse, forcing you to provide these services yourself, make sure your budget can handle the costs if you plan to rent the building anyway.

Will we need an accountant to keep our books?

No, but unless one of your members has some bookkeeping background, you'll need an accountant to set up a simple set of books and show your more financially inclined members how to keep them. After that, those particular members can probably handle the books themselves.

How do we go into business as a co-op?

First, decide which you want to be—a partnership or a corporation. For information on incorporation, see Chapter 15. Briefly though, there are two basic reasons for incorporating: limited liability and tax benefits.

What is limited liability? Limited liability means that if your organization goes bankrupt, creditors of the corporation can only claim the assets of the corporation if there are any—they can't ask you and your fellow members to pay debts out of your own pockets. Under a partnership, your personal assets can be claimed by creditors. Nevertheless, limited liability will probably not offer any real advantage to a co-op. Since co-ops are predicated on the idea that dues and initiation fees should cover costs, it's unlikely that enormous debts will be incurred.

Will the co-op benefit from tax advantages? Incorporation won't bring about any tax advantages unless the business is making a considerable profit, a fact that should eliminate incorporation from your consideration. Co-ops hardly ever make a profit unless they charge relatively high commissions, and even then profits can't be expected for the first few years. If business begins to boom later on, you and the others in the co-op should ask an accountant about the advantages of incorporation. But, in the beginning, incorporation seems an unnecessary expense.

Should we investigate incorporation anyway? Yes, it might be wise to check out the possibility of incorporation with a lawyer. Your particular situation might for some reason demand limited liability. Also, if your co-op is a large one with new members joining and old ones resigning with frequency, the corporate form of business might be more appropriate—partnerships usually dissolve when partners leave, meaning that a new partnership must be formed every time this happens.

How do we form a partnership?

Find out from the County Clerk's Office what forms must be filled out or what applications must be made—they vary from region to region.

Next, work out a written agreement to be signed by all members that spells out the terms of partnership. Basically this means that you'll want to include:

1. The name of the partnership.

2. The purpose for which it was organized, which will probably be to exhibit and sell art.

3. How you want to limit the powers of individual partners. For instance, you might say that all expenditures over a certain amount must be approved by all partners.

4. How dues and fees are to be paid.

5. How profits and losses are to be shared—they'll usually be shared equally between partners.

6. How assets (fixtures, equipment, and so on) are to be divided if the co-op dissolves.

This is a rudimentary outline of what goes into a partnership agreement. It would be far better to get a lawyer to do it properly for you.

Is the partnership agreement enough in itself?

Yes, but, you might want to draw up a contract similar to the dealer-artist agreement discussed in Chapter 5 *in addition* to the partnership agreement. The agreement, which would represent a contract between the co-op and its members, would clarify what each member can expect from the co-op.

Can a co-op be a nonprofit organization?

Yes, co-ops can file as nonprofit organizations either as corporations or as unincorporated associations (the equivalent of partnerships) in their states. This means that they've been established for purposes other than financial gain and that no part of their assets, income, or profits can be distributed to their members (unless paid in the form of salaries). A nonprofit organization can organize for numerous purposes, but presumably a co-op might be founded as a cultural or educational group. Indeed, many co-ops whose prime purpose is exhibition file as nonprofit organizations because they see themselves as educational institutions.

Does this mean a co-op is eligible for funding?

That depends on what kind of funding you're talking about: public funding from the federal government, state and local governments, or private funders. Federal public funders, such as the National Endowment for the Arts, are required by law to fund only nonprofit organizations that have been declared tax-exempt by the I.R.S. However, this is not always the case on a state or local level. Some state arts councils, for example, can legally fund nonprofit organizations that are not tax-exempt.

Private funders, such as foundations, can give money to anyone they please, but they are strongly encouraged to fund tax-exempt groups by the Internal Revenue Code, which provides that only contributions to tax-exempt groups are deductible for income tax purposes. Because of this, private funders rarely fund nonprofit organizations not declared tax-exempt.

Is it easy for a nonprofit co-op to become tax-exempt?

Unfortunately, it's almost impossible. Despite the fact that the requirements for nonprofit status and tax-exempt status are almost identical, the I.R.S. rarely accepts co-ops as truly nonprofit organizations. While the state simply takes a co-op's word for the fact it's nonprofit, the I.R.S. investigates. And only those groups that don't engage in any selling efforts and are primarily engaged in education activities, such as conducting classes and workshops, qualify, eliminating 99 out of every 100 nonprofit co-ops.

7. The Original Print

- Definitions
- Practices
- Legislation
- Documentation

The current printmaking boom—etching, lithography, silkscreen, engravings, woodcuts, and even linoleum block prints—erupted back in the late 50s when a number of entrepreneurs appeared on the scene. These businessmen and women operated professional printmaking shops and/or publishing facilities. The latter became important since the prime function of publishers is to distribute work for sale. Thus the publisher often is not involved in the printmaking process and prefers to buy work wholesale from workshops or artists who make their own prints.

The point of both these operations—publishing and printmaking shops—was to offer buyers of modest means an opportunity to derive an esthetic experience from an original artwork at prices they could afford. Although the collectors might not be able to pay thousands of dollars for a painting, they probably could spend a few hundred (or less) on a print. But as the print's popularity increased through the years, the esthetic experience offered by the medium lost ground to its investment potential as the motivating factor for buying. The collector jumped at the possibility that he could buy cheap and sell dear, and he frequently leapt into the arms of unscrupulous dealers and printmakers selling, for example, signed, limited editions guaranteed to double in value next year, and triple the following year. Unfortunately, many of them bought what they thought were valuable lithographs or etchings only to find they were the humble possessors of reproductions. Because these abuses and others, the public now clamors for laws to protect the unwary consumer.

The purpose of this chapter, then, is to highlight some of the problems involved in the print medium and describe the legislation a few states have enacted to deal with them.

What does "original print" mean?

There are myriad opinions on the subject, but let's take a quick look at the official definition of the United States Customs Department and a definition adopted and later dropped by the Print Council of America (PCA).

The Customs Department—it gets involved because it charges duty on reproductions but not on original works of art—defines original prints as including "only such as are *printed by hand* from plates, stones, or blocks etched, drawn, or engraved by photochemical or other mechanical processes."

What is the PCA's definition?

In 1961, the Print Council of America proclaimed that:

An original print is a work of graphic art, the general requirements of which are: (1) The Artist alone has made the image in or upon the plate, stone, woodblock or other material for the purposes of creating a work of graphic art. (2) The impression is made directly from that original material by the artist or pursuant to his directions. (3) The finished print is approved by the artist.

Why was it dropped?

Modern technology has multiplied the ways that printmakers make prints, so it's almost impossible to tell what is a pure, unadulterated original print. Even a not so recent example will demonstrate what I mean. To create a series of prints known as *Miserere,* Georges Rouault had some preliminary drawings made into plates by a photomechanical process. After the plates were completed, he worked on them with printmaking tools. On the one hand, he violated the requirements of the PCA's definition by allowing his drawings to be reproduced mechanically, and, on the other hand, he satisfied them by manually manipulating the photogravure plates.

Who are considered printmakers?

It's important to note that today we have two distinct categories of printmakers. In the first category are those artists who do everything themselves. They perform every step of the process from creating the image; deciding on the paper, inks, and so on; placing the image on the stone or plate; to printing the prints on—very frequently—their own presses.

Artists in the other category rely heavily on the craft skills of professional (master) printers and, many times, on the recommendations of their publishers as to sizes, shapes, colors, and even the images themselves. The difference between the groups was acutely summed up by Cecile Shapiro and Lauris Mason in *Fine Prints: Collecting, Buying, & Selling*:

The difference between the two methods of producing prints might be compared to home cooking and restaurant meals—one, from menu planning, to marketing, to preparation, to serving, to cleaning-up is done by an individual. The other depends upon secondary staff at every step along the way. Some home cooks are dreadful, while others are superb; the same can be said of restaurants. But one difference is certain: the latter is more expensive than the former and must cater to the taste of a broader clientele.

Despite the fact that the do-it-yourself group sometimes feels that artists in the second category are not quite kosher—not "real" —they must be considered so if they work closely with the professional printer. The only time their genuineness could be questioned is when an artist contributes nothing more to the process than a drawing, which is then copied, placed on the stone or block, and printed by someone else. In this instance, the work would be considered a reproduction.

What is a master printer?

A master printer is a professional printer who prints original etchings, lithographs, silkscreens, and so on, for other artists who supply him with a finished plate, stone, or screen. The artist may work with the master printer in developing color possibilities, or he may give the master printer a *bon à tirer* (see below).

What is your definition of an original print?

One workable definition of an original print is a work of art created solely for the print medium and no other. The reason a person makes an original print is because he's seeking a particular kind of effect that only a woodcut or an etching or whatever can give.

What is a reproduction?

It's an exact duplicate of a work that already exists in another form. If you take a drawing, for example, photograph it, make a metal plate of the photograph, and reproduce it, you have a picture of a picture—a reproduction.

The essential difference between a reproduction and an original print centers on the word "original." As Carl Zigrosser, author of one of the definitive books on the subject, *A Guide to the Collecting and Care of Original Prints* put it:

One may ask with reference to a color reproduction: Where is the origi-

nal? and receive the correct answer that the original is a painting by So and So in the collection of such and such a museum. But one cannot give the same answer with reference to an artist's etching. There is no mythical original of which the print in question would be a replica. One cannot consider the copperplate the original nor the preliminary drawing study with its sketchy lines, granted that the artist has made one (often he has not). These are but the preliminary steps in the production of the finished etching, which is the perfect embodiment of the artist's creative intention. The print itself is the original.

Are prints always called "original prints"?

Actually, the word "original" is fast falling from favor as a descriptive term. After all, a print by its very nature cannot be original in the sense of being unique. But "original" is being replaced by lawyers and legislators with equally fuzzy terms, such as the "fine print" or the "fine art print."

Joseph Rothman, former Special Assistant Attorney General of New York State in charge of art fraud and author of legal drafts that have found their way into the print laws of several states, believes that "the word original should be totally outlawed as a deceptive act if used in connection with the word print unless called multioriginal."

Nevertheless, for the sake of consistency, such artworks will be referred to in this book as original prints.

What are the most common abuses that consumers complain about?

The most obvious one—with regard to original prints—is the practice of leading the customer to believe, without actually saying so, that he's buying an original print when he's actually purchasing a photomechanical reproduction. Usually this is done through the use of the words "signed," "numbered," and "limited editions," all of which may actually be applicable to an edition of reproductions but are usually associated with original prints. Other abuses explained below are connected with the practices of signing and editioning.

What is a signed print?

A print that has been signed by its creator below the image in pencil. This relatively recent practice was popularized by Whistler, who signed prints with his Butterfly mark.

What is the significance of the signed print?

According to Zigrosser: "The signature has come to stand for, among other things, a guarantee of printing quality, a stamp of good workmanship, similar to the hallmark on silver."

How does signing a print become a misleading act?

There's nothing misleading about signing an original print after it's been printed. The signature attests to the quality, which may vary from one print to another because they are made by hand. Not so with reproductions. By the very nature of the process, all photomechanically produced reproductions are the same. No useless okay by the artist is needed to vouch for quality. When an artist signs a reproduction, therefore, he's probably doing one of two things: trying to deceive the public into believing that the reproduction is an original print, because original prints bear signatures; or adding an autograph which by its presence alone will make the reproduction seem more valuable. There's nothing illegal about the latter, as long as the work is clearly marked a reproduction; it's simply a marketing device.

Are there any other misleading signing practices?

Yes. Signing the stone or plate so it looks like an individual autograph on each print, and signing blank papers before printing are dubious practices. Both actions preclude the artist's approval.

If a master printer prints work for me, should I sign it?

Yes, but sign it differently. The PCA recommends that if you print the work yourself, you should write after your name, "imp." (*impressit*—he printed it). If a master printer executes it, the work should be signed, "John Artist del Peter Printer."

What is a numbered print?

When a print bears a number, the number supposedly indicates when in a series that particular print was printed. For example, a print marked 7/35 should mean that it was the seventh print made in an edition of 35.

What's the significance of numbering prints?

There's very little significance to numbering prints. The sole purpose of this fairly recent—yet well established—practice seems to be to provide a means to increase the marketability of a work. Collectors often assume that the earliest numbers are the best, but this isn't necessarily so. In a small edition, all impressions may be of equal quality.

Furthermore, numbering may be a meaningless gesture. Printmakers, particularly those making color images, often don't bother to keep track of the order in which they print. And sometimes, with multicolored prints, an artist will print all 40 or 80 prints one color at a time. When that color dries, he'll start printing the next one. It would be the rare printmaker indeed who would be so meticulous as to maintain the proper sequence when making a four-color print, much less one of 10 or 15 colors.

What is a limited edition?

A limited edition is one in which the artist promises to make just so many impressions and no more. Limited editions are still another product of the twentieth century. Historically, artists made prints from the same plate as long as it held up and a market for them existed. For example, records show that 73,000 impressions of a single Currier and Ives lithograph were sold.

Do artists abuse limited editions?

Yes, sometimes they do. As a general rule, the smaller the edition, the more valuable the print. Some people reduce the numbers in individual editions artificially while actually printing larger editions to make more money in the end. First, there's the practice of producing separate editions of the same image from the same plate. This tactic, while not considered fraudulent, leads to confusion. Suppose, for example, a publisher issues two editions of 40 prints each, using the same plate but two different types of papers. Isn't the total size of the edition 80? Not everyone thinks so. Paper is a crucial factor in printmaking—many reputable people would deem two such editions legitimate.

Second, and less acceptable, are those editions of the same image made from the same plate that differ only by the use of Roman numerals on one edition and Arabic numerals on the other.

Other potentially deceptive acts are associated with the selling of restrikes, artist's proofs, prints made after an artist's death, and other proofs.

What are restrikes?

Prints made from a plate, or whatever, after the original edition was issued. Restrikes are perfectly valid legally as long as they aren't sold as prints from the original limited edition. To prevent this from happening, the plate should be cancelled.

What do you mean by cancelled?

To destroy the master design or alter it in such a way that no more prints can be made from it after the original limited edition has been made. For example, an etcher might etch either his name into the plate or a line across the image. Evidence that the plate has been cancelled is given by making a print, called a cancellation proof, from the defective plate.

What's wrong with selling prints made posthumously?

Again, there's nothing fraudulent about making and selling prints after the artist's death as long as the buyer knows that he's buying a work that the artist could not approve.

What are artist's proofs?

Artist's proofs are a very small number of prints from an edition reserved for the artist's personal use. They are not numbered, but are marked A/P. Because of their personal association with the artist, these prints have added value in the eye of the collector. Unscrupulous artists and publishers have taken advantage of this fact by printing large numbers of prints marked artist's proofs. They then raise the prices accordingly, and, at the same time, reap the benefits of increasing the total number of prints to sell.

What is considered an ethical number of artist's proofs?

This has never been established by custom or law, although from time to time art groups have advocated limiting the number to 10% or 12% of each edition.

What other prints might be offered for sale?

Printer's proofs, *hors commerce,* trial proofs, and prints from different states. All perfectly valid as long as they aren't labeled and sold as something else.

What's a printer's proof? A proof bearing the artist's signature, indicating that he has found the plate satisfactory, and used as a standard against which other prints from the edition are compared. A printer's proof is also known as a *bon à tirer* (literally, a print good to print).

What's a hors commerce? A sample copy for salesmen, not counted as part of the edition, and not intended for sale.

What's a trial proof? Proofs pulled before the *bon à tirer* that aren't satisfactory. Trial proofs are rarely preserved or offered for sale, although they may be very interesting because artists frequently draw revisions on them, using them as working notes.

What's a state? A state is any stage when the plate is altered. Trial proofs are states, as are changes made after a *bon à tirer* is pulled. An artist may print an edition and then decide he wants to rework the plate and make new prints from the altered plate. The new edition would be another state. States are usually indicated by lower-case Roman numerals. For example, i/iv means the first of four states.

Was there ever an attempt to limit the size of a limited edition?

No. No law, custom, or ethic dictates the size of a limited edition. It's up to the artist and publisher.

What states have laws governing printmaking practices?

As of this writing, California, Illinois, and New York.

What does the New York law say?

The least stringent of the laws, the New York one refers only to "signed" prints. It says that any fine print (legislators substituted the word "fine" for "original") offered for sale as a "signed" print must have been signed by hand after it has been printed.

Many lawyers and legislators would like to expand the New York law. The Committee on Art of the New York City Bar Association, for example, would like to extend the legislation to deal with limited editions. The committee believes that buyers should be told if there are copies other than those indicated on the print itself or on the bill of sale. In other words, if there are other editions using different papers or inks or numbered in a different way (for instance, in Arabic and Roman numerals). The committee also recommends disclosure of the total number of artist's proofs if they exceed 12% of the limited edition.

What are the penalties for violating the New York State law? The buyer is entitled to the return of the purchase price, and, in the unlikely event that he could prove damages, i.e., financial or otherwise in excess of the purchase price, he could sue for them.

What does the Illinois statute say?

The Illinois law applies only to dealers and fine prints printed after July 1, 1972, and offered for sale unframed for $50 or more, or framed for $60 or more. It also applies both to fine prints and reproductions if they're described as signed, numbered, and/or limited editions. The bill requires the disclosure of the following facts:

1. The name of the artist and the year when printed.

2. Whether the print is an etching, engraving, woodcut, or lithograph.

3. Whether the edition is being offered as a limited edition, and, if it is, the total size of the edition (exclusive of trial proofs).

4. Whether the plate has been destroyed, effaced, altered, defaced, or cancelled after the current edition.

5. The series number of the current edition—if there were any prior editions from the same plate—and the total size of all prior editions.

6. Whether the edition is a posthumous edition or restrike, and, if so, whether the plate has been reworked.

7. The name of the workshop, if any, which printed the edition.

If the dealer does not know all the details, he must specifically state which ones he is ignorant of. Disclaiming such knowledge eliminates the dealer's responsibility for standing behind his product.

What happens if the dealer violates the Illinois law? If the dealer violates it unknowingly, the purchaser can sue for the purchase price plus interest; if the purchaser can prove that the dealer deliberately violated the law, the purchaser may recover three times the purchase price plus interest. Both actions must be brought within one year of discovery and not more than three years after the print was bought. The dealer, if convicted, can also be fined up to $1,000 by the state.

What does the California bill provide?

Almost the identical provisions as the Illinois statute with these exceptions: it applies to prints printed after July 1, 1971, which sell unframed for $25 or more, or framed for $40 or more, and to both artist and dealers.

Information to be disclosed in both sales promotional material and sales receipts includes:

1. The name of the artist and the year when printed.

2. Whether the edition is being offered as a limited edition exclusive of trial proofs, and, if so: the number of signed or numbered

impressions, or both, in the edition; the number of unsigned or unnumbered impressions, or both, in the edition; the number of artist's, publisher's, printer's, or other proofs, if any, outside the regular edition; and the total size of the edition.

3. Whether the plate has been destroyed, effaced, altered, defaced, or cancelled after the current edition.

4. The total number of states—if there were any prior states of the same print—and a designation of the state of the print in question.

5. The series number of the subject edition—if there were any prior or later editions from the same plate—and the total size of the other editions.

6. Whether the edition is a posthumous edition or restrike, and, if so, whether the plate has been reworked.

7. The name of the workshop, if any, where the edition was printed.

What are the penalties for violating the California law? The same as the penalties for violating the Illinois statute, except there is no provision for a fine if the artist or dealer is convicted.

Are other states contemplating legislation?

Florida is considering it at the time of this writing, and some California legislators are trying to revise their law to put more punch into it. They want to extend the statute to other art forms, such as photographs, collages, and sculptures produced in an edition of two or more impressions, and to provide stiffer monetary penalties. They would also like to require the seller to give more detailed information.

Are these laws fair?

That depends on your viewpoint. Many artists and dealers strenuously object to the paperwork involved and the precise descriptions demanded, particularly since a dishonest dealer can protect himself from breaking the law by claiming that he doesn't know the details of a print, while the honest person can be penalized if he makes a mistake. They also argue that sufficient laws already exist to protect the consumer from fraud.

Are just artists and dealers against these laws?

No, in an article in *American Artist* magazine, Betty Chamberlain quotes Una Johnson, former curator of prints at the Brooklyn

Figure 11. Whether you live in a state that demands print documentation or not by law, it's a good idea—particularly from a marketing point of view—to furnish a certificate of authenticity to collectors. The example shown gives sufficient information, but, if you want to, add additional information about the print process itself.

CERTIFICATE OF AUTHENTICITY

ARTIST:

Born:

Studied:

Exhibitions:

Awards:

Collections (or comments):

AUTHENTICATION: This is to certify that the print entitled _____ is an original by _____ numbers of colors _____ paper _____ year printed _____ number of authorized signed prints in the edition _____ artist's proofs _____ publisher's proofs _____ unsigned proofs _____ number of other editions _____ size of other editions _____ has plate been cancelled? _____ Printer: _____

_____   _____
Authorized Signature   Date

Museum, as saying, "It is impossible to make a law to protect a buyer who is an absolute dope. Legislation can wind up hamstringing precisely the wrong people—honest artists and dealers." And Gilbert Edelson, himself a lawyer and one-time legal adviser to the Art Dealers Association of America, feels that "dealers, if required [to follow] too many and too complicated procedures, will simply stop selling prints, and this will only hurt the artist."

What's an artist to do, then?

If you object to the legislation, organize as California artists did in 1975 to defeat the amendment described above. But whether you object to certain legislation or are even affected by it, sooner or later you'll probably have to confront the issue on an individual basis.

The consumer has a right to know such facts as whether there are any other unaccounted for prints floating around besides those he thinks comprise a limited edition. So you'll be doing yourself a favor by providing some documentation of the work. Most dealers and printmakers automatically furnish such information without being commanded to do so by law. An example of such documentation is found in Figure 11.

8. The Artist and the Publisher

- Original print publishers
- Fees
- Contracts
- Reproduction publishers
- Fees
- Contracts

Having delved into the murky topic of original prints and reproductions, let's backtrack a little to look at the problems you may run into before your work ever gets off the press. What I'm referring to are the deals you make with publishers of original prints and reproductions (meaning those to be framed and hung on the wall, not those published on greeting cards, for example, or in books). Despite the prestige of original prints, there's no stigma attached to producing high-quality reproductions as long as they don't pretend to be original prints.

No matter what printing process is used, however, the issues that should be incorporated into publishing contracts are pretty much the same for both original prints and reproductions. But in order to avoid confusion, they're discussed separately below—original prints first.

After reading this chapter go back to Chapter 4. Agreements between artists and publishers closely resemble those made between artists and clients commissioning the creation of artwork. Chapter 4, then, should be reread before signing on the dotted line of a publishing contract to refresh your memory with respect to general contract considerations, such as start and finish dates, death clauses, and so on. The discussion here is limited strictly to specific issues involved in publishing.

Who is a publisher?

A publisher is simply a person who "issues or causes to issue" printed works for sale, according to the dictionary. This means that a publisher doesn't have to be either a printer or a retailer, although both can qualify for the title if they can bring the work before the public.

Who usually publishes original prints?

The artist, the artist in partnership with someone else, or a businessperson who commissions (or sometimes buys) an edition.

As publisher, how will I sell my original prints?

To the public directly, through galleries, or sometimes through wholesalers.

If I sell original prints to galleries, how much should I charge?

If you sell only a few works, you would charge about 50% of the retail price. If you sell the whole edition, 35% to 40% of the retail price would be equitable, although you may have to settle for less if you're relatively unknown.

If I consign original prints to galleries, what commission will they charge?

You can expect a dealer to charge up to 50% of the retail sales price. Commissions on original prints are usually higher than on unique works.

Is it better to sell or consign original prints to galleries?

Because of the fragility of original prints, it's usually a better idea to sell outright. Otherwise you take the risk of getting the work back damaged.

Should I have a contract with a gallery if I consign original prints?

Yes, if you consign work, a contract similar to the artist-dealer contract shown in Chapter 5 would be appropriate.

If I sell original prints to a wholesaler, how much should I charge?

If you sell to a wholesaler, once again the price is based on how many pieces you offer. A few pieces would justify your asking 25% of the retail price (50% of the wholesale price). If you sell the whole edition, you might have to go to as low as 10% of the retail price.

Who do artists usually co-publish original prints with?

An artist and his dealer often team up to produce an edition. Each makes an equal investment in the project. In other words, the artist will either execute the image on the stone or plate and print the edition or supervise the printing in a workshop, while the dealer provides the money for materials and possibly printing costs, if the artist works in a print workshop. Profits are split 50-50, although some dealers will subtract distribution costs (what it costs them to sell your work around the country) before profits are divided.

Who else do artists co-publish with?

Joint ventures are also fairly common between artists and the owners of print workshops. In these cases, you may find no money changing hands at all. What frequently happens is that the artist supplies the image and works on the stone at the workshop. When the edition has been printed, the printer takes half and the artist takes the other half. Both are free to do what they want with their part of the edition, although they should have an agreement promising to uphold an agreed-upon retail price.

Fifty-fifty arrangements are less likely to occur with a straight-forward wholesale publisher (described below). But if your name is big enough, you could still demand to split the profits down the middle after printing and sales costs have been eliminated.

Who usually commissions original prints?

Three types of businesses. Their functions frequently overlap, but in general they represent the three basic vehicles for bringing an original print before the public.

1. A print workshop. The owner may plan to wholesale the work through galleries or retail it through advertising. Gemini G.E.L. and Universal Limited Art Editions, which publish the works of such superstars as Robert Rauschenberg and Jasper Johns, are examples of workshop publishers—though they may also be examples of 50-50 joint ventures.

2. A wholesale publisher. Although he may have printing facilities, his major role is to sell prints to galleries and other retail stores. Occasionally, he may sell some work directly to the consumer through advertisements in periodicals and by direct mail.

3. A dealer. He will sell the prints through his own gallery and possibly wholesale them to other galleries.

Should my agreement with a publisher of original prints be in writing?

Of course. It might be an informal letter of a couple of paragraphs setting forth the financial arrangements. A better idea would be to draw up a more comprehensive contract including the usual clauses referring to the scope of work and start and completion dates, plus the following specific clauses: remuneration; artist's proofs; responsibilities; rights and copyright; effacement; and termination (see below).

If a publisher commissions me to make an original print, how will he pay me?

Either with a flat fee or a royalty.

How do publishers arrive at a flat fee?

Everyone has his own method. Some publishers may pay a flat fee for the entire edition equivalent to what you would get for a work on paper, such as a drawing. Other publishers will offer an arbitrary sum based on their estimate of your sales potential and the costs of printing and distribution.

How do they work out royalties?

Royalties are payments that are paid after the work is sold rather than when it's done. There are no hard and fast rules here either. One wholesale publishing company offers artists one-sixth of a mutually agreed-upon retail price, with half of this amount being paid to the artist on delivery of work and the other half paid as the prints are sold.

Royalties, if an edition sells out, should amount to more than a flat fee. This is only as it should be—after all, by not accepting money up front, you are in essence subsidizing the publisher until sales start coming in.

What are ideal flat fees and royalties?

The whole point of both flat fees and royalties is that ideally they should be roughly equivalent to the same old formula of 25% of the retail price. But only big names will be able to command this percentage. If you're an unknown, expect to go as low as 10%, maybe even lower. Another company told me they offer a flat fee that would equal a 5% royalty, but they supplement this fee with free transportation to and from New York from anywhere in the country plus room and board for two to three weeks while the artist works in their workshop. Don't forget, of course, that percentages will also be lower if you don't do the printing yourself.

Which is better?

Unless you're confident that the edition will sell out, and even appreciate in value, sending prices up before it sells out, a flat fee is probably better than royalties. You'll get your money immediately without waiting months or years for it, or maybe not getting it at all.

In any case, most publishers will offer flat fees rather than royalties, unless they have some pressing reason for not wanting to pay you immediately.

Do I get paid for preliminary sketches for the project?

In any special commission, you should ask for payment for preliminary work, so if the project falls through, you won't be caught short. This sum may represent additional compensation or—more commonly—it will be an advance against royalties or the final fee.

Are advances returnable if the original prints don't sell?

They shouldn't be, so make sure your contract says they aren't returnable unless you fail to complete the work.

When will I be paid a flat fee for a commission?

A flat fee for a commission of original prints should be treated the same way as that for any special project. Therefore, you should request a schedule of payments. It might run something like this: first payment on execution of the contract; second payment when you approve the trial proof for printing; and final payment when you sign the prints.

When will I be paid royalties?

Royalties are generally paid every six months, and, in your contract, you should have a clause granting you the right to inspect the publisher's financial records concerning your work.

How many artist's proofs should I be entitled to?

Whether paid a flat fee or royalties, you should also be entitled to a certain number of free artist's proofs—10% to 12% of an edition of original prints is the general rule.

What responsibilities will the publisher have?

It goes without saying that publishing, promoting, and selling the prints are the publisher's responsibilities. He might also agree to provide equipment, materials, working space, and technical assistance, including a master printer. In fact, you might want to stipulate that your agreement will be terminated, if the services of a particular master printer aren't available to you.

What responsibilities will I have?

You will be required to assist with proof correction (if you don't do the printing yourself) until you approve the *bon à tirer*, which the printer will use as a standard with which to judge the quality of succeeding prints. And you will be required to hand sign the prints.

What rights will I give the publisher?

You'll give him the right to publish, promote, and sell your work.

Who owns the copyright?

Unless you agree in writing to the contrary, you own it. So make sure your copyright notice is placed in the stone or fixed by hand later. Your contract should also require the publisher to register the copyright with the Copyright Office in your name (Chapter 2).

What do you mean by an effacement clause?

In order to protect yourself against future accusations that your limited edition of original prints exceeded the limit, your contract should have an effacement clause. It should state that the publisher agrees to efface the stones or plates (if you don't do the printing and cannot efface the stone yourself) so overruns on the edition, restrikes from the original plate, and reprinting on different papers won't occur. The contract should further require the publisher to furnish you with a cancellation proof, a print made on the damaged plate, as proof of effacement.

What should be in a termination clause?

It should provide that all rights you granted the publisher (to publish, sell, promote) revert to you on termination. And if you gave him the copyright, be sure to demand that it be transferred back to you on termination. Finally, you might want your contract to give you the opportunity to purchase the plate, if it doesn't belong to you and the contract terminates before the edition is complete.

Who usually publishes reproductions?

In general, retail dealers and small printers don't get involved in publishing reproductions. Reproductions are usually made by wholesale publishers who sell to retail stores or through advertisements. These businesses frequently have their own printing plants, but sometimes they contract the work out to outside printers. Occasionally, an artist will publish his own reproductions, which he pays a printer to make, and sell them through retail outlets.

If I publish reproductions, what should I charge a retail store?

About 50% of the retail price.

What should be in a contract with a publisher of reproductions?

Most large publishing firms offer relatively inflexible contracts, which you may not be able to change unless you're a proven moneymaker. If you're not, don't sign just any contract—make sure the terms put forth in the following clauses suit you: remuneration; publication rights; return of original art; revisions; and insurance. See below for details.

How do reproduction publishers pay?

Sometimes with royalties, but usually with flat fees (see above).

What is an average royalty on a reproduction?

Since editions of reproductions are generally very large, from 1,000 to 5,000, the royalty would be much smaller per print than that paid on a limited edition of original prints. Two and a half percent to 5% of the wholesale price, therefore, would not be out of line; neither would even half that if royalties are based on retail price. This means that if an edition of 3,000 reproductions sold wholesale for $10 and your royalty was 2.5%, you would earn $750 if the edition sells out.

What would an average flat fee be?

There's no such thing as an average fee. But many publishers will pay a flat fee that is somewhat in the neighborhood of the amount you would make in royalties if the edition sells out. So if you were asked to do an edition similar to the one described in the previous paragraph, you would probably be offered $650 or $700.

Are artist's fees for reproductions based on reputation?

Somewhat. But unlike publishers of original prints who pay big names more than unknowns, publishers of reproductions base their fees to a large extent on their enthusiasm for the work itself and their estimate of its sales potential in terms of a pleasing image rather than on the artist's reputation.

When do publishers pay flat fees and royalties?

Flat fees are generally paid within 30 days of delivery of the original artwork, and royalties every six months—so get the timing of these payments in the contract. And once again, make sure you have a clause granting you the right to inspect the publisher's financial records regarding your work.

Who owns the copyright on the original artwork?

You do, unless the publisher demands it and you're willing to give it up. If you retain it, make sure to put proper copyright notice on the painting or drawing (see Chapter 2) and register it.

Who owns the copyright on the reproductions?

Again you do, unless you're willing to give it up. If you keep it, your contract should require the publisher to place copyright notice on the reproductions and register it with the Copyright Office in your name.

Should I give up my copyright?

If giving up the copyright seems unfair to you, you have the option of not signing the contract. But the deal might be lucrative enough to make selling your copyright worthwhile. Nevertheless, you might try to amend the contract so if your contract terminates, copyright will revert to you. Better still, if you have enough clout, you should try to grant only limited publication rights.

What do you mean by limited publication rights?

This means you limit the right to reproduce your artwork to an edition of only a certain number of reproductions. This doesn't concern an edition of reproductions that's advertised as a limited edition—if this is the case, the publisher is bound to reproduce only a certain number of reproductions and then efface the plate just as a publisher of original prints does.

When reproductions are not limited in this sense, theoretically the publisher can reproduce your work indefinitely—and without further compensation to you unless you're being paid royalties. But if you're working on a flat fee basis, you should grant publication rights for only a limited number of reproductions, say 5,000. Then if the publisher wants to reproduce more, he would have to pay you another fee.

Will the publisher want to copyright this limited edition of reproductions?

Yes, he might want to, if you grant him the copyright.

Why would he want to copyright in his own name?

Even though he has the rights to only one edition, he does have a vested interest in the reproductions, and he may not want to rely on you to sue if infringement occurs, figuring that most artists like to avoid legal confrontations.

Who owns the painting or drawing after it has been reproduced?

That's up to you and the publisher and should be clarified in your agreement. Chances are the publisher only wants the rights to reproduction, but there's no guarantee he'll give the work back unless it's clearly stated in the contract.

Can the publisher request that I make changes in my image?

That depends on what's in the contract. Many companies will demand this right. On the other hand, if your reputation is secure, you ought to be able to eliminate this clause, substituting one of your own that prohibits such requests.

Who carries insurance on my artwork?

While the publisher has it, he should, so make sure it's in the contract.

What's an example of a good contract with a publisher?

Look at the one shown in Figure 12. It's an example of a contract used by a leading publishing house that gives the artist a fair break.

Figure 12. This is an actual example of a contract used by a leading publisher (the name has been changed). It's shown here because it represents a fair contract from the artist's standpoint.

CONTRACT WITH PUBLISHER

Dear Mr.

Graphics Unlimited ("GU") has acquired from _____ ("the Artist") the right to reproduce a painting entitled "Arabesque" ("the Work") upon the following terms and conditions:

(1) The Artist hereby grants to GU the exclusive right throughout the world to publish, manufacture, advertise, distribute and sell color reproductions of the Work ("the Reproduction").

(2) Each Reproduction shall be approximately _____" in size, excluding margins.

(3) In consideration hereof, GU shall pay to the Artist upon execution of this Agreement, as a nonrefundable advance against the royalty hereinafter specified, the amount of $_____.

(4) GU shall pay to the Artist a royalty of 1.2% of retail price per copy for each Reproduction sold by GU.

(5) GU may cause the Work to be reproduced by such method and by such entities and means as GU in its sole discretion may select.

(6) GU shall furnish to the Artist, without charge, six (6) Reproductions and the Artist may purchase additional Reproductions at fifty percent (50%) of the retail price of each Reproduction.

(7) The Artist shall deliver the Work to GU simultaneously with the execution of this Agreement. GU shall retain the Work and shall proceed promptly to have plates made. The Work shall be returned to the Artist within 180 days of the date of this Agreement. While it is in the possession of GU, the Work shall be insured against all risks.

(8) Each Reproduction will carry a legend indicating the size and medium of the Work, and the name of the Artist. If the Artist so advises GU in writing within five (5) days after the date of this Agreement, the legend on each Reproduction will include the nationality and date of birth of the Artist.

(9) The ownership of the copyright in the Reproduction shall at all times reside in GU and the ownership of the copyright in the Work shall at all times reside in the Artist.

(10) The Artist warrants originality, authorship and ownership of the Work; that the Artist has the full power to enter into this Agreement; that neither the Work nor the Reproduction has been heretofore used or published; that no right in the Work or Reproduction has heretofore been assigned, licensed or transferred; and that the use or publication of the Reproduction by GU will not infringe upon any copyright, proprietary or other right of any third party. The Artist agrees not to authorize others to use or publish the Work or the Reproduction during the term of this Agreement.

(11) This Agreement is to continue in effect for the term of the copyright on the Reproduction.

(12) GU shall keep accurate books and records with respect to all transactions herein contemplated, which shall be available for inspection and copying by the Artist at reasonable times and upon reasonable notice during regular business hours in order to verify any statement or accounting rendered hereunder.

(13) If GU shall have sold more than fifty (50) Reproductions during the prior six (6) months, GU shall account to the Artist ninety (90) days following each June 30 and December 31 during the term hereof, each such accounting to be accompanied by that amount, if any, therein shown to be payable.

(14) This Agreement contains the entire understanding of the parties and shall be construed under and in accordance with the laws of the State of _____.

Please confirm that the foregoing accurately and completely sets forth our entire understanding by signing and returning the enclosed copy of this letter.

Very truly yours,
Graphics Unlimited

By _____
James Brown, President

Confirmed and Agreed to:

_____
Artist

9. The Artist and the Museum

· Lending
· Insurance
· Donating
· Selling

Every artist dreams of the day when he has the opportunity to exhibit his work in a prestigious museum. The usual ways to achieve this goal are to be invited by the museum to take part in an exhibition, to be selected for a juried exhibition, or to sell or donate work to a museum. (You can also bequeath work and rent through museums, but the former topic will be taken up in Chapter 16 and the latter was discussed in Chapter 3.)

Once your work has been accepted by a museum, you may be too elated to think about the legal and financial details involved in this honor, but you should keep the following things in mind.

If I'm invited to lend work for exhibition, will I get a contract?

Probably. Most museums have standard contracts, such as the one in Figure 13, detailing the terms concerning the loan of a work for an exhibition. Each term may be subject to negotiation. And if you don't get a contract automatically, ask for one.

In general, what do museum loan agreements cover?

An exact description of the work received for loan, the length of the loan, plus clauses detailing:

1. Loss or damage—who's responsible at what times.

2. Value—how much the work is really worth (see below).

3. Insurance coverage—who provides it at what times (see below).

4. Option to buy, if any.

5. Restoration and repair—who will supervise and pay for them.

6. Framing. The museum is probably not going to pay for this, even when you've been invited to exhibit.

Figure 13. This is an example of the type of agreement you should receive from a museum when you lend work for an exhibition. Before you sign such a contract, be sure to check the conditions on the back.

WHITNEY MUSEUM OF AMERICAN ART / LOAN AGREEMENT

945 Madison Avenue, New York, N.Y. 10021 (212) 794-0600

Please complete, sign and return. The blue copy is for your records.

EXHIBITION

Area
Code

Lender_____ **Telephone (Business) (** **)**_____
(Home) (**)**_____

Address_____
(Unless otherwise instructed below, work will be shipped from and returned to this address)

Credit_____
(Exact form of lender's name for catalogue, labels and publicity)

Name of Artist_____ **Born**_____ **Died**_____
(year) (year)

Address of Artist_____

Title of Work_____

Medium or Materials and Support_____

Size: Painting, drawing, etc. (excl. frame or mat): H_____ W_____ Outer dimensions of frame: H_____ W_____

Sculpture (excl. pedestal) or relief: H_____ W_____ D_____ Approx. Wt._____

Pedestal: H_____ W_____ D_____ Approx. Wt._____ Detachable?_____

Date of Work_____If date appears on work, where?_____

Signature If work is signed, where?_____

Is Work for Sale?_____ **Selling Price**_____ (See conditions on the reverse)

Insurance Value (U.S. Currency) $_____
(See conditions on the reverse; insurance cannot exceed selling price, if any)

Do you prefer to maintain your own insurance?_____If so, estimated premium_____

Framing: Is the work framed?_____If necessary, may we reframe or remat the work?_____May we substitute plexiglas for glass?_____.

The work will be returned to the lender in its original frame or mat unless other arrangements are made with the Museum in writing.

Photographs: Which of the following are available: Black and white photographs for catalogue reproduction and publicity? (If known, please give negative number)_____ Color separations or plates?_____ Transparencies?_____

Color slides, post cards or other reproductions for sale?_____

Unless permission is declined here, it is understood that this work may be photographed, telecast and reproduced for publicity purposes connected with this exhibition and for illustration in the Museum's catalogue and other publications, and that slides of it may be made and distributed for educational use.

Special Instructions: Ship from_____ Return to_____ Other_____

Duration of Loan: ☐ at Whitney Museum only; ☐ at Whitney Museum and subsequent tour.

THE CONDITIONS OF THIS LOAN AS STATED ABOVE AND ON THE REVERSE ARE ACCEPTED.

Signed:_____ Date:_____
(Lender or authorized agent)

CONDITIONS

1. The Whitney Museum of American Art (the "Museum") will exercise the same care with respect to the work of art referred to on the reverse (the "work") as it does in the safekeeping of comparable property of its own.

2. The work shall remain in the possession of the Museum and/or the other museums participating in the exhibition for which it has been borrowed (the "participating museums") for the time specified on the reverse, but may be withdrawn from such exhibition at any time by the Director or Trustees of the Museum and/or of any of the participating museums. The work will be returned only to the owner or lender at the address stated on the reverse unless the Museum is notified in writing to the contrary. If the legal ownership of the work shall change during the pendency of this loan, whether by reason of death, sale, insolvency, gift or otherwise, the new owner may, prior to its return, be required to establish his legal right to receive the work by proof satisfactory to the Museum.

3. The Museum will insure the work wall-to-wall under its fine-arts policy for the amount specified by the lender on the reverse against all risks of physical loss or damage from any external cause while in transit and on location during the period of this loan; provided, however, that if the work shall have been industrially fabricated and can be replaced to the artist's specifications, the amount of such insurance shall be limited to the cost of such replacement. If no amount shall have been specified by the lender, the Museum will insure the work at its own estimated valuation. The Museum's fine-arts policy contains the usual exclusions for loss or damage due to war, invasion, hostilities, rebellion, insurrection, confiscation by order of any Government or public authority, risks of contraband or illegal transportation and/or trade, nuclear damage, wear and tear, gradual deterioration, moths, vermin and inherent vice, and for damage sustained due to and resulting from any repairing, restoration or retouching process unless caused by fire and/or explosion. The lender agrees that, in the event of loss or damage, recovery shall be limited to such amount, if any, as may be paid by the insurer, hereby releasing the Museum, each of the participating museums, and the Trustees, officers, agents and employees of the Museum and of each of the participating museums from liability for any and all claims arising out of such loss or damage.

4. If the lender chooses to maintain his own insurance, the Museum must be supplied with a certificate of insurance naming the Museum and each of the participating museums as an additional assured or waiving subrogation against the Museum and each of the participating museums. If the lender shall fail to supply the Museum with such a certificate, this loan agreement shall constitute a release of the Museum and of each of the participating museums from any liability in connection with the work. The Museum cannot accept responsibility for any error or deficiency in information furnished to the lender's insurer or for any lapses in coverage.

5. The Museum assumes the right, unless specifically denied by the lender, to examine the work by all modern photographic means available. Information thus gathered will remain confidential and will not be published without the written consent of the lender. It is understood that the Museum will not clean, restore, or otherwise alter the work without the consent of the lender.

6. The Museum's right to return the work shall accrue absolutely at the termination of the loan. If the Museum, after making all reasonable efforts and through no fault of its own, shall be unable to return the work within sixty days after such termination, then, the Museum shall have the absolute right to place the work in storage, to charge regular storage fees and the cost of insurance therefor, and to have and enforce a lien for such fees and cost. If, after five years, the work shall not have been reclaimed, then, and in consideration for its storage, insurance and safeguarding during such period, the work shall be deemed an unrestricted gift to the Museum.

7. If the work is for sale and is sold during the period of this loan, the lender shall pay the following amount to the Museum to be used exclusively for the Museum's Art Purchase Fund: 5% of the selling price on a sale to another institution; on any other sale, 10% of the first $25,000 of the selling price and 5% of the selling price, if any, in excess of $25,000.

7. Reproduction rights. You'll probably want to grant them for catalogs and publicity work.

8. Sale price, if your work is for sale. Although museums don't usually sell work for artists, you're likely to find this occurring during regional juried shows.

If there's a purchase prize, how much should it be?

A purchase prize for an open exhibition should be at least equal to two-thirds of the amount you can expect to sell the work for. If your prints, for example, sell for $150, the purchase prize should be at least $100. If it isn't, it won't be worthwhile competing for unless you think the prestige will make up for the financial loss. If that isn't the case, then when you enter the show, indicate on the entry blank that you don't wish to be considered for the prize.

Who carries insurance if a museum invites me to exhibit?

The museum should, but if you already carry insurance on your work, they may agree to reimburse you for your insurance payments for the time they possess the work. Museum coverage is usually "wall to wall," meaning that they insure work from the time it leaves the wall of your studio (or gallery or whatever) until it returns. Occasionally, a museum may refuse to insure work if it's too fragile.

If a museum refuses to insure work that's not fragile, you should refuse to lend it unless they specifically agree in the contract that they'll compensate you fully in the event of loss, damage, or theft.

Who sets the valuation on my work for insurance purposes?

As a general rule, you will. However, if the museum feels you've made an unreasonably high valuation, they may insist on a more realistic value, and they may demand that the value exclude your dealer's commission.

Museums sometimes balk at valuations placed on works made from an artist's model by an industrial operation, such as a steel fabricating plant. The Whitney Museum of American Art, for example, says in its agreement, "That if the work shall be industrially fabricated and can be replaced to the artist's specifications, the amount of such insurance shall be limited to the cost of such replacement."

If I leave work to be considered for open exhibition, will it be insured?

No. When you leave work for museum officials to consider for inclusion in a show, you'll receive a receipt. (The same holds true if you leave work for them to consider buying or accepting as a donation.)

The receipt usually informs you that the museum will not insure the work nor pay for shipping and packing costs. Indeed, should you not pick up the work when notified, the receipt may state that the work will be shipped to you collect or stored at your expense.

On the more positive side, museums are liable by law for loss or damage if they fail to exercise proper care of the artwork (see Chapter 11 on bailments).

Will it be insured if selected for inclusion in the show?

Yes. When your work is selected for an exhibition, you'll be asked to sign a loan agreement—just as you are if you're invited to exhibit—which should promise to insure the work.

Will a museum charge a commission if it sells a work?

It will probably take a minimal commission; 10% would be about average.

If I donate artwork, can I take a tax deduction?

Yes, but if the work you're donating to a museum is your own, you may only deduct the cost of the material used to create the work—not the fair market value.

Only people donating works of others can claim a deduction of the fair market value. Before 1969, the tax law allowed artists as well as many other people to deduct the fair market value of their donations from income. The Tax Reform Act of 1969 amended this law because of the many abuses committed by politicians and other big names who donated their papers and then claimed large tax deductions.

What's the result of this tax law?

The result of this reform has been a disaster for our cultural institutions. When the I.R.S. refused to allow deductions, artists refused to part with their work. For instance: in the two-year period of 1968 and 1969, various artists made 125 donations of their own work to the Museum of Modern Art (MOMA) in New

York. In the four-year period of 1972–1975, MOMA received only 29 donations. Other museums reported similar losses, which could not be compensated for through purchases because of the increasingly poor financial position of museums.

Because of this, both legislators and artists have been battling every year since for reform of the reform.

If I donate a work of art, can I demand permanent display?

Museums don't like gifts with strings attached. In fact, most museums refuse to accept donations at all if restrictions are placed on them. So unless you're extremely influential, this demand—as well as any others, such as how work is to be displayed—will probably be denied.

Can I demand to get first chance to buy back a work I sell?

Probably. This provision, of course, would come into effect only if the museum later decides to sell your work. According to a museum survey article in *American Artist,* many museums routinely agree to this. So you would do well to incorporate this requirement into your sales agreement.

Can I borrow back my work for exhibitions?

Yes, most museums will go along with this practice. But if you want to insure its cooperation, make it one of the terms of sale after finding out what the museum's policy on this is.

If I sell a work, can I dictate display terms?

Not unless your clout is extraordinary—otherwise, you probably won't be able to get such a requirement into your sales agreement.

If I sell my work, will the museum want the copyright?

It may, but most likely it will simply want to be granted reproduction rights so it can reproduce the work for postcards and so on.

Will I get royalties for reproductions?

As a matter of courtesy, museums sometimes pay the artist a royalty on reproductions suitable for framing and on reproductions used on Christmas cards—although not usually on postcards —regardless of who owns the copyright, or even if the work is in the public domain. They'll also generally share royalties with an artist if they sell the reproduction rights to someone else. The only time they don't pay royalties is when the reproductions are made for educational purposes, such as slides for slide shows or book illustrations.

Despite their generosity, however, it's a wise idea to keep the copyright, in case you want to sell reproduction rights to others. So, on your sales agreement, make it clear that you retain the copyright.

How much of a discount will a museum ask for when buying?

Ten percent is the usual museum discount, although it might ask for more.

10. The Content of Art: Can It Get You Into Trouble?

· Libel
· Invasion of privacy
· Flag desecration
· Obscenity

Times change, and so do fashions in art and law enforcement. In modern times Supreme Court justices have watched a lot of movies in the dark, and they have rarely come out smiling. Thus, our perhaps not blind, but bleary-eyed, justices have pronounced from time to time—contradictorily—on the constitutional status of art. Art is protected by the First Amendment but obscenity is not. Nor is libel, invasion of someone's privacy, or desecration of the Stars and Stripes. The First Amendment guarantees everyone in this country freedom of speech, and art is legally considered either pure speech (for example, a mural or still-life oil) or symbolic speech (for instance, a sculpture or construction using the flag). In general, an artist of serious intent can rest assured that he won't be charged criminally or civilly with wrongdoing because of what he puts on canvas or on a wall or in a gallery window even when the imagery involves sex or nudity or public controversy.

But there are limits. The twists and turns of obscenity law still lead back to the issue of local community standards. Technically, that is now an issue to be decided by juries in individual cases (and under the guidance of a judge's instructions). But there won't be a trial at all if the local police don't first exercise their own judgment and decide the offending display—be it innocent nudity or immodest mischief—is not art but rather obscenity. And who can say when the high-mindedness of local community standards may become the moving force in a police vigilante action to "clean up" the community by seizing art or prosecuting artists? It doesn't happen every day, but it can. And the same legal vagueness and practical uncertainty are also present in the areas of libel, privacy, and flag desecration.

What is libel?

Everyone has the right to a good professional and private reputation, i.e., a reputation free from false and malicious injury by others. Causing that injury by public utterance—a speech, a newspaper article, or an artwork—may be libel. If you paint a libelous picture but hide it in your studio, you won't be accused of libel because the offended party can't say he lost his good reputation in the eyes of his business associates or the general public. But if it's exhibited or published, you may be in for trouble.

What sort of artwork would be libelous?

Work that ridicules or demeans someone or depicts him falsely in some way so his reputation suffers. For the sake of example, a libelous work might depict someone as a drunk or with a sexual problem. Or if you paint specific members of your local medical society dripping with blood and gore and grinning from ear to ear, these doctors will no doubt scream libel.

What if it's true?

If the depiction is a completely accurate portrayal and you can prove it, you'd win your case if sued for libel. But proving what's actually true—not just what seems to be true—may be harder than you think.

How often are fine artists sued for libel?

Frankly, I've never heard of a case—but that doesn't mean it can't happen. If you've painted a movie actress who is famous for playing *ingenues* as a common prostitute and called the picture *A Star on the Street,* it would be a good idea to hesitate before showing it in public. You may not have meant it as a personal slur, but simply as a comment on the age-old combination of careerism and sex, but that doesn't matter. A libel suit might be brought even though you had no intention of maligning her.

What artists run the biggest risks of being sued for libel?

Cartoonists. In their exaggerated, humorous, or satirical treatments of public figures, they frequently walk a fine line between what's libelous and what's described as "fair comment."

What is fair comment?

The privilege of fair comment applies to statements in either writing or artwork about well-known public figures or about unknown individuals who are unexpectedly thrown into public life (such as victims of crimes). Fair comment is similar to the right to freedom of the press. Anyone in the news can be legally subjected to a certain amount of ridicule or contempt by writers and artists, as long as the depiction remains a reflection about the person's performance in public life. When it goes beyond this, fair comment no longer applies. For example, a cartoonist might fairly depict a hawkish congressman as a warlord, but he'd better not portray him as susceptible to bribery and controlled by organized crime, unless he's prepared to prove it.

Fair comment also protects art critics against suits by artists who don't like the way their art was reviewed. So forget about suing someone who said in print that your latest exhibition was a real bomb—you placed your work in the public spotlight, and it's open to fair comment.

What is invasion of privacy?

Under some state laws, the right to privacy prohibits the use of the name or image of any person for commercial or advertising purposes without his written consent. When this right is violated, you have invasion of privacy. The purpose of these laws it to prevent unscrupulous persons from exploiting the valuable names and pictures of people—usually public figures—to increase the sale of products without paying adequate compensation for use.

What does this mean to artists?

It means that commercial artists and photographers must get permission from their subjects before their artwork goes into an advertisement or on a commercial product. If you've painted a recognizable picture of Cher, for example, which is to be used on T-shirts, you'll invade her privacy if you don't get her permission.

How do invasion of privacy laws affect the fine artist?

The impact of these laws on fine artists is much less clear than for commercial artists and photographers because there have been hardly any cases. This in itself indicates that very little danger exists for the artist creating a work of art not intended for advertising or commercial purposes. In fact, at least one court has found that a serious work of art cannot represent an invasion of privacy with respect to a person depicted.

If I paint portraits of famous persons for magazine covers, must I get their permission?

No. Even though the picture will appear on a commercial product, you are protected by the doctrine of fair comment discussed above. You're allowed to paint any public figure or private individual if he's somehow newsworthy as long as you don't libel him.

What if I paint portraits of public figures from photographs, for sale?

This could be invasion of privacy. Technically, you're painting these particular people because of the financial benefit involved, so you might be considered to be commercially exploiting them for your own gain. On the other hand, you'd probably be able to claim protection under the doctrine of fair comment. It doesn't seem as though any cases have resolved the issue, perhaps indicating its unimportance as a practical matter.

If a commissioned portrait I painted is rejected, should I get permission before I exhibit or sell it?

To be on the safe side, yes, get permission from the client, though it's not likely that the person who commissioned you would sue you for invasion of privacy. Nor could he sue you on these grounds in all states. In New York State, for example, the mere exhibition of a portrait is not sufficient to bring suit for invasion of privacy. But since state laws differ, why not protect yourself by getting permission in writing from your client.

When would I sue someone for invasion of privacy?

When your name is used for commercial or advertising purposes. Take the example of the case of Harry Neyland v. the Home Pattern Co., Inc. Briefly, Neyland had authorized a magazine called *Arts and Decoration* to reproduce his painting. Sometime later, an ad promoting patterns for embroidered pillows appeared in the *Ladies' Home Journal,* a magazine published by the Home Pattern Co. One of the designs resembled the painting in *Arts and Decoration.* The composition was altered slightly, but the text of the ad baldly stated "The C. W. Morgan [a square-rigger] on the pillow comes straight from the painting by Harry Neyland."

Neyland sued for infringement of copyright on the painting, but he didn't stop there. He sued for invasion of privacy because his name had been used for purposes of trade, and he won.

When else should a fine artist worry about invading the privacy of his clients?

Anytime you plan to list the names of your private collectors in magazine copy, catalogs, programs, and so on, get written permission first. The collectors may not want their names published and could bring action against you if you do.

What's flag desecration?

The act of desecrating the American flag has never been defined once and for all, although many state and federal laws prohibit it.

What do these laws prohibit?

Most laws forbid mutilation and other unconventional uses of the flag, as well as casting contempt on it. The wording of a New York State statute is typical of these acts. It says: "Any person who . . . shall publicly mutilate, deface, defile, or defy, trample upon or cast contempt upon [the flag] either by words or act . . . shall be guilty of a misdemeanor."

Don't flag desecration laws violate the first amendment?

Sometimes. The courts have found certain ones unconstitutional, particularly those that prohibit the placement of symbols or writing on the flag.

Other courts have held that these statutes are justified in order to prevent a breach of peace or to protect the flag as a symbol representing national sovereignty.

Nevertheless, most flag desecration cases occurred during the Vietnam War—when many artists used the flag in unorthodox ways to symbolize protests against the U.S. military policy—and the sound and fury over flag desecration has abated. The famous *Radich* flag desecration case, which dragged through the courts for seven years until 1974, indicated that freedom of speech, as guaranteed by the First Amendment, should receive a higher priority than laws condemning flag desecration. This case should set a precedent for some years to come, unless the country is propelled into some new international catastrophe.

What did the court say in this decision?

The flag and that which it symbolizes is dear to us, but not so cherished as those high moral, legal and ethical precepts which our Constitution teaches. When our interests in preserving the integrity of the flag conflict with the higher interest of preserving, protecting and defending the Constitution, the latter must prevail, even when it results in the expression of ideas about our flag and nation which are defiant, contemptuous or unacceptable to most Americans. United States ex rel. Radich v. Criminal Court of the City of New York.

What is the legal definition of obscenity?

The courts have been attempting to define obscenity for years and have never come to any conclusions, although they do offer guidelines.

What are these guildelines?

Prior to 1973, material was obscene if:

1. The dominant theme of the material taken as a whole appealed to a prurient interest in sex;

2. The material was patently offensive because it affronted contemporary community standards relating to the description or representation of sexual matters; or

3. The material was utterly without redeeming social value.

In 1973, these guidelines changed.

What are the guidelines now?

Now material is obscene if:

1. The average person, applying contemporary community standards, would find that the work, taken as a whole, appeals to the prurient interest;

2. The work depicts or describes in a patently offensive way sexual conduct specifically defined by the applicable state law; or

3. The work taken as a whole lacks serious literary, artistic, political, or scientific value.

That last clause gives a lot more leeway in curbing free expression than the previous restriction that material had to be "utterly without redeeming social value."

Furthermore, this historic decision, Miller v. United States, handed over to local and state authorities the power to decide what is obscene. According to Chief Justice Burger:

It is neither realistic nor constitutionally sound to read the First Amendment as requiring that the people of Maine or Mississippi accept public depiction of conduct found tolerable in Las Vegas or New York City. People in different states vary in their taste and attitudes and this diversity is not to be strangled by the absolution of imposed uniformity.

What are the chances that a fine artist will be arrested for obscenity?

Not very great. Works of art are usually considered to represent serious attempts to express artistic concepts and sentiments and are thus protected by the First Amendment. So, despite the fact that your work contains nudes or even explicit sexual references, it's not likely that you would be arrested for obscenity. Law enforcement groups are more concerned with cracking down on sexually explicit books and magazines that are thrust on the public by aggressive sales campaigns.

Nevertheless, with every community in the country getting into the act of defining obscenity, it can happen.

Do you have an example? Yes, in August, 1974, Maine artist Russell Aharonian began work on a mural commissioned for a mall in Portsmouth, New Hampshire. In the past, Aharonian's mixed-media work had frequently included themes that some might consider erotic, and the shopping mall collage-mural was to be another step in the development of his work.

Except that he didn't get very far. On the day he began to work, some passersby noticed that some of the artist's collage-photos were of nudes, and they felt the photos were erotic. By the end of the second day, their objections had brought out the police, who asked Aharonian to stop work. He did so. The police then seized various materials and covered the uncompleted mural with a huge dropcloth. A week later, when Aharonian returned to Portsmouth to reclaim his materials, he was arrested and charged with violation of the New Hampshire obscenity statute.

Sounds incredible, doesn't it? That a respected artist in the process of creating a work of art based on his own imagery could be charged with obscenity. It wasn't as if he were deliberately trying to titillate with pornographic images; the thought that he was being obscene had probably never entered his mind, much less that he was committing a crime for which he could be arrested.

Aharonian's was not a landmark obscenity case. The police had pulled a real boner by seizing his materials without first fulfilling certain legal requirements (see below). Because of this technicality, the charge against him was dismissed and the question of whether his work was obscene never had to be decided.

Nevertheless, Chief Justice Burger was right that standards differ from Mississippi and Maine to New York and Las Vegas. So unless your purpose is to stir up controversy, if your work depicts nudes or genitalia or is in some way erotic, you might think twice before you spend time and money mounting a show in an unfamiliar place, especially if the work is to be shown to minors or a captive audience.

Why does the presence of minors make an exhibition of my work more dangerous?

Some states prohibit the sale to minors of sexually provocative materials. In New York, for example, it's a crime to sell or offer for sale any art object depicting nudity, sexual conduct, or sado-masochistic abuse to anyone under 18. And in 1973, Chief Justice Burger said that the states could prohibit "dissemination" of obscene material if there was a significant danger of juveniles exposure as a result. "Dissemination" was not defined, but it could conceivably mean exhibition of artwork.

What do you mean by a captive audience?

A captive audience is composed of people who, because of a specific situation, have no other choice but to look at the obscene material. Court cases involving captive audiences usually refer to people who receive but don't solicit sexually explicit materials through the mails, an enterprise most fine artists won't be engaged in.

But here's a case that hits closer to home, where a captive audience transformed an act of free speech into an act against the community.

How did this happen? In 1970, an art instructor at the University of Massachusetts accepted an offer for a 24-day exhibition of his works in a heavily traveled corridor in the Student Union. After the show was hung, considerable controversy arose over its sexual nature, and college authorities removed it after five days. The instructor charged the officials with invasion of his constitutional rights and sued for an injunction to order the officials to make the space available to him for the remaining 19 days. Said the instructor: "Art is as fully protected by the Constitution as political and social speech."

The court disagreed. It said, rightly or wrongly:

There are words that are not regarded as obscene in the Constitutional sense that nevertheless need not be permitted in every context. Words that might properly be employed in a term paper about Lady Chatterley's Lover *or in a novel submitted in a creative writing course, take on a very different coloration if they are bellowed over a loudspeaker at a campus rally or appear prominently on a sign posted on a campus tree.*

And then the Court concluded: "Freedom of speech must recognize at least within limits, freedom not to listen." Or in this case, freedom not to look.

Can policemen seize my work if they think it's obscene?

Yes, but only if they have prepared for seizure with proper actions—procedural steps that the New Hampshire police in the Aharonian case evidently didn't think about. Before any seizure or confiscation of exhibited works of art for obscenity, an impartial hearing must be held to decide whether there are grounds for seizure. And before the hearing, you should have advance notice and time to engage a lawyer. The notice should inform you of who is making what charges against you and, particularly, your work. Then you and your lawyer appear before an impartial judge to argue your case. At the hearing, the law enforcement officers who testify that the work is obscene must have seen the work—they can't rely on the word of others. Then the judge decides whether the work is obscene. Only after that can your work be seized; otherwise seizure is unconstitutional even if the police come armed with a search warrant.

What should I do if the police seize my work before a hearing?

If they're determined to have their way, don't resist them physically. Instead, protest orally that they're violating the First Amendment by not allowing you a hearing, and ask them to make a note of this in their records. As you saw from the Aharonian case, you now have a great defense. An impartial hearing is a must, no matter what.

What's my chief protection against charges of obscenity, libel, and so forth?

The First Amendment. Countercharging that your accusers violated your right to freedom of speech is often used as a defense. The First Amendment can also be used when you want to sue someone who censors or confiscates your work. Being arrested on an obscenity charge, for example, is a pretty rare event. But having some community or educational body censor your work isn't. From time to time, the newspapers report on a town council demanding the removal of an exhibition of nudes. The people involved don't want the artist arrested—they just want the exhibit taken down. In this case, you could charge them with violating "those high moral, legal and ethical precepts which our Constitution teaches" and *your* First Amendment right to freedom of speech.

11. Insurance: Getting What You Need

· Insurance on artwork
· Valuation
· Insurance on the studio
· Workmen's compensation
· Group plans

The following quote comes from one of the definitive books on art law, *Art Works*: "Insuring works of art should be separated into three categories: (a) insurance for collectors; (b) insurance for dealers; and (c) insurance for museums." So far so good, but what about insurance for artists? Not one mention is made of insuring an artist's work, although much of the book is devoted to the problems of the creators of art.

Another quote, this one taken from *The Art Letter*, explains why. In an item entitled, "A How-To Guide to Fine Arts Insurance: Getting the Best Coverage at the Lowest Price," the editors, after discussing how others in the art world should go about buying insurance, conclude with a brief paragraph about the plight of the artist:

Unlike most museums, galleries, and collectors, artists don't often have the luxury of deciding whether and to what extent they wish to insure their own art in their studios. Artists' insurance is hard to get, because the insurance companies consider it too risky. The sad consequences of this were felt by 83 artists who were burned out of their home/studios . . . in Boston's Jamaica Plains section. No artwork was salvageable and no insurance . . . helped to cushion the loss. 'Most insurance companies won't handle artist's insurance or the rates are too high,' observed Tom Harris, one of the uninsured victims. The reason for this is that the security and construction of many artists' studios are poor from the perspective of insurance companies, and the companies find it difficult to assign values to works by artists who have not established a market.

In other words, if you haven't sold enough work over a long enough period of time so you have plenty of evidence of what your work is worth, an insurance company cannot value it.

And that in a nutshell is why artists get short shrift on the subject of insurance. Nevertheless, it's an important subject to examine along with the other types of insurance that relate to your profession. Nonrelated insurance coverage for health and life isn't within the scope of this book, but, at the end of the chapter, the names of organizations that offer individual artists protection under group policies in these areas are listed.

What kinds of insurance should an artist consider?

Insurance on your artwork, on your studio, and on employees. Each will be described below.

What kind of insurance should I get for my artwork?

That will depend on the sort of risks you have. A risk can be anything that threatens your artwork, such as fire, theft, water damage, or vandalism. If your studio is in a wood building surrounded by other wood structures, you would want to insure against fire. If you live in a high-crime area, you'd want a policy for theft. You can insure against risks by purchasing individual policies for fire, theft, or whatever, or buying one all-risk fine arts policy.

What's an all-risk fine arts policy?

Although "all-risk" isn't a precise definition of this kind of insurance, it does protect your artwork against all of the major threats most people worry about—fire, theft, water, vandalism, and so on. Its standard exclusions are usually limited to such risks as war, nuclear damage, insects, vermin, wear and tear, gradual deterioration (from the weather, for example), damage to fragile items, and damage due to repairing or restoring.

Is it more economical to buy an all-risk policy or individual policies?

There's no question that one individual policy—for example, for fire—will be cheaper than an all-risk policy. But the premiums (the annual cost of the insurance policy) on several policies—one for fire, another for theft, and a third for vandalism—may cost more than one all-risk policy. In any event, shop around. Call up several different insurance agents or brokers and ask them the prices of different policies.

Is it a good idea to insure for just one risk?

It's very possible that you might want to insure only against fire.

Most artists feel fire is the greatest threat to their work, and, to keep costs down, they opt for fire insurance only. An insurance broker told me, for instance, of an artist whose work sells in the six figures who buys fire insurance only. Why? He recently bought a bank building to use for studio and storage space. With his paintings locked up in vaults, he's not worried about burglary or other dangers. But you don't need your own bank to regard fire as your biggest and perhaps only real risk.

How much is fire insurance?

Premiums on fire insurance policies depend on building construction and other factors affecting the likelihood of fire. Obviously, the greater an insurance company thinks your risk is, the higher the premiums it's going to charge. Fire insurance for studios in regions like southern California that are periodically ravaged by forest fires or buildings such as old New York City factories will command a pretty steep price. Some may go as high as $2 per $100 of work meaning that if you had $10,000 worth of work in your studio, you might have to pay a premium of $200 a year.

And if you live in a particularly fire-prone building or area, you may find that insurance companies won't want to insure you at all.

How expensive is an all-risk policy?

Only your insurance broker knows for sure. Living in a building considered a bad risk by an insurance company from the standpoint of fire, for example, will escalate costs. To generalize is impossible, but one broker told me premiums could go as high as $6 per $100.

Does a fire insurance policy cover my work out of the studio?

No, it doesn't. A simple fire insurance policy covers work only when it's in the studio. Therefore, before you lend work to a gallery or museum, you should make sure they have an insurance policy that would cover your loan.

Does an all-risk fine arts policy cover my work out of the studio?

It can. Your policy can be written to extend coverage on artwork when it's in your studio, when it's traveling to shows, and when it's at its destination. In other words, you can extend coverage every time your work leaves the studio if you so desire.

An all-risk fine arts policy is a form of inland marine insurance, which is a type of insurance that can be tailored to fit your needs (unlike fire insurance). Inland marine may be an unfamiliar term to you, but it's a common type of property insurance. Originally written to protect goods in transit, inland marine insurance now covers a potpourri of valuable properties, such as jewelry, furs, and works of fine art. Collectors, for example, insure their artword under a form of inland marine insurance called a "personal articles floater."

What's a personal articles floater?

A personal articles floater is a type of insurance that covers individual pieces, each of which must be appraised and its value written into the policy.

Does a collector always use a personal articles floater?

No, he might insure his artwork under his homeowner's policy, which insures his residence and its contents as a whole against a number of risks for a lump sum—$50,000 for the house and $30,000 for the contents, for example. But if he wants broader coverage against more risks or if he sends part of his collection to exhibitions from time to time, he would get a personal articles floater. Also, if the collector, wants to make sure a claim for loss or damage of a work is paid in full, he would get a personal articles floater for fine arts.

Can I insure my artwork under a personal articles floater?

No. A personal articles floater, which is relatively cheap compared with the all-risk fine arts policies bought by artists, is not suitable for you—your work is classified as business, rather than personal, property.

You could easily take out a personal articles floater; I know brokers who do insure artist's unsold work this way. They reason that the insurance carrier won't know whether the work is business property or work you plan to keep personally. Unfortunately, though, a problem arises when you try to collect a claim. If the claim is small, you might get away with this subterfuge. But if it's large, you can expect a penetrating examination by the insurance company, followed by the rejection of your claim.

Why do I have to establish a value for my work?

For two reasons. First you must establish a value for work in order to buy an all-risk policy. Most all-risk fine arts policies insure individual pieces in the same way that artwork is insured under a personal articles floater. This means that a value must be assigned to each work before it can be written into a policy. If you can't establish the value of your artwork, you won't be able to insure it with an all-risk policy.

Second, if you buy fire insurance instead of the all-risk policy, you must establish a value to guarantee that claims will be paid. Establishing a value prior to the purchase of a fire insurance policy isn't necessary—theoretically, you can buy fire insurance for any amount you want as long as you're willing to pay the premiums.

Can you illustrate this? Suppose you have at any one time 20 paintings in your studio, and you think they're worth $500 a piece. You will probably be able to buy a fire insurance policy that insures them for $10,000 easily. But should you have a fire, the insurance company won't necessarily pay $10,000 if all the work is destroyed. The company isn't going to accept your word on what the work is worth—it will demand objective proof of its value.

How do I establish this value?

If you sell regularly and you or your dealer can produce the bills of sale to prove the prices you're accustomed to charging and getting, you should have no problem establishing values.

If you don't sell regularly, you might as well forget about insuring your artwork.

What do you mean by selling regularly?

There's no way of knowing what an insurance company will call a consistent sales record. When you buy insurance, you have to negotiate with the insurance company officials over terms, and they hold the upper hand. They can, for example, decide that your work isn't worth insuring at all because of the hazardous conditions you live in. And in the same vein, they may decide that a brief sales record of a small number of works isn't a consistent sales record. You can point out that a three-year record of 10 sales a year of $1,000 paintings can't be compared to the sales record of some other products and that 10 paintings isn't a bad sales record in the art market. And you may convince them. The point is you have to sell them on the fact that your work is valuable and should be insured. If they don't agree, you'll have to forget the insurance.

How do I prove that work has been lost or destroyed?

By keeping accurate records as outlined in Chapter 3. Otherwise, you'll have no proof of work when it has been destroyed by fire or stolen or whatever. So as soon as a work is finished, photograph it and assign it an inventory number. Then record the date completed, the size, medium, tentative selling price, and so on. *And be sure to store these records in a safe place outside your studio.*

How much should I insure my work for?

If you can't afford—or don't want—to pay the premiums on a policy that would totally insure your work, decide how much work you think you can afford to lose. In other words, figure out how easy it will be to replace lost or damaged work.

But if you plan to carry fire insurance only, before you decide to insure for less than the full value, consider the concepts of co-insurance and how much you're *really* insuring your work for.

How much am I really insuring my work for?

You probably think that when you insure $20,000 worth of work against fire for less than the full value, for $15,000, for example, and all the work is destroyed in a fire, you'll receive $15,000. That's true. But you might also believe that if only part of the artwork is destroyed by fire, say $10,000 worth, the insurance company will pay you $10,000. Not true.

Many states have laws requiring you to insure a certain percentage of the value of the property—usually 80% or 90% in order to receive the full amount for a partial loss. If you don't comply with the state requirement, you'll bear some of the loss, thus becoming a co-insurer of a certain percentage of the work.

What's a co-insurer?

If you don't comply with state requirements, you'll end up paying some of your partial loss yourself (co-insurance). To figure out what that amount or percentage is, divide the amount of insurance you bought by the amount of insurance required by law (ask your agent) and multiply the resulting percentage by the amount of the partial loss.

For example, suppose your artwork is valued at $10,000. If, according to state law, you must insure 80% of it to receive the full amount of a partial loss, you should insure it for $8,000. But if you only insure your work for $6,000 and then sustain a fire loss of $4,000, the insurance company will pay only $3,000. ($6,000 divided by $8,000 = 75% and 75% of $4,000 = $3,000). This means you're a co-insurer of 25% of the partial loss.

If I don't insure my work, can I deduct its loss from my income tax?

If a work is stolen or destroyed by fire or whatever, you can deduct from your income tax only the cost of the raw materials that went into the work. Thus, if your work sells for about $1,000 each, but each one costs only $50 to make, you can only deduct $50 each if your work is destroyed in a fire.

If I have insurance, can I deduct the loss from my income tax?

On the contrary. Any insurance money you receive for a claim that exceeds the cost of raw materials must be reported as income on your tax return. So if an insurance company pays you $500 for a painting that cost you $5 for paint and canvas, you'll have to report $495 as income. Of course, your insurance premiums are deductible from your tax as a business expense.

How much will my dealer insure my work for while it's in his gallery?

That depends on your agreement. He may not insure it at all, or, if he does, it may be for less than the retail selling price. You should aim for an agreement that states that he'll insure the work for what it's worth to you, i.e., retail price minus his commission. And you should ask to be named a payee of his insurance policy.

When I lend work to a museum for an exhibition, what about its insurance?

Be sure to ask if the museum will insure your work; whether its policy is all-risk; and whether its coverage is wall-to-wall? If the answers are negative, and you have an all-risk fine arts policy, you might want to ask your insurance broker to extend your coverage to insure the work while it's in transit and/or at the museum. If you have only fire insurance and want to extend your coverage, ask your broker to see if he can get some inland marine insurance on your artwork that will protect it while it's traveling and while it's at the exhibition.

What is wall-to-wall coverage?

Wall-to-wall coverage means that under the museum's all-risk fine arts policy, work is insured from the moment it leaves your wall until it returns.

If I lend a museum work with no contract, is the museum responsible for it?

Yes, even if it's not provided for in a contract, the museum can't shirk all responsibility. Under the law, anyone who agrees to hold someone else's property in a situation where both parties benefit from the arrangement is responsible for the loss or damage of the property if he's guilty of negligence (failure to exercise reasonable care). This situation is called a "bailment" in legal terms.

When else does a bailment exist?

There are many situations that qualify as bailments, but here are two that would have particular relevance for the artist: when you leave a painting for framing or restoration, and when you leave a portfolio or work at an advertising agency.

Is a bailment created if I leave work at a museum or with a dealer for consideration for a show?

Yes, but it might be considered a different type of bailment than the one discussed above, which benefits both parties. You can also have a bailment where one party agrees to hold someone else's property but only *one* of the parties benefits. In this case, the holder of the property is responsible for loss or damage only if he is guilty of gross negligence, which is harder to prove than plain negligence (see below). A museum or gallery might argue that if you simply left work for consideration, the bailment existed only for your benefit. Most courts, however, would probably find that because of the nature of their business, museums, galleries, agencies, and so on all benefit from the ability to see potentially acceptable work. If that were the decision, you would have to prove negligence—not gross negligence.

What's the difference between negligence and gross negligence?

A matter of degree. Negligence may be considered as the failure to exercise reasonable care; gross negligence would be the complete failure to exercise any care. Once again there are no hard and fast rules that define these terms on a practical basis. But an example of negligence might occur if work left for consideration by a museum was not put safely away but left in a hallway where it was damaged. Gross negligence usually occurs only under the most extreme circumstances. To take a rather absurd example, gross negligence would occur if the museum decided to store your work in the incinerator room, where it was destroyed.

Can I insure my studio at the same time I insure my artwork?

Yes, if you plan to buy fire insurance only. Your fire insurance policy would describe the property insured by the policy as your studio and its contents,which consist principally of fine artwork. If you want to insure your studio against other risks, you'll have to buy separate policies.

What kind of insurance do I need for my studio?

First of all, let's get a few facts straight. Your studio is a place of business, and all places of business should be protected by property insurance and casualty insurance.

What is property insurance? Property insurance protects against loss or damage to buildings and/or their contents. Fire insurance is property insurance; so is burglary insurance.

What is casualty insurance? Casualty insurance protects against bodily injury to anyone on your property and is called liability insurance. If you have clients or tradesmen coming to your studio who might fall down stairs or slip on wet paint or injure themselves in some way, you'll want a business liability policy.

How do I get these types of insurance?

There are several ways to acquire these types of insurance coverage. Let's assume that your studio and your home are separate. As mentioned above, if you plan to insure your studio and your artwork for fire only, you could buy one fire insurance policy for the building and contents and one business liability policy.

If you want to insure the studio against a number of risks—fire, burglary, and water damage—you might be able to buy a combination of these property insurances plus business liability. This combination is called a commercial package policy. Most commercial package policies exclude property held for sale. Since your art is for sale, you won't be able to insure it under the commercial package policy—you'll have to purchase a separate policy for your artwork.

What if my studio is in my home?

If you own or rent a home, you'll undoubtedly cover it with a homeowner's policy. Homeowner's insurance is also a combination or a package of property insurance policies plus personal liability.

Now, if your studio is in your home and represents a smaller portion than the living quarters, you would probably be eligible for coverage on your studio by attaching to your homeowner's policy an "incidental studio endorsement," in insurance jargon.

Similarly, if your studio is in a loft and takes up most of the space, leaving just a small living area, you might opt for a commercial package with an "incidental residence endorsement." In either case, you must insure your artwork separately.

Is there another time I would buy business liability insurance?

Yes, if you're planning a large-scale project for which you're assuming the risks. Painting a mural on the outside of a building is a prime example of such a project, as injury might occur to the public if a paint can falls on a passerby or a car, or if a scaffold collapses. In fact, if you're planning to use scaffolding, your state laws may demand insurance against both bodily injury and property damage. Check out these scaffolding laws with your local authorities, starting first by inquiring at your city hall or asking someone at the firm that's renting you the scaffolding equipment. Then describe your project in detail to your insurance broker and ask him to get you short-term insurance for the duration of the project.

When would I want workmen's compensation insurance?

When you hire someone. By state law, you're required to provide Workmen's Compensation insurance on all employees in case they're injured on the job. Information can be obtained from your state Department of Labor.

Do I have to insure volunteers?

It's hard to say. According to *Mural Manual,* a book describing the ins and outs of public mural painting:

Even if the team is all volunteer, you may well be liable if any team member is injured. This is a 'gray area' that you should go over with a lawyer in relation to your project. You may find it necessary to buy Workmen's Compensation or some other type of insurance to cover volunteer workers.

Is a group health or life insurance plan better than an individual policy?

Sales and administrative costs are significantly less when an insurance broker sells one plan to a group of many individuals rather than many plans to single parties. Furthermore, a group plan allows the insurance company to spread its risks over a far broader base than it does with an individual policy. For both these reasons, insurance companies charge individuals participating in group plans much smaller premiums.

What organizations offer artists group insurance plans?

For life insurance, contact:

Artists Equity Association (AEA), 2813 Albermarle Street, N.W., Washington, D.C. 20008.

Foundation for the Community for Artists, 32 Union Square East, New York, New York 10003.

For health insurance, write to:

American Crafts Council, ACC Insurance Program, IGP Administrators, 2100 M Street, N.W., Washington, D.C. 20037.

Artists Equity Association, 2813 Albermarle Street, N.W., Washington, D.C. 20008.

Artists Equity Association of New York, 1780 Broadway, New York, New York 10019.

Boston Visual Artists Union, 3 Center Plaza, Boston, Massachusetts 02108.

Foundation for the Community for Artists, 32 Union Square East, New York, New York 10003.

Graphic Artists Guild, Group Plans, Shepherd-Taylor, 270 Madison Avenue, New York, New York 10016.

Society of Illustrators, Group Insurance Plans, 747 Third Avenue, New York, New York 10017.

To compare, write these groups for more information. In some cases, it is not necessary to be a resident of the area in which the organization is located, although you must be a member.

12. Bookkeeping Made Easy

· Informal records
· Formal records
· Cash accounting
· Expenses

Chapter 3 discussed the records you should keep to catalog your work as a reference on costs, techniques, collectors, and so on, and to offer as proof in case of loss or theft or infringement of copyright. But these records represent only half of your bookkeeping chores—another kind of record must also be kept for tax reasons.

Before launching into a discussion of tax records, however, let me point out that I realize that most of you probably have a job to supplement the income you make as a self-employed artist. And to compute your taxes, you'll want to keep records pertaining to your job, like the stubs from your salary checks as well as records involving your personal life, such as medical bills. This book, however, deals only with records kept on income made and expenses incurred from your self-employment.

Why should I record business income and expenses?

Records of business income allow you to figure out your yearly taxable income.

Records of business expenses are the supporting evidence you need to back up claims for tax deductions if you are ever questioned by the I.R.S. Furthermore, they're invaluable as an aid to making a complete list of deductions. Without them to jog your memory, you may forget about certain expenses altogether when you're preparing your tax return.

What do you mean by tax deductions?

The I.R.S. allows you to deduct business expenses connected with your self-employment from your income before you compute the tax on it.

What kind of records back up deductions?

According to the *Audit Technique Handbook for Internal Revenue*

Agents, you are required to keep two types of documents: informal records and formal records.

What are informal records?

Informal records are all the papers you receive in the course of business. These would include cancelled checks, bank statements, and bills and receipts you receive for goods and services you've bought. If you're meticulous, you'll save movie stubs from films seen in connection with your artwork and cash register receipts for supplies, no matter how small the amount.

You may need several records to document an expense. A check alone isn't always accepted as proof by the Internal Revenue Service, particularly if the amount includes nonbusiness expenses, so make sure you get an itemized bill or receipt whether you pay by cash or check. In any case, all receipts and bills should record the appropriate dates, describe the time or service paid for, and be stored in a safe place. They can also be cross-referenced with checks. For example, on every bill you pay you might want to write, "Paid by Check No. ____ on 6/6/78."

Should I have a separate bank account for my self-employment?

Absolutely. There's no better way to maintain accurate records than to deposit all income earned through self-employed activities in one account and pay for all expenses out of that same account. Otherwise, business and personal records can get mixed up. And if you support yourself from self-employment, write yourself checks from your business account for personal use, putting notations on your checks of what you're doing. In this way, you'll have a record of withdrawals made to finance personal expenses without cluttering up your business account with checks written for personal items.

Should I pay most expenses by check?

Definitely. The endorsed cancelled check may serve as a receipt as long as it isn't written out to you or cash. So don't cash a check first and then pay a bill.

And while we're on the subject of checks, an easy record-keeping device is the voucher check. Voucher checks, which are available from your bank, provide spaces for the date of the bill, the items covered by the check, and their individual costs.

How do I keep receipts and bills?

Myriad ways exist. One efficient system is to set up an alphabetical file with such headings as "Entertainment," "Supplies," "Travel," and so on. Another way would be to collect receipts and bills by the month.

Should I keep receipts from trips? Yes, but this doesn't have to be difficult. Gathering receipts when you go on a trip can be easy if you put them all in one envelope as you go along. When you return home, file them alphabetically or simply summarize the contents of the envelope on the outside, seal it with the receipts inside, and put it in the proper monthly file.

What about receipts for tolls and gasoline? They can be collected in a similar way by keeping an envelope in your car at all times, along with a memo pad for recording mileage, and other expenses, such as parking, when receipts aren't available.

What kind of formal records must I keep?

Records that list or summarize income and expenses should be kept by either single-entry bookkeeping or, if necessary, double-entry bookkeeping.

What is single-entry bookkeeping?

Single-entry bookkeeping is any system that lets you list all of your expenses as they're incurred so you can add them up at the end of the year. All you need to say about most expenses is what they were and how much they cost. Expenses for travel and entertainment must be accompanied by a few more details, which will be discussed a little later.

Where do I record this list of expenses?

In a simple pocket diary, if you like. Though it might seem that a diary would be just about the poorest possible way to substantiate tax deductions—after all, what's listed there depends on what you elect to write—it has the stamp of approval from both Congress and the I.R.S. The Internal Revenue Code and the I.R.S. regulations both also mention a diary as the accepted way to substantiate entertainment expenses of less than $25 that aren't backed up by receipts.

More elaborate file systems can be found at any stationery store. Some systems provide separate columns for recording travel and entertainment expenses; others may combine a log to record monthly expenditures and income plus a filing system for your informal records.

What is double-entry bookkeeping?

Double-entry bookkeeping is a much more complicated system involving ledgers and journals in which every item is entered twice—once as a debit and once as a credit—so the books are always in balance. The only reason you would undertake such a sophisticated system would be if you run a business, such as a craft store, where you would be recording checks from different accounts and making many dispersements to pay expenses.

In other words, it's the number of transactions that dictate the type of bookkeeping system you would use. The more transactions, the greater the chance of error in recording. The chief advantage of a double entry system is that it checks itself—any errors in arithmetic or recording are revealed by "unbalanced" books and can be corrected at the end of each accounting period. Despite this advantage, it's unlikely a fine artist would need to go to the trouble to use a double-entry bookkeeping system.

When do I record income and expenses?

This depends on the accounting method you plan to use; the cash basis method or the accrual method.

What's cash accounting?

Cash accounting is the simplest, most frequently used, and best method of accounting for artists keeping single-entry books. Under this accounting system, you record income when you receive it and expenses when you pay them. So if you sell a painting in November but your client waits until February to pay, you record the income in February. Expenses are treated the same way. If you buy supplies in December but hold off payment until January, the expense would be reported in January.

What is accrual accounting?

Under the accrual method, income is recorded when "earned," not when received, and expenses when incurred, not paid. "Earned" here means that by your performance you've "earned" the right to receive payment. If you sold a painting to a client in November, you've earned the income then. Even if he doesn't pay until January or if he pays in installments, your records must show that income was received in November.

The purpose of accrual accounting is to match up expenses more accurately with the income they produce, but cash accounting is more convenient and allows greater flexibility in adjusting income for tax purposes.

Is there any reason I might have to use accrual accounting?

Yes, if you run a business that involves the maintenance of large inventories—if you make and retail, for example, large unnumbered editions of ceramics—the I.R.S. might require you to adopt at least a partial accrual accounting system. But until the I.R.S. demands this or your accountant believes for some reason that accrual accounting will improve your tax position, forget it. As a general rule, you have nothing to gain from accrual accounting.

How can cash accounting help my tax position?

If you want to increase your income to eliminate the possibility of the I.R.S. calling your art a hobby (see Chapter 13), you could put off paying bills while asking clients to pay early. In other words, you might be able to persuade collectors to whom you sold your work in December to pay right away, instead of waiting for the first of the following month. At the same time, you could delay paying for that new kiln you just bought until after the first of the year. This might result in a profit for the year, and the I.R.S. will not classify you as a hobbyist if you have a profit in two out of five consecutive years. If, on the other hand, you want to reduce your taxable income, you could reverse the process by asking clients to delay payment until after January 1, while you pay as many bills as possible.

But here's a word of caution. Dating your checks "December 31" doesn't automatically entitle you to claim the deduction for that year. To be valid, your checks must be *in the mail* before or on December 31.

Are there any bills I can't pay in advance?

You can pay anything in advance, but you can't claim a deduction for the prepayment of interest on loans, premiums on business insurance, or rent. They can only be deducted in the year they were incurred.

What expenses do I record?

Record the following:

1. Legal and accounting fees relating to your self-employment.

2. Premiums for business property insurance and casualty insurance.

3. Supplies.

4. Postage.

5. Publications and professional journals that keep you abreast of professional developments.

6. Books that relate to your work.

7. Admission to theaters, films, museum exhibitions, and other artistic events that relate to your work.

8. Training in classes necessary for maintaining or improving skills.

9. Promotional expenses (ads, brochures, press releases, photography, and so on).

10. Capital expenditures (explained below).

11. Rent, utilities, and upkeep of a rented studio, if separate from your house; or mortgage interest payments, property taxes, upkeep, and utilities on a separate studio you own. (See below for how to divide up the expenses if you live and work in the same building).

12. Telephone bills. (These too must be separated from personal bills.)

13. Local transportation.

14. Travel.

15. Entertainment.

What are capital expenditures?

Any item bought for business reasons which has a useful life for you of more than one year. The purchase of a building, a car, a camera, an easel, are all examples of capital expenditures. Inexpensive items, even if they last a lifetime—such as palette knives—aren't considered capital expenditures.

What makes capital expenditures different from other expenses? They can't be deducted in one year, but must be deducted over a number of years. (This is called depreciation and will be discussed in Chapter 13.) Nevertheless, even though the full price can't be deducted right away, record the purchase in your records so you won't forget it.

How do I divide up expenses for a studio in a space used for both work and living?

This can be done in one of two ways: by rooms or by square footage, whichever is more advantageous to you. For example, the deduction for a one-room studio in a six-room house or apartment might be calculated as one-sixth the rent and expenses. But if the room used for the studio equals one-third of the square footage of the house, you would deduct 33%. Therefore, in the latter case, if your rent is $300 a month, you would claim $100 plus one-third of the utilities and upkeep as a business expense.

What if I own my own home? If you own your own home, you can claim as a business expense a portion of the depreciation (discussed in Chapter 13), the mortgage interest payments, the property taxes, plus a portion of the utilities and repairs, such as plumbing, roofing, and guttering. But don't be greedy—the I.R.S. won't accept all repairs as business expenses. If, for example, you have your driveway repaired, the I.R.S. will consider this a legitimate expense only if clients visit your home-studio on a regular basis and leave their cars in your driveway. But if you use the studio solely to paint in and receive no business visitors, driveway repair is not a legitimate expense. (Not everyone can deduct studio expenses—be sure to read about them in the next chapter.)

How do I divide up telephone expenses?

To figure out how much of your phone is used for business v. personal expenses, keep a pad by the phone for two months— neither your busiest nor your slowest business month—and write down all the calls you make, both local and toll. Ask your family to do the same. At the end of the months, figure out the ratio of business calls to total calls for *each month.* Then take the average of the percentages. If one month 60% of the calls were for business, and the other month only 50% were business calls, you would claim 55% of your phone bills as a business expense.

Should I have a separate business phone? If business calls predominate, maybe you should have one, as it can be totally deducted. This precaution might be a good idea since I.R.S. agents have been known to be real sticklers on the subject of telephone expenses.

What do you mean by local transportation?

Any business travel in a local area that does not represent commuting back and forth to your studio. So if you have a separate studio, driving to it in the morning and back in the evening is not deductible. If your studio is located in your house, however, and you go out on appointments—to your dealer, then a framer, and finally a client—travel to your first appointment and back from your last one as well as all transportation in between is a deductible expense. (This is assuming, of course, that you have no other job to commute to.)

A notation in your diary describing such travel might look like this:

June 15
Appointment with Mrs. Jones in Larchmont for portrait sitting.
Tolls and parking, $6.75; gas, $5.00 (cash).

Can't I claim other expenses for my car?

Yes. Besides gas, oil, tolls, and parking, you can also deduct depreciation (see Chapter 13) and percentages of the maintenance, insurance, tires, and so on. Just make sure you get receipts for all these expenses.

If I use my car for business and personal reasons, how do I divide up these expenses?

Naturally, it would be best if you could keep a log of every single time you took your car out of the garage, but even the I.R.S. doesn't expect that. What you should do is take a sample of two or three weeks of driving during the year. Simply keep a pad handy in the car or use your diary when you're making the test, and write down all the vital information—what the use is for, whether it's business or personal, and the mileage (see Figure 14). At the end of the time period, you'll see what percentage of your travel is personal and what's business. Just divide the total number of miles traveled during the period by the number of miles traveled for business purposes to determine the percentage of business use of the car.

Isn't there an easier way to calculate car expenses?

Yes. You might simply keep a yearly record of the number of miles you travel. If your car is used strictly for business, mark down the number of miles on your odometer at the beginning of the year and again at the end. Then, when you figure out the expense, multiply the mileage by the I.R.S. automobile mileage allowance (which increases once in a while to try to keep up with inflation). The I.R.S. mileage allowance is a cost estimate of what you spend per mile on gas, oil, maintenance, insurance, depreciation, tires, car washes, and so on.

Which way is better?

The mileage allowance is much easier to figure out, although it

Figure 14. By making a simple entry into a diary every day for a month or two, you can validate your auto expenses in the eyes of the I.R.S. This is an example of the list you might make in your car for a set time period.

Mileage start   18,239
1. Home to studio   5
2. Studio to gallery   12
3. Gallery to framer   24
4. Framer to Mr. Jones' house (collector)   15
5. Mr. Jones' house to home   10
Mileage end   18,305

Business   51
Non-business   15

$\frac{51}{66}$ = bus. %

isn't as generous as it should be, and I.R.S. authorities say that if you put a lot of mileage on for business—say, 30,000 to 40,000 miles a year—you should make the computation both ways and pick the most advantageous calculation.

When I travel, what expenses should I record?

Air, bus, train, and other fares to get you to and from your destination; taxis and other fares while you're there; your own automobile expenses, if you brought your car; food; lodging; tips; cleaning; telephone; and anything else you can think of. In other words, anything that costs you money while you're on a business trip.

Expenses under $25 need not be backed up by receipts (try to get them anyway, if you can), but all food expenses over $25 and all lodging no matter what the cost must be documented by receipts that include the names of hotels and restaurants plus addresses and itemized costs.

How do I describe travel expenses in my records?

A description of travel expenses should include a day-by-day listing of expenses, plus the means of travel, and the reason for travel. A record of incidental expenses under $25 for the first day of a two-day trip might look like this in your diary:

June 28
Trip to Original Prints Atelier in Chicago to approve and sign edition of prints.
Tolls to airport, $1.50. Porter, $1. Taxis in Chicago, $6.55. Bellhop and room-service tips, $3. Lunch, $4.50.

What if the trip is both business and personal?

If the trip is primarily a business trip, you would record the fare to and from your destination plus all other expenses, just eliminating those that relate solely to the personal part of the trip. If, for example, you spent Monday through Friday talking to dealers and clients and the weekend visiting relatives, returning home on Monday, you should record everything but your hotel and food bills for the weekend.

If the trip is made primarily for personal reasons, record only the expenses involved in transacting business when at your destination, such as restaurant bills, taxi fares, and so on.

Trips combining business and pleasure outside the United States are sometimes governed by more stringent regulations. If you're planning a trip abroad, check with the I.R.S. to see how much you can claim as a deduction.

What if my spouse comes along? Eliminate his or her expenses even if it's solely a business trip. But you don't have to go overboard. If, for example, you take a $50 double room, you could claim as a legitimate expense the single-room rate, which might run $35. You don't have to split the bill down the middle.

What about days that I'm away but can't conduct business?

Providing they aren't used for personal reasons, you can deduct expenses for these days if they're the results of unavoidable lay-overs, holidays, and weekends between business days.

Should I record expenses for a trip made to secure new galleries in distant cities?

By all means record them, although you may run into resistance on the part of the I.R.S. in accepting them as a deduction, even though seeking out new business through travel, entertainment, or whatever is a legitimate business expense. If you're making a profit from your self-employment, you probably won't be questioned about this. But if you're not making a profit, you may be considered a hobbyist (see Chapter 13) and not a professional artist. In this case, the I.R.S. may reject your right to business expenses that exceed the income you earn from selling art. To counteract these charges, back up your claim with another type of informal record not mentioned before: letters.

What kind of letters? Letters to and from dealers, clients, publishers, and so on, that discuss the purpose of your trip. So if you write letters to galleries saying you'd like to show them your work on a certain day, stash the carbon copies away in your informal records file along with their responses. Letters help establish the legitimacy of your expenses and should be retained not only by the not-yet-profitable artist but by the successful artist as well.

Should I record travel expenses for trips made to distant places to pursue my art?

Yes. If you decide, for example, to paint landscapes of the national parks, go ahead and record the expenses involved. Once again, however, you may run into the problem of justifying them to the I.R.S. if you're not making a profit.

Should I record day-trip meals?

No. You can't deduct out-of-town dining unless you stay overnight. Of course, if you take a client out to dinner, you could probably deduct the cost as an entertainment expense.

How do I record entertainment expenses?

Note the amount spent, the date, persons entertained, their business affiliations, where entertained, type of entertainment, and reason for the entertainment. Furthermore, since the I.R.S. requires that these expenses must be "directly related to or associated with the active conduct of your trade or business," you must be able to show an expectation of income or other business benefits as a result of the occasion. And the I.R.S. means it. While the law allows you to claim the cost of entertainment if you have a reasonable expectation of new clients, for example, in practice internal revenue agents require some evidence that the entertainment did in fact produce some new collectors of your work, i.e., sales to these people. If this doesn't happen and you don't end up with new collectors, you might lose the deduction.

Entertainment expenses, such as business dinners, may be curtailed soon in a new reform law. Check with the I.R.S. for changes.

How long should I keep my records?

For tax purposes, bills, receipts, and diaries justifying noncapital expenditures must be kept a minimum of three years after the date you file the tax return reporting them. Records of capital expenditures (real estate, cars, equipment, and so on) should be retained as long as you own the property.

13. How to Pay Your Income Taxes

- · Schedule C
- · Business income
- · Business expense
- · Home-studio deduction
- · Depreciation
- · Getting help
- · Hobby-loss problem

Okay, you've played by the rules all year long, scrupulously hoarding every scrap of evidence documenting payments and income, and faithfully recording them in your diary. Now it's almost April 15 and time to transfer these figures on to your tax return. But, first, let me say something about tax returns in general.

When you file an income tax return, you use Form 1040, *The U.S. Individual Income Tax Return* (see Figure 15). For some people, this one form is enough. But a number of other people, because of circumstances peculiar to their personal lives or the way they make money, must fill out one or more schedules and other forms to accompany Form 1040. For example, if you had enormous medical bills in any one year, you would itemize them on Schedule A, rather than take the standard deduction on Form 1040. You also deduct interest on mortgage payments and other taxes, such as property taxes, on Schedule A.

This chapter will teach you how to handle those portions of the tax return that deal with your self-employment. Primarily, this involves Schedule C, the *Profit or (Loss) from Business or Profession* statement (see Figure 16). This is the schedule on which you enter income from self-employment and itemize business deductions. Several other schedules and forms will also be mentioned in the appropriate places in this and the following two chapters. The schedules and forms are essentially worksheets, and the figures arrived at on them are all eventually transferred to Form 1040. Then Form 1040 is filed, along with the completed schedules and forms attached to it.

Figure 15. Form 1040 is the U.S. Individual Income Tax Form Return. Although this is a 1976 Return, Form 1040 remains basically the same every year.

Form **1040**	Department of the Treasury—Internal Revenue Service **U.S. Individual Income Tax Return**	**1976**	This space for IRS use only

For the year January 1–December 31, 1976, or other taxable year beginning _____ , 1976 ending . _____ , 19 ___ .

Please print or type

Name (If joint return, give first names and initials of both)	Last name	Your social security number
Present home address (Number and street, including apartment number, or rural route)	For Privacy Act Notification, see page 5 of Instructions.	Spouse's social security no.
City, town or post office, State and ZIP code	Occu-pation Yours ▶ Spouse's ▶	

Filing Status

1 ☐ Single **(Check only ONE box)**
2 ☐ Married filing joint return (even if only one had income)
3 ☐ Married filing separately. If spouse is also filing give spouse's social security number in designated space above and enter full name here ▶
4 ☐ Unmarried Head of Household. See page 7 of instructions to see if you qualify ▶
5 ☐ Qualifying widow(er) with dependent child (Year spouse died ▶ 19). See page 7 of Instructions.

Exemptions

6a Regular ☐ Yourself ☐ Spouse Enter number of boxes checked ▶
b First names of your dependent children who lived with you _____ Enter number ▶
c Number of other dependents (from line 7) . ▶
d Total (add lines 6a, b, and c) . . . . . ▶
e Age 65 or older . ☐ Yourself ☐ Spouse Enter number of boxes checked ▶
  Blind . . . . ☐ Yourself ☐ Spouse
f TOTAL (add lines 6d and e) . . . . . ▶

7 Other dependents:

(a) Name	(b) Relationship	(c) Months lived in your home. If born or died during year, write B or D.	(d) Did dependent have income of $750 or more?	(e) Amount furnished for dependent's support
				By YOU. If 100% write ALL. $	By OTHERS ..including dependent. $

8 **Presidential Election Campaign Fund** . . ▶ Do you wish to designate $1 of your taxes for this fund? . . Yes ☐ No ☐
If joint return, does your spouse wish to designate $1? . . Yes ☐ No ☐
Note: If you check the "Yes" box(es) it will not increase your tax or reduce your refund.

Income (Please attach Copy B of Forms W-2 here)

9 Wages, salaries, tips, and other employee compensation (Attach Forms W-2. If unavailable, see page 6 of Instructions.)* | 9
10a Dividends (See pages 9 and 16 of Instructions) _____, 10b less exclusion _____, Balance ▶ | 10c
(If gross dividends and other distributions are over $400, list in Part I of Schedule B.)
11 Interest income. {If $400 or less, enter total without listing in Schedule B} {If over $400, enter total and list in Part II of Schedule B} . . . . | 11
12 Income other than wages, dividends, and interest (from line 37) . . . . | 12
13 Total (add lines 9, 10c, 11 and 12) . . . . | 13
14 Adjustments to income (such as moving expense, etc. from line 42) . . . . | 14
15a Subtract line 14 from line 13 . . . . | 15a
b Disability income exclusion (sick pay) (attach Form 2440) . . . . . | 15b
c **Adjusted gross income.** Subtract line 15b from line 15a, then complete Part III on back. (If less than $8,000, see page 2 of Instructions on "Earned Income Credit.") . . . | 15c

Tax, Payments and Credits

16 Tax, check if from: ☐ Tax Table ☐ Tax Rate Schedule X, Y or Z ☐ Schedule D ☐ Schedule G ☐ Form 2555 **OR** ☐ Form 4726 | 16 (If box on line 3 is checked see page 10 of Instructions)
17a Multiply $35.00 by the number of exemptions on line 6d . . . . | 17a Enter larger of a or b ▶
b Enter 2% of line 47 but not more than $180 ($90 if box 3 is checked) | 17b
| 17c
18 Balance. Subtract line 17c from line 16 and enter difference (but not less than zero) | 18
19 Credits (from line 54) . . . . | 19
20 Balance. Subtract line 19 from line 18 and enter difference (but not less than zero) . . | 20
21 Other taxes (from line 62) . . . . | 21
22 Total (add lines 20 and 21) . . . . | 22
23a Total Federal income tax withheld. (attach Forms W-2, or W-2P to front) | 23a
b 1976 estimated tax payments (include amount allowed as credit from 1975 return) . | 23b
c Earned income credit. (from page 2 of Instructions) | 23c
d Amount paid with Form 4868 . . . . . | 23d
e Other payments (from line 66) . . . . . | 23e
24 **TOTAL** (add lines 23a through e) . . . . ▶ | 24

Pay amount on line 25 in full with this return. Write social security number on check or money order and make payable to Internal Revenue Service.

Due or Refund (Please attach Check or Money Order here)

25 If line 22 is larger than line 24, enter **BALANCE DUE IRS** . . . . ▶ | 25
(Check here ▶ ☐, if Form 2210 or Form 2210F is attached. See page 10 of instructions.)
26 If line 24 is larger than line 22, enter amount **OVERPAID** . . . . . . ▶ | 26
27 Amount of line 26 to be **REFUNDED TO YOU** . . . . ▶ | 27
28 Amount of line 26 to be credited on 1977 estimated tax ▶ | 28 |

Under penalties of perjury, I declare that I have examined this return, including accompanying schedules and statements, and to the best of my knowledge and belief it is true, correct, and complete. Declaration of preparer (other than taxpayer) is based on all information of which preparer has any knowledge.

Sign here

| Your signature | Date | Preparer's signature (and employer's name, if any) | Date |
| Spouse's signature (if filing jointly, BOTH must sign even if only one had income) | Identifying number (see Instructions) | Address (and ZIP code) |

Figure 16. Schedule C. The statement of Profit (or Loss) from Business or Profession *is where you report expenses and losses from your work as a self-employed artist.*

SCHEDULE C (Form 1040) Department of the Treasury Internal Revenue Service	**Profit or (Loss) From Business or Profession** (Sole Proprietorship) Partnerships, Joint Ventures, etc., Must File Form 1065. ▶ Attach to Form 1040. ▶ See Instructions for Schedule C (Form 1040).	**1976**

Name of proprietor   Robert Artist   Social security number

A Principal business activity (see Schedule C Instructions) ▶ .... Artist .... ; product ▶ Painting

B Business name ▶ Robert Artist

C Employer identification number ▶

D Business address (number and street) ▶

City, State and ZIP code ▶

      C

E Indicate method of accounting: (1) XX Cash (2) ☐ Accrual (3) ☐ Other ▶   Yes | No

F Were you required to file Form W-3 or Form 1096 for 1976 (see Schedule C Instructions)?   X

    If "Yes," where filed ▶

G Was an Employer's Quarterly Federal Tax Return, Form 941, filed for this business for any quarter in 1976?   X

H Method of inventory valuation ▶   — —   . . Was there any substantial change in

the manner of determining quantities, costs, or valuations between the opening and closing inventories? (If "Yes," attach explanation). . .   X

Income

1 Gross receipts or sales $ .... Less: returns and allowances $ .... Balance ▶	1	10,000
2 Less: Cost of goods sold and/or operations (Schedule C-1, line 8)	2	2,000
3 Gross profit	3	8,000
4 Other income (attach schedule)	4	
5 Total income (add lines 3 and 4)	5	8,000

Deductions

6 Depreciation (explain in Schedule C-3)	6	900
7 Taxes on business and business property (explain in Schedule C-2) . . .	7	35
8 Rent on business property	8	2,000
9 Repairs (explain in Schedule C-2)	9	
10 Salaries and wages not included on line 3, Schedule C-1 (exclude any paid to yourself) .	10	
11 Insurance	11	
12 Legal and professional fees	12	200
13 Commissions	13	
14 Amortization (attach statement)	14	
15 (a) Pension and profit-sharing plans (see Schedule C Instructions)	15(a)	
(b) Employee benefit programs (see Schedule C Instructions)	(b)	
16 Interest on business indebtedness	16	
17 Bad debts arising from sales or services	17	
18 Depletion	18	

19 Other business expenses (specify):

(a)	Automobile	1,000	
(b)	Telephone	300	
(c)	Promotional material	1,000	
(d)	Travel	600	
(e)	Publications	100	
(f)			
(g)			
(h)			
(i)			
(j)			

(k) Total other business expenses (add lines 19(a) through 19(j))	19(k)	3,000
20 Total deductions (add lines 6 through 19(k))	20	6,135
21 Net profit or (loss) (subtract line 20 from line 5). Enter here and on Form 1040, line 29. **ALSO** enter on Schedule SE, line 5(a)	21	1,865

SCHEDULE C-1.—Cost of Goods Sold and/or Operations (See Schedule C Instructions for Line 2)

1 Inventory at beginning of year (if different from last year's closing inventory, attach explanation) . . .	1	
2 Purchases $ .... Less: cost of items withdrawn for personal use $ .... Balance ▶	2	
3 Cost of labor (do not include salary paid to yourself)	3	500
4 Materials and supplies	4	1,500
5 Other costs (attach schedule)	5	
6 Total of lines 1 through 5	6	2,000
7 Less: Inventory at end of year	7	
8 Cost of goods sold and/or operations. Enter here and on line 2 above	8	2,000

Did you claim a deduction for expenses of an office in your home? . . . . XX Yes ☐ No

SCHEDULE C–2.—Explanation of Lines 7 and 9

Line No.	Explanation	Amount	Line No.	Explanation	Amount
	Unincorporated business tax	$ 35	7		$

SCHEDULE C–3.—Depreciation (See Schedule C Instructions for Line 6)

If you need more space, use Form 4562.

a. Description of property	b. Date acquired	c. Cost or other basis	d. Depreciation allowed or allowable in prior years	e. Method of computing depreciation	f. Life or rate	g. Depreciation for this year
1 Total additional first-year depreciation (do not include in items below)———————————————→						
2 Other depreciation: Transportation	1/2/75	5,400	–	Straight line		900

3 Totals . . . . | | 5,400 | . . . . | | | 900

4 Less amount of depreciation claimed in Schedule C–1, page 1 . . . .

5 Balance—Enter here and on page 1, line 6 . . . . | | | | | | 900

SCHEDULE C–4.—Expense Account Information (See Schedule C Instructions for Schedule C–4)

Enter information with regard to yourself and your five highest paid employees. In determining the five highest paid employees, expense account allowances must be added to their salaries and wages. However, the information need not be submitted for any employee for whom the combined amount is less than $25,000, or for yourself if your expense account allowance plus line 21, page 1, is less than $25,000.	Name	Expense account	Salaries and Wages
	Owner		
	1		
	2		
	3		
	4		
	5		

Did you claim a deduction for expenses connected with:

(1) Entertainment facility (boat, resort, ranch, etc.)? . . ☐ **Yes** ☐ **No**   **(3)** Employees' families at conventions or meetings? . . ☐ **Yes** ☐ **No**

(2) Living accommodations (except employees on business)? ☐ **Yes** ☐ **No**   **(4)** Employee or family vacations not reported on Form W–2? ☐ **Yes** ☐ **No**

☆ U.S. GOVERNMENT PRINTING OFFICE : 1976—O-218-055 94-0743750

What income is reported on Schedule C?

Almost anything you take in as a self-employed person. For example: fees from the sale of completed art, for commissioned work, and for demonstrations and lectures, and the value of artwork received in a trade with another artist. You would also report royalties, fees you receive for selling or licensing copyrights on your work (see Chapter 2), and insurance proceeds from the loss or destruction of work (see Chapter 11). Some grants and many prizes and awards are taxable, but they're usually reported on Form 1040 itself, not Schedule C.

What grants are taxable?

Taxable grants are those that: (1) are paid as compensation for past, present, or future services, or (2) allow you to pursue your studies or researches, but are given primarily for the benefit of the employer.

What's an example of a grant that represents compensation for services? A grant that requires you to teach for a certain number of hours would be an example of a grant subject to tax. However, if this requirement is also a requirement of a college or graduate school degree program, it isn't taxable.

If teaching is a requirement of the grant (but not of the degree program), must I pay tax on the whole grant? No, only on the amount for which you're being compensated. Suppose, for example, you receive a $3,000 grant with the stipulation that you must teach 50 hours. If the going hourly rate at your institution for teaching is $10, $500 would be taxable; $2,500 would not.

What's an example of a grant primarily benefiting the grantor? An obvious one would be if the advertising agency you work for as an artist gives you a grant to study a particular type of drawing.

Determining whether a grant primarily benefits the grantor isn't always this easy, however. For example, suppose you receive a grant from a private foundation to travel in Europe to enhance your skills as a painter. Suppose also that the foundation reserves the right, if it wants it, to reproduce any painting made during your travels for its annual report. Although the right to reproduce wasn't a condition of the grant, the I.R.S. nevertheless might take a hard line on this, declaring that the foundation benefited from the grant.

If you're unsure whether the grant you receive is taxable or not, check with a lawyer and the granting agency.

When don't I pay tax on a grant?

If you are a degree candidate and you don't fall into either category mentioned above, you don't have to pay any tax on your grant. If you're not a degree candidate but you don't fit either of the above categories, you may exclude a portion of the grant from your taxable income.

If I'm not a degree candidate, what portion can I exclude?

You may exclude $300 a month from your taxable income for a total of 36 months. These 36 months don't have to be consecutive.

What if I receive less than $300 a month for more than 36 months? You can't exceed the 36-month limit. Grants for 48 months, for instance, would be fully taxable for the last 12 months.

What if I receive more than $300 for less than 36 months? You'd have to pay tax on the amount that exceeds the $300 limitation.

Are prizes and awards taxable?

Yes, unless they meet *all* of the following conditions:

1. The prize or award is made primarily in recognition of religious, charitable, scientific, educational, artistic, literary, or civic achievement;

2. You're selected without any action on your part to enter the competition, or whatever; and

3. You're not required to render substantial future services as a condition for receiving the prize.

An example of an untaxable prize might be as follows: the editors of the *American Artist* magazine decide to give a cash prize to the artist who has made the most outstanding artistic contribution to his or her community. The only artists the editors will consider are those who have appeared in the magazine some time in the past five years. The recipient of the award won't have to pay tax because the award is made in recognition of artistic achievement; he doesn't "enter" the contest; and he promises no future services to the magazine.

Is artwork I exchange with another artist income?

According to the law, it is and you must include it as income on Schedule C. And even if you aren't eager to include it as income, it may prove a wise move in the future.

Why would it be wise to report this income?

Because if the work you receive appreciates in value and you donate it to a museum as a collector would, you'll be able to take a larger tax deduction than if you didn't report it. If you can prove that you, in effect, bought the work by reporting it as income, you may be able to claim a deduction for its market value at the time you donate the work. In other words, if the work was worth $200 when you got it and $2,000 when you donate it, you can claim a deduction based on the larger figure. The reason for this is that the law says you can take a charitable deduction for the value of works purchased and held for more than one year before donation to a museum.

Not so, if you've merely received a gift. The recipient of a gift is treated like the artist himself—eligible for nothing more than a deduction for the raw materials that went into the work. And you probably wouldn't be able to claim that either, since the artist probably deducted the cost of them during the year he made the work.

How do I estimate the income I receive in an exchange?

When you exchange work, find out how much the work you receive would sell for, and subtract the cost of materials in the work you gave. The result is your income.

What business expenses may I deduct on Schedule C?

All ordinary and necessary expenses, meaning those that can be expected to arise with a degree of regularity and are appropriate and helpful in the profession of being an artist. In other words, all those expenses mentioned in Chapter 12: supplies, postage, promotional material, travel, entertainment, telephone, studio expenses, and so on.

Some of these, as mentioned in the last chapter, such as telephone, car, and studio expenses, must be broken down into nondeductible personal expenses and deductible business expenses before the right amounts can be reported on your tax return. Others, those known as capital expenditures, must be depreciated, i.e., deducted over a number of years.

But before I get into depreciation, let me explain the limitations on deducting studio expenses mentioned in Chapter 12.

Why might I not be able to deduct all my studio expenses?

You can, if your studio is separate from your house. But the 1976 Tax Reform Act changed the law to make it much more difficult to deduct home-studio expenses (which include not just expenses involving the studio itself but also telephone and utilities).

The law says that you can deduct expenses only up to the point at which they equal your income from self-employment. This means that if you rent your home-studio and you earned $1,000 last year from self-employment, all you can deduct for rent, telephone, utilities, and upkeep is $1,000, even if you spent more.

The law goes on to say that if you own your own home and your studio is a part of it, you can deduct expenses only up to your income from self-employment minus certain deductions you'd be allowed anyway. These deductions are real estate taxes and mortgage interest payments.

How does this work? Suppose you earn $3,000 from self-employment, your home mortgage interest is $3,000 a year, and real estate taxes are $2,600. Other home expenses, such as the cost of heating, water, telephone, electricity, air conditioning, and similar expenses and depreciation (see below) amount to $7,200 for the year. If your studio takes up one-fourth of your house, you'll be able to claim one-fourth of the real estate taxes and mortgage interest payments as business expenses. One-fourth of $5,600 ($3,000 plus $2,600) equals $1,400.

Because you can write this expense off as a deduction anyway, you must subtract $1,400 from your $3,000 self-employment income to get the amount you can claim for expenses: $1,600.

One-quarter of the other home expenses ($7,200) comes to $1,800, but since you can only deduct $1,600, you won't be able to claim the remaining $200.

How else does the Revised Tax Law limit home-studio deductions?

It says that your studio must be used exclusively—and on a regular basis—as the principal place of your self-employed business. By exclusively, the law means that your studio can't double as a bedroom or living room.

If I have a regular job, can my studio be a principal place of business?

Yes. You can have as many principal places of business as you have businesses. For example, if you teach, your school is your principal place of business for your teaching career, while your studio is your principal place of business for your art career.

What if I'm a teacher required by my school to maintain an art career?

Even though your school may demand that you maintain your professional art career, you can't write your studio expenses off as business expenses for that reason alone. The law still requires that you make enough income from self-employment to equal studio expenses before you deduct.

How do I depreciate capital expenditures?

As mentioned in the last chapter, capital expenditures are items with useful lives of more than one year. Because they last for a long time, they can't be deducted totally in the year they are purchased—the deduction must be spread over a period of years. These spread-out deductions are called depreciation deductions. The principal ways to compute depreciation are: the straight line method, the 200% declining balance method, and the sum-of-the-years digit method. The straight line method is easiest to calculate; the others allow you to deduct the item in large initial amounts. After you read about all three, you'll be able to decide which one is best for you.

How does straight line depreciation work?

Straight line depreciation is determined by dividing the purchase price of the item less salvage value (defined below) by the remaining useful life (defined below).

What is the useful life of an item?

The useful life of anything is the number of years you expect to use it. The I.R.S. accepts most reasonable estimates based on your assessment of how long the item will be of use to you. For example, while a reasonable estimate of the life expectancy of a camera might be five years, the amount of stress you subject your camera to might dictate that you buy a new one every three years. If so, three years would be the useful life of the camera. If you're still in the dark about the useful life of items you purchase, ask someone at your nearest I.R.S. office. They have tables listing their estimates of the average useful lives of many items.

What is salvage value?

It is the item's worth after its useful life is up. For example, suppose you decide a camera has a useful life to you of five years, and, at the end of that time, it still has a market value of $100. In other words, you could probably sell it for $100 at that time. Its salvage value, then, is $100.

If its salvage value is less than 10% of the purchase price, however, you can skip it altogether when calculating straight line depreciation.

How do I calculate straight line depreciation?

First, a few things must be said about salvage value and useful life. In straight line depreciation, if the salvage value is 10% or more of the item and the item has a useful life of three years or more, the I.R.S. allows you to reduce salvage value by subtracting 10% of the purchase price from it. And if the item has a useful life of six years or more, you can take a larger initial deduction, which is explained below.

Now here's a step-by-step analysis of straight line depreciation:

1. You buy a camera for $500 on January 1.

2. You decide that the camera will have a useful life of five years and a salvage value at the end of that time of $100.

3. Since the salvage value ($100) is more than 10% of the purchase price of $500, you subtract 10% of the $500 from the purchase price, increasing the amount to be deducted to $450 from $400 (purchase price minus salvage value).

4. You divide the $450 by five (the camera's useful life) to arrive at your yearly depreciation deduction of $90. Every year for five years, you'll take a $90 deduction for your camera.

What if I don't buy my camera on January 1?

You can calculate first-year depreciation a couple of ways. If you just make the one capital expenditure—the camera—you start depreciating when you get it. So if you buy a camera in March, you would depreciate the camera in the first year by five-sixths of the yearly depreciation, since you used it for 10 out of 12 months. In the example above, your first year depreciation for that camera would be $375 ($450 times 5/6).

What if I buy more than a camera?

If you made a number of capital purchases—the camera, a car, a press—the I.R.S. allows you to lump them all into half-yearly increments. This means that for items bought between January 1 and June 30, you can claim a whole year's deduction on all of them, no matter when they were purchased. For items bought between July 1 and December 31, you can take one-half of one year's deduction.

What if the item has a useful life of six years or more?

If the item has a useful life of six years or more and represents an investment of $10,000 or less (or $20,000 or less on a joint return), you can deduct an additional depreciation deduction—20% of the cost—besides the regular first-year depreciation deduction. If you take this deduction, you don't consider salvage value. The end result is that you can take a bigger deduction in the first year than if the item had a useful life of less than six years.

What's an example of this? The best example is a step-by-step analysis:

1. You buy a brand new van on July 1 for $6,400 to transport art to shows.

2. You expect the van to have a useful life of 8 years. (The figures used here aren't meant to be particularly realistic; they were chosen so the computations would come up with nice round figures.)

3. Figure out 20% of $6,400.

4. Subtract this amount—$1,280—from the cost of the van to give you the amount to be depreciated.

5. Divide the remaining cost of the van—$5,120—by the useful life (8 years) to get your yearly depreciation: $640.

6. Since the van was purchased on July 1, this year's depreciation would be half of the yearly depreciation, $320.

7. Add the additional first-year depreciation of $1,280 to the half-yearly depreciation for the first year ($320), and you have the total amount you can deduct in the first year you own the van—$1,600. (For the following seven years, you'll deduct $640. If you used the straight line method without the additional first-year deduction, you would deduct $800 every year for eight years—$6,400 divided by 8, assuming no salvage value.)

Can I always take this additional first-year depreciation?

Yes, even if you use the other two methods of calculating depreciation—the 200% declining balance method and the sum-of-the-years digits method. However, to simplify calculations, I won't include the additional first-year depreciation in the computation of the other two methods discussed below.

How does the 200% declining balance method work?

This method can be used only with items having a useful life of three years or more. Although it doesn't take salvage value into consideration in the computation, you'll see in a moment that you can't forget it entirely.

Compute the 200% declining balance on a $6,400 van with a life expectancy of 8 years as follows:

1. Compute the percentage of the original price that you would be able to deduct each year under the straight line method. This would be the number of years of useful life (8) divided into 1— i.e., 1/8, or 12½%.

2. Double this percentage (this is where the 200% comes in): 12½% times 2 equals 25%.

3. Starting with the original price in the first year, this percentage (25%) is deducted from the remaining balance in each succeeding year—for the first year, 25% of $6,400 equals $1,600, which is your deduction. The remaining balance is $6,400 minus $1,600, or $4,800. The second year, you take 25% of $4,800, which equals $1,200, your second deduction. The remaining balance this time is $4,800 minus $1,200, or $3,600. The third year, you take 25% of $3,600, or $900, which is your deduction. The remaining balance is $3,600 minus $900, which is $2,700. And so on.

Now about salvage value. In the 200% declining balance method, you can't depreciate below salvage value. Depreciation must stop when the remaining balance equals salvage value, preventing you from depreciating the entire amount.

What is the sum-of-the-years digit method?

To calculate this method—which is also restricted to items with a useful life of three years or more—add up all the numbers in the figure you use for useful life. This does sound funny, but if the useful life is eight years, you add 1, 2, 3, 4, 5, 6, 7, and 8, which equals 36. Each year a fraction is used whose denominator is this sum, 36, and whose numerator is the remaining years. The cost of the item is then multiplied by this fraction each year to obtain the depreciation deduction.

Thus the first-year deduction for that van would be 8/36 times $6,400, or $1,422. The second-year deduction would be 7/36 times $6,400, or $1,244. The third-year deduction would be 6/36 times $6,400, or $1,066. And so on.

What if there's salvage value?

Treat it as you do when you use the straight line method—subtract salvage value from the original cost.

Can I switch from one method of depreciation to another?

The I.R.S. allows you to make one switch: from the 200% declining method to the straight line. If you want to make any other switch, you'll have to request I.R.S. approval on Form 3115.

Why would I want to combine those two methods?

If you calculate deductions using both the straight line and the 200% declining balance method over the life of your purchase, you'll see that the 200% declining balances gives you bigger deductions in the early years, but less in the later years than you would get by using the straight line method.

For example, with the straight line method, each year you could deduct $800 on your van assuming no salvage value (remember, this isn't taking the 20% additional first year depreciation into consideration). But if you used the 200% declining method, see what happens:

Year	Deduction	Balance	Year	Deduction	Balance
1	$1,600	$4,800	5	$506	$1,519
2	1,200	3,600	6	380	1,139
3	900	2,700	7	285	854
4	675	2,025	8	213	641

And you never fully depreciate the entire cost of the van, as you would with the straight line method.

The best thing to do is switch from the declining balance to straight line method in the year it becomes profitable to do so. Then, simply take the remaining balance not yet depreciated and divide this evenly among the remaining years, unless there's salvage value.

When would I switch?

The following table gives you the best year in which to switch from the 200% declining balance to the straight line method, assuming there's no salvage value.

Useful life	Last year to use declining method	Useful life	Last year to use declining method
3	2	9	5
4	3	10	6
5	3	11	6
6	4	12	7
7	4	13	7
8	5	14	8

Therefore, using our example of the $6,400 van with the eight-year useful life, here's how the deductions would look. (Don't be confused by the fact that the deduction is the same in the fifth and sixth year; this is a coincidence.)

200% Declining Method			Straight Line Method		
Year	Deduction	Balance	Year	Deduction	Balance
1	$1,600	$4,800	5	$506	$1,519
2	1,200	3,600	6	506	1,013
3	900	2,700	7	506	507
4	675	1,519	8	506	—

What if there's salvage value?

Subtract it from the remaining balance before you apply the straight line method. The result might prove that switching would be unwise. For example, suppose the van had a salvage value of $800. You would subtract this from the balance at the end of the fifth year ($1,519), leaving you with $719. This would give you a deduction of $237 in each of the three remaining years—it's clearly not worthwhile switching.

How does sum-of-the-years digits method compare with the combination?

The initial deductions offered by the sum-of-the-years digits method aren't as large as the combination of the 200% declining balance and straight line methods, but they're offset by greater deductions in the middle years. Compare the two columns below (assuming no salvage value).

Year	Combination: 200% declining balance for 5 years and straight line for 3 years	Sum-of-the-year digits method
1	$1,600	$1,422
2	1,200	1,244
3	900	1,066
4	675	888
5	506	711
6	506	533
7	506	355
8	506	178
	$6,400	$6,397

Which method is best?

There's no best method of depreciation; there is only a best method for you, and that depends on when you want to take the largest deductions. For example, if your income is good in the year you make your capital expenditure and you expect it to remain so for the next year or two, you might want to deduct as much as possible now to reduce your taxable income. This means that you'd opt for the combination of the declining and straight line methods.

But, if you think your income will continue to grow significantly over the next five years, you might choose the sum-of-the-years digits method which allows you larger deductions in the middle years.

On the other hand, if you have a hobby-loss problem, explained later on in this chapter, you might want to report as much taxable income as possible. In this case, straight line would be the method of choice.

How do I depreciate equipment that I buy used?

First, figure out how long the item will be useful to you. For example, if you plan to use a two-year-old camera for another three years, three years would be its useful life. Then you can compute the depreciation by any of the methods mentioned above with one change. The 200% declining balance changes to a 150% declining balance when used items are depreciated. Going back to our example of the $6,400 van, had it been purchased used, you would deduct $18^3/_4\%$ from the declining balance, instead of 25%.

What about equipment bought for personal use earlier but now used for artwork?

For such used equipment—saws, drills, and so on—determine what they're worth today (if less than the original cost) and their remaining useful life. Then depreciate.

What if the item breaks down before its useful life is up?

Deduct the entire amount left to be deducted in the year it breaks down.

How do I depreciate my home-studio?

Figure out how much your whole house depreciates each year, and then claim a percentage of it as a business depreciation deduction. The percentage will be the same percentage you used to calculate other business home-studio expenses.

Here are the steps you would use to figure out the overall depreciation rate of your house:

1. Start with the purchase price of the house or the amount you spent to build it.

2. Subtract the land value, because land can't be depreciated. (You can get this amount from your tax assessor.)

3. Add in the cost of any major improvements, like a new furnace.

4. Divide the results by the expected useful life.

How do I determine its useful life?

Ask a real estate appraiser or the county assessor what he thinks. Or make the estimate yourself, using as a criterion how many years you think you could rent the house to someone else. Your estimate will take into consideration improvements and repairs. The average life of a new house is usually 30 to 40 years.

What method of depreciation do I use to depreciate my house?

Straight line. But there are two important differences in the way you depreciate a house and other capital equipment. First, you cannot claim the 20% additional first-year depreciation on a house. Second, you cannot reduce the salvage value of a house by 10% in your calculation.

Do I get any other tax breaks for capital expenditures?

Yes, you also can get an investment credit for equipment (but not buildings) in the year you buy the item. An investment credit is a real bonus because, unlike a business deduction which is deducted from taxable income, an investment credit is deducted from the tax itself.

The credit does not appear on Schedule C; rather, it is reported on Forms 1040 and 3468, which explains the credit.

Investment credits works like this:

1. If the item has a useful life of seven years or more, you can claim an investment credit of 10% of the purchase price of the item. (The percentages change from time to time, so be sure to check them out with the I.R.S. in the year you plan to claim them.)

2. If it has a useful life of more than five years but less than seven, you can claim an investment credit of $6^2/3\%$ of the purchase price.

3. If it has a useful life of more than three but less than five years, you can claim an investment credit of $3^1/3\%$ of the purchase price.

Therefore, if you owed $3,000 in taxes in 1977, the investment credit from your $6,400 van would reduce them by $640 to $2,360.

What is the hobby-loss problem?

This entire chapter discusses deducting expenses incurred from self-employment from income earned from self-employment, both of which are reported on Schedule C, the profit or loss statement. If income is greater than expenses, the profit from self-employment is reported on Form 1040 and added to other income you earn from a job, investments, or whatever. If expenses exceed income on Schedule C, the loss is also reported on Form 1040 and subtracted from other income. You can do this because, as a professional artist in the business of making and selling art, you are like any other businessman who, if he spends more than he makes in the course of business, can deduct the loss from total taxable income.

The hobby-loss problem arises when the I.R.S. decides to dispute the legitimacy of your right to claim a business loss on the grounds that you are not a self-employed professional out to make a profit but a mere hobbyist. A hobbyist in the eyes of the I.R.S. isn't interested in making a profit since he's not really in business and is, therefore, not entitled to deduct a business loss from total taxable income.

Can a hobbyist deduct anything?

Yes, he's allowed deductions for expenses from the hobby up to the amount of income the hobby produces. For example, suppose a doctor takes up painting on Sundays and becomes proficient enough to sell $500 worth of work in one year to his colleagues. He spent $1,000 pursuing his hobby, but all he can claim is $500.

The problem, then, is to convince the I.R.S., if you're audited, that your loss is legitimate because you have a profit motive.

What do you mean by "audited"?

An audit is an examination of your tax return by an I.R.S. official to see if you paid the correct amount of taxes.

What happens if we disagree?

If, after the audit, the official thinks you didn't pay the right amount but you think you did, you can request a meeting with an I.R.S. supervisor. If you and the supervisor disagree, you can appeal the decision to the district conference of the I.R.S. and then to the appellate division. If you still don't agree, you can take your case to the United States Tax Court.

At any of these stages after the initial examination, you and the I.R.S. can decide to compromise. In other words, a dispute over taxes isn't a cut-and-dried affair. If the I.R.S. says you owe $500 in unpaid taxes and you believe you don't owe them anything, it may be wiser to negotiate a settlement somewhere in between rather than incur heavy legal and accounting fees trying to prove you're right.

Another way to handle a tax dispute if the amount in question is less than $1,500 is to sue the I.R.S. in the Tax Court's small tax claims division. In this court, you don't need a lawyer to present your case (although it's helpful), and the decision is final—you can't appeal it.

How can I prove a profit motive?

The easiest way is to report a profit on Schedule C for any two out of five consecutive years ending with the taxable year in question. This will satisfy an I.R.S. requirement. So if by December 31, 1978, you've reported a profit on Schedule C in any two years since January 1, 1974, don't worry. The I.R.S. will accede to the fact that you're a legitimate business.

And making profits may not be as hard as you think. If you adopt the cash method of accounting recommended in Chapter 12, manipulation of income and expenses by delaying payment on expenses until after the first of the year and trying to collect as many fees before the old year runs out may result in a profit. It may be a small one, but so what? Two years of small profits and three of somewhat larger losses boosts you into the professional category; five years of small losses won't.

Can I prove a profit motive if I don't make profits in two out of five years?

Yes. The two-out-of-five-year requirement is a relatively new way to prove a profit motive. It came in with the Tax Reform Bill of 1969 to make it easy for taxpayers to make their case. Unfortunately, some auditors tend to see this measure as the only criterion.

But they are wrong. The regulations of the Internal Revenue Code set forth a number of factors which are used to determine whether or not there's a profit motive involved in any activity, and these factors have been backed up and elaborated on by court cases.

You don't have to qualify for every factor, nor will any one be crucial. Each case is decided on the sum total of the circumstances that affect your self-employment.

What are these factors?

The following six things:

1. The manner in which you carry on your business. This means that if you keep records in a businesslike manner, as I described in Chapter 12, and engage in other activities—entering competitions, traveling to art shows, exhibiting in art galleries and museums, publicizing your work—you'll be all right on this score.

2. Your expertise. Expertise may be indicated by extensive study; gallery and museum exhibitions; gallery representations; awards and prizes; recognition as a talented artist in catalogs, newspapers, magazines, museum journals, and other publications that write critically about artists; and the ability to hold a teaching position in your particular field of art.

3. The amount of time you spend working as a self-employed artist. The I.R.S. has never spelled out what it considers a significant amount of time to be. Working full-time would be ideal, of course, meaning devoting yourself solely to making and selling art and not working at any other job. But if you have a job that allows you to work on a regular basis as a professional, the I.R.S. should accept this. For example, in at least one case, the Tax Court ruled that four hours a day was enough. This doesn't mean that a smaller amount of time wouldn't also be sufficient, only that four hours satisfied that court in that particular case. The real point is that you must work on a consistent basis.

4. A prior history of critical or financial success—despite intervening periods when you didn't work or earn a profit—is a plus. For example, suppose you had established your reputation as an artist, but then married, had children, and devoted yourself entirely to being a mother. If you return to your artwork later when your children are older, your old reputation should stand you in good stead in case of an audit.

5. Your history of income with respect to the activity. Selling more each year or selling at higher prices should impress the examiner hearing your case.

6. Your financial status. Here's where it pays to be poor. A lack of other substantial income reported on your income tax should indicate that you need income from your art, and that you can't afford a hobby. This should put you in a better position to prove your case than someone who makes a lot of money from other sources.

Do you know of someone who didn't measure up to these factors?

One of the most frequently quoted cases is that of Johanna K. W. Hailman, a rich Pittsburgh socialite who painted about 600 paintings throughout her life. Although she was recognized as a leading artist in western Pennsylvania and elsewhere, during her lifetime she sold only 50 works. These were priced between $700 and $1,500, and she refused to sell for less. All told, her income for an 18-year period from 1936 to 1954 was $7,200, while she reported expenses totalling $131,140. In 1954, the I.R.S., who for many years had compromised on expenses by allowing her an annual $3,000 deduction, decided enough was enough. It said her losses were excessive and held that she didn't intend to conduct her activities as a professional.

The Tax Court agreed, concluding that since expenses were 18 times as great as receipts, only independent wealth permitted her to continue the activity—including the setting of high prices and the retention of most of the artworks. Therefore, said the Court, her activity must be classified as a hobby pursued without the requisite profit motive.

Do you know a case of someone who overcame being classified a hobbyist?

Yes, the following case was excerpted from "The Hobby-Loss Challenge: For Many Artists Their Biggest Headache," by Tad Crawford in *American Artist*. It puts into perspective how the I.R.S. factors for determining a profit motive can work for you.

Anna Maria de Grazia, who painted under the name Anna Maria d'Annunzio, was the granddaughter of Gabriele d'Annunzio, the famous Italian writer and military hero, and was raised in Italy, where she became interested in painting in 1940. During World War II she served as a guide for the Allied Forces, but she continued her painting until 1944, when polio forced her to learn how to paint with her left hand rather than her right. In 1942 she won first prize in an exhibition by young painters in Florence and the same year placed third in a contest open to all Italians.

Giving up her art from 1943 to 1947, she resumed painting and exhibiting from 1948 to 1951. During this period she was admitted to the Italian painters union upon the attestation of three professional artists that she was a professional artist. In 1952, after moving to the United States, she married Sebastian de Grazia, and she neither painted nor exhibited until 1955, when she became a naturalized citizen. By 1957 she had studied with the artists Annigoni, Carena, and Kokoschka and had received recognition in a book on Italian painting in which her self-portrait and biographical background appeared.

She resumed painting in 1956 and 1957, supported by the modest income of her husband, who was a visiting professor at Princeton University. In 1957, after working in Princeton in a rented house and trying unsuccessfully to acquire a New York gallery, she felt her studio facilities inadequate and left in May to paint at the Piazza Donatello Studios in Florence. Her decision to go to Florence was prompted by familiarity with the art world in Italy.

Despite her return to Italy, she was still interested in getting a New York gallery and was told that a show at any prestigious gallery in New York would require numerous paintings. To achieve her goal, she began to create a significant body of work, painting four hours a day in 1957 and devoting additional time to stretching and preparing canvases and transacting business with art dealers and framemakers. By the end of 1957 she had completed 12 or 15 paintings, with ten more in progress. After 1957 she exhibited successfully, having a number of solo shows in Italy as well as exhibiting in Princeton and New York City.

In 1957 her paintings earned no income, but she incurred $5,769 in expenses; in 1958 she made $500, while her expenses were $6,854; in 1959 she earned $575 and spent $5,360; and in 1960 income amounted to $710, while expenses totaled $4,968. She did not keep formal business books but did have records relating to her receipts and expenses as an artist.

The I.R.S. challenged her deduction of $5,769 in 1957 on the grounds that she had been merely pursuing a hobby, or preparing to enter a business or trade, but had not been engaged in the business or trade of being an artist in that year.

The Tax Court disagreed with the I.R.S. It concluded that she had been in the business or trade of being an artist in the year 1957. The Tax Court considered the following facts as significant of her profit motive: she began painting in her youth and won prizes for her work; she struggled to overcome the handicap imposed by polio; she studied with recognized artists; she received recognition from the Italian painters union and in critical publications; she had exhibitions both prior and subsequent to 1957; she worked continually and unstintingly at her painting and necessary incidental tasks; she had no other sources of income so that losses were a financial strain; and she had constantly increasing receipts in the years after 1957.

The Tax Court also rejected explicitly the argument that she had merely been preparing to enter a trade or profession, stating that the history of her art activities onward from 1940 rebutted any such contention. In a notable section of the decision, the Court wrote, "It is well recognized that profits may not be immediately forthcoming in the creative art field. Examples are legion of the increase in value of a painter's work after he receives public acclaim. Many artists have to struggle in their early years. This does not mean that serious artists do not intend to profit from their activities. It only means that their lot is a difficult one."

Should I get professional help if I'm audited?

Yes. Get a lawyer or CPA to accompany you to your audit hearings. Don't appear by yourself. Sure, you can go it alone, but it will probably cost more in the long run. And don't count on the friendly neighborhood bookkeeper or tax preparer who filled out your return. These people can only answer questions about the work they did on your return. They can't negotiate settlements or take cases through the various levels of appeal. Lawyers and CPAs, on the other hand, can develop the factors of your case favorably, and their presence at initial conferences with I.R.S. agents may clear up your difficulties immediately.

Is there anything else I can do to help my case?

Make sure your lawyer or CPA is familiar with the hobby-loss problem. In particular, make sure he has read the de Grazia case. And for a complete set of legal references, refer him to the bibliography accompanying "Hobbies, Horses and the Struggling Artist," by Tad Crawford and Hedrick L. Lidstone in *Art and the Law* (see the bibliography).

14. More On Taxes

· Estimated taxes
· Self-employment tax
· Unincorporated business tax
· Sales tax

You may think you've read everything you ought to know about taxes in this book already. Or maybe just more than you want to know. But unfortunately as a self-employed artist, you're faced with the possibility of filling out even more forms than those already discussed. So here's more on taxes.

As a self-employed person, do I have to pay taxes in advance?

Yes. The last chapter discussed all about filling out Form 1040 and its accompanying schedules and forms for return with your check to the I.R.S. on or before the April 15th deadline. But paying taxes isn't quite that easy for the self-employed person. You do have to file a tax return on April 15th for the previous year's income. But you also have to file returns and pay taxes during the year in which you're earning you're income.

What's the point of this?

What the I.R.S. is actually doing is asking you to be your own employer and withhold wages to be remitted as taxes as if you were employed by someone else. According to the law, anyone who earns more than $500 not subject to withholding tax must file Form 1040 ES. This is true of both fully self-employed people and the self-employed who also have jobs. Form ES consists of an estimated tax worksheet and four declaration vouchers. The first declaration voucher reports the amount you think you'll owe in taxes for the current year. Full payment of that amount may be paid at that time or in installments on April 15th, June 15th, September 15th, and January 15th. Payments are sent to the I.R.S. along with the other three vouchers. Either way, 80% of your actual tax must be paid by January 15th. If it isn't, the I.R.S. can penalize you.

How do I know how much to pay?

By April 15th, you'll know how much you have made the first three months of the year and what expenses you've incurred. By using the worksheets that come with the voucher, you can estimate your tax for that period. Then it's a simple matter of multiplying by four to get your estimated tax for the year. The I.R.S. doesn't expect you to hit the figure on the nose—all it cares about is that you have paid 80% of it by January 15th. If your income falls off or increases drastically during the year, you can adjust payments to accommodate the change by January 15th.

What if I haven't paid 100% of my tax bill by January 15th?

If, by January 15th, you have paid 80% of your tax but still owe the government more, just send the remainder with your regular tax return (Form 1040) for the previous year on or before the April 15th deadline—like employees do if their employers haven't withheld enough taxes from their wages.

What if I've overpaid by January 15th?

If you overpay, note this on Form 1040 and indicate on your declaration voucher that you either want this overpayment credited against the first payment of the estimated tax due for the current year or spread out over each of the four installment payments. Or you can simply ask for a refund.

Must I pay estimated income taxes if 80% of my taxes are withheld from another job?

No. And even if you find that your art income soars during the latter part of the year, meaning that 80% won't be paid by January 15th by withholding, you can still rectify the situation by filing a declaration voucher with a payment on this income by January 15th.

As a self-employed person, must I pay social security tax?

Yes. If you were employed, your employer would deduct a certain amount from your check to pay the social security tax. But since you're self-employed, you must pay the tax yourself. The tax is called the Self-employment Tax and is reported on Schedule SE.

If I'm employed as well as self-employed, must I pay self-employment tax?

Possibly. Every year the I.R.S. establishes how much of your income is subject to a social security tax, whether it's the self-employment tax or the social security tax taken out of your paycheck by your employer. If you don't earn that amount in wages, your net income from self-employment is subject to social security tax up to the amount of the difference.

Could I ever overpay the social security tax?

Yes, if you have two jobs in one year, and earn more than the maximum amount subject to social security tax and both employers deduct the tax, you would overpay. If that happens, just deduct the overpayment on Form 1040.

What other taxes may I have to pay?

It's possible you may have to pay a state unincorporated business tax. Since corporations have to pay taxes, many states reason that it's unfair that unincorporated businesses get away tax-free. To equalize the situation, they impose an unincorporated business tax. And they impose it on you. Even if you think of yourself as just a painter or a sculptor, if your state has·such a tax, its tax department sees you as a business if you're earning money from your art, and it taxes you as a business over and above your personal income tax. So find out if your state has an unincorporated business tax. It usually isn't much, and it's better to pay it now rather than wait for your state tax department to catch you for nonpayment.

Must I collect sales tax on artwork I sell?

Yes, if you sell art as a retailer, most state laws require you to charge and collect a sales tax.

Who is a retailer?

You're a retailer if you sell your art to the person who plans to use it and not resell it. In other words, if a collector comes into your studio and buys a piece of art to hang on his wall, you've just made a sale on the retail level and must charge a sales tax.

If I sell or consign work to a gallery, am I responsible for the sales tax?

No. A sales tax is collected only once—on the final sale. If you sell or consign work to a gallery—or a frame shop—the owner becomes the retailer, so he's responsible for collecting the tax. You are, in effect, only a wholesaler selling goods for resale.

Who collects the sales tax at art shows and exhibitions?

Whoever handles the sales. If you do personally (or someone

who's helping you out does), you'll have to collect the tax; if all sales go through the sponsor of the show or festival, it's his responsibility.

How do I collect the sales tax?

First, you must register with your state sales tax department, which will possibly require you to put down a minimum deposit. Then it will issue you a sales permit and a resale number and supply you with the appropriate forms to be filled out and returned to it when you remit the tax. In most states, sales tax returns are filed quarterly.

Next, record all sales taxes on your sales invoices, and report them in your bookkeeping system along with income. (Make sure you keep these records accurately in case you're ever audited.) Then every three months, or whatever the appropriate time period is, total the taxes collected as indicated in your records and send a check for that amount to the state sales tax department along with the return bearing your resale number.

What if I sell work at out-of-state art shows?

If that state has a sales tax, you must collect it. And rumor has it that tax agents lurk about the booths of artists who sell well at out-of-town shops and fairs to see if they're complying with the law. The best course of action, then, is to apply to the sales tax department of that state for whatever forms or permits it requires for out-of-staters setting up temporary shop within its boundaries.

What else is a resale number good for?

A resale number also allows you to buy at wholesale prices and avoid paying sales tax on certain supplies. A tax can be charged on goods only once—at their final sale. This means materials and supplies purchased for incorporation into another product are not taxable. In other words, canvas, paint, stone, clay and so on should not be taxed when sold to you—providing you've applied for and received a resale number—because they will be taxed again when they end up as the final product, the artwork.

What supplies aren't tax-exempt?

Supplies that don't end up in the final product you plan to sell, such as brushes, knives, and easels.

How do I avoid the sales tax on tax-exempt supplies?

When you go into an art supply store, tell the clerk that supplies are tax-free for you and show him your resale number. He marks on the sales invoice that the sale is a "resale," records your resale number, and leaves the tax off the bill.

15. How To Reduce Taxes

- · Assigning royalties
- · Income averaging
- · Retirement plans
- · Incorporation

Nobody wants to pay more taxes than necessary, and no discussion of taxes would be complete without mentioning some of the ways you can reduce them. In this chapter, therefore, four tax-saving devices are discussed. This is not meant to be a definitive list of ways to reduce taxes—your tax lawyer or accountant can most probably suggest others, particularly if your income is large and you're able to make nontaxable investments, for example. So be sure to ask for help in planning a tax strategy that will keep the amount you have to pay in taxes as low as possible.

How can I reduce the amount of taxes I must pay?

By assigning royalties, income averaging, retirement plans, and incorporation.

What do you mean by assigning royalties?

As explained in Chapter 2, you can transfer your copyright to others either by giving it away or selling it. Now, suppose you own the copyright on a work that has been reproduced in a large edition. The edition is selling well and will probably be reissued—and you're being paid a royalty on each sale. If you're in a high income bracket, the amount of taxes you'll have to pay on these royalties may be considerable.

But if you give your copyright to one of your children, he'll be paid the royalties, not you. Since he's probably in a very low income bracket, his taxes on these royalties will be considerably less.

But before you rush into any copyright assignments, get the advice of your lawyer. There may be other legal and tax reasons why it would not be advisable.

What is income averaging?

Income averaging is a method provided by federal tax law that can reduce taxes if your career is characterized by large increases in income every now and then. And as everyone knows, an artist's income is up one year—down the next. Suppose, for example, that your taxable income for four consecutive years was $6,000, and then in the fifth year, thanks to a sell-out one-person show, it soared to $20,000. Income averaging would let you treat the extra income in the fifth year as if it had been earned evenly over all five years.

In other words, if you pay taxes without averaging on the example used above, the tax bill for your taxable income for the five years ($44,000) would come to $9,685 (assuming you're single). But if you're eligible for income averaging, your total tax bill would amount to $9,066, approximately what you would have paid if you earned $8,800 each year for a five-year income of $44,000.

What is the time period to which I can apply income averaging?

Five years—no more and no less.

How do I know if I'm eligible for income averaging?

To be eligible:

1. You must have been a U.S. citizen or a resident alien for the entire five-year period.

2. You must have furnished at least half of your own support in the previous four years.

3. Your average taxable income during the previous four years must have been at least $3,000.

4. Your taxable income in the fifth year must exceed 120% of your average taxable income for the prior four years by more than $3,000.

What do you mean by that last statement? As an example, suppose that in the four previous years, your taxable income was $7,000 in the first year, $8,000 in the second, $4,000 in the third, and $5,000 in the fourth year. The sum of these amounts is $24,000, and the average income for these years is $6,000.

Since your taxable income must exceed 120% of your average income for the prior four years by more than $3,000, first you would figure 120% of $6,000, giving you $7,200. Then you would add this amount to $3,000. So your taxable income would have to be at least $10,200 before you would be eligble to income average.

Would I save much on taxes if I made that minimum income?

No. You won't save any at all if you income average with $10,200 as your high year. The table below tells you how much your taxable income must be in order to save at least $100 in taxes.

If your average taxable income for the previous four years is	You must earn this much in the fifth year to save at least $100 in taxes
$ 4,000	$11,333
6,000	11,333
8,000	15,333
10,000	19,333
12,000	19,333
14,000	22,500
16,000	22,500

How do I income average?

The computation is rather complicated, and, if you think you're eligible for income averaging, you may want to ask an accountant or call the I.R.S. for help. But for an idea of how it works, look at Figure 17 for Schedule G, the schedule on which income averaging is reported.

How do retirement plans reduce my tax?

If you're eligible to set up your own retirement plan, the money you invest in it is deducted from gross income, reducing the amount of tax you'll have to pay. It's taxable later, of course, when you start withdrawing funds for your retirement. But by then you'll probably be in a lower tax bracket and the taxes on your investment will be less. Furthermore, the interest, dividends, or whatever you earn from your investment is likewise not taxable until withdrawn. These retirement plans are known as Keoghs (Keogh is the Congressional Representative who initiated this retirement program) and Individual Retirement Accounts (I.R.A.s).

What are Keoghs and I.R.A.s?

They're investment plans offered by banks, financial organizations, and insurance companies (the most common types will be discussed below) that are especially endorsed by the I.R.S. for the purpose of encouraging individuals to create their own retirement plans. These plans may be identical to other investment plans, but before you put your money into one of them, make sure it is labeled an I.R.A. or Keogh. Opening a savings account, for example, is one way to create an I.R.A. or Keogh retirement plan. But you can't deposit your money in just any savings account—in order to make sure that the amount you deposit is tax

Figure 17. If your home income fluctuates widely, you may be able to reduce the amount of taxes you owe in peak years by income averaging, which is reported on Schedule G. Once again this is a 1976 form and the figures are based on 1976 tax rates.

SCHEDULE G (Form 1040) Department of the Treasury Internal Revenue Service	**Income Averaging** ► See instructions on pages 3 and 4. ► Attach to Form 1040.				**1976**
Name(s) as shown on Form 1040 Mr. Single Artist				Your social security number	

Taxable Income and Adjustments

	(a) Computation year 1976	(b) 1st preceding base period year 1975	(c) 2d preceding base period year 1974	(d) 3rd preceding base period year 1973	(e) 4th preceding base period year 1972
1 Taxable income (see Specific Instructions on page 4) . .	$20,000	$6,000	$6,000	$6,000	$6,000
2 Income earned outside of the United States or within U.S. possessions and excluded under sections 911 and 931 (see Specific Instructions on page 4)					
3 Excess community income and certain amounts received by owner-employees subject to a penalty under section 72(m)(5) (see Specific Instructions on page 4) . . .					
4 Adjusted taxable income (line 1 less line 3). If less than zero, enter zero	$20,000				
5 Base period income (line 1 plus line 2). If less than zero, enter zero		$6,000	$6,000	$6,000	$6,000

Computation of Averagable Income

6 Adjusted taxable income from line 4, column (a)	6	$20,000
7 30% of the sum of line 5, columns (b), (c), (d), and (e)	7	7,200
8 Averagable income (line 6 less line 7)	8	$12,800

Complete the remaining parts of this form only if line 8 is more than $3,000. If $3,000 or less, you do not qualify for income averaging. Do not fill in rest of form. **G**

Computation of Tax

9 Amount from line 7			9	7,200
10 20% of line 8			10	2,560
11 Total (add lines 9 and 10)			11	9,760
12 Excess community income included on line 3, column (a)			12	
13 Total (add lines 11 and 12)			13	9,760
14 Tax on amount on line 13*			14	2,034
15 Tax on amount on line 11°	15	2,034		
16 Tax on amount on line 9°	16	1,392		
17 Difference (line 15 less line 16)	17	642		
18 Multiply the amount on line 17 by 4			18	2,568
19 Tax (add lines 14 and 18). Enter here and on Form 1040, line 16. Also check Schedule G box on Form 1040, line 16 . . . .⸳.			19	4,602

*If the amount on which the tax is to be computed is $20,000 or less use the Tax Table; if more than $20,000 use Tax Rate Schedule X, Y, or Z.

deductible, you must deposit your money in a savings account the bank says is a specially designed I.R.A. or Keogh retirement plan.

Who's eligible to set up a Keogh plan?

A person is eligible for a Keogh plan if he's self-employed. He can be either fully self-employed or partially self-employed and partially employed by someone else. But he can make a contribution to a Keogh plan only from that portion of his income that is derived from self-employment.

Who's eligible to set up an I.R.A.?

A person is eligible for an I.R.A. if:

1. He's employed but his employer doesn't offer a retirement plan.

2. He's employed, but not yet eligible for his company's retirement plan.

3. He's self-employed and doesn't have a Keogh plan.

How much money can I invest in a Keogh plan?

You can contribute 15% of your earned income a year up to $7,500. Earned income for a self-employed person means net income after business expenses have been deducted. So if you earned $18,000 from self-employment after deductions, you could invest $2,700 in a Keogh plan, leaving only $15,300 to pay taxes on.

How much money can I invest in an I.R.A.?

Much less than you can contribute to a Keogh. You can contribute 15% of earned income up to $1,500 if you're single, or $1,750 if you're married and your spouse doesn't work. If you and your spouse work and are both eligible for an I.R.A., both of you can contribute 15% of your separate incomes up to a limit of $1,500 for each. Each spouse's contribution is computed separately. Earned income here means net income from self-employment and/or a salary from a job that doesn't offer a pension plan. So if you're single and earn $18,000, all you can contribute is $1,500 if you choose an I.R.A.

When can I make withdrawals from the retirement plan?

You may begin withdrawing from your retirement plan when you reach age 59$^{1/2}$, and by age 70$^{1/2}$ you must have withdrawn some of it. If you haven't, the entire plan may become taxable. The I.R.S. will tell you the minimum amount you must withdraw from different plans to keep the unwithdrawn amount untaxed.

Can I ever withdraw money before I am 59½?

Yes, if you become disabled. Or if you die, the funds in the plan go into your estate.

What happens if I withdraw money before 59½ and I'm not disabled?

You must include the amount of the withdrawal in your income in the year you withdraw it and pay income tax on it. In addition, you must pay a 10% penalty tax on the interest earned on the amount withdrawn prematurely.

What kind of retirement plans can I invest in?

There are a number of ways you can invest your money in retirement plans. Some people, for example, invest in the stock market through plans offered by their stockbrokers.

But most people invest in five general types explained below: individual retirement bonds; time deposits; retirement annuity policies; endowment and retirement income policies; and mutual fund shares. All are available to people setting up either I.R.A.s or Keoghs.

What are individual retirement bonds?

They're bonds issued especially by the federal government for I.R.A.s and Keoghs. They may be purchased in person or by mail from Federal Reserve banks and their branches or from the Bureau of the Public Debt, Washington, D.C. 20026.

Retirement bonds are available in denominations of $50, $100, and $500, and the law currently guarantees an interest rate of 6% per year, compounded semi-annually, until you turn 59½. This means that if you purchase $1,500 of these bonds a year for 35 years, at the end of that time, the value of your investment will be $177,181 on your investment of $52,500.

There are no charges involved in purchasing retirement bonds.

What are time deposits?

Time deposits are savings accounts offered by commercial banks, savings banks, and savings and loan associations. When you open a time deposit account, you deposit at least the minimum amount of money required by the bank and you must keep your money in the account for a stipulated length of time in order to earn a certain guaranteed rate of interest. Interest rates are higher for deposits made for longer periods of time. For example, a 90-day time deposit will be several percentage points lower than a 10-year time deposit. In other words, in a time when interest rates are neither very high nor very low, a 90-day time deposit might earn $5^1/4\%$ while a 10-year time deposit might earn $8^1/4\%$.

What happens if I withdraw my money before the time is up? If you withdraw your money before the time deposit is up, you'll be penalized by the bank. This means that it may either pay a lower interest rate on the amount you withdraw and/or charge you a termination fee. Some banks also charge administrative fees.

What should I ask when I open a time deposit account? Before you open an account, shop around and ask these three questions:

1. Does the bank charge a fee for administration?

2. What interest rates does the bank offer (rates can vary from bank to bank)?

3. What penalties will it impose for early withdrawal?

What are mutual fund shares?

When you buy shares in a mutual fund, you are buying into the ownership of a mutual fund company, just as you would buy into General Motors, if you bought shares of stock in that company.

What are mutual funds?

They're a type of financial organization that purchases a wide variety of stocks and/or bonds in order to make money from the dividends on these investments as well as from their sale when it becomes profitable to sell them. Because of the great diversity of their investments, buying shares in a mutual fund company should be less risky than if you personally invest in stocks and bonds. Moreover, a mutual fund can increase your investment much more than retirement bonds and time deposits. On the other hand, if the managers of the mutual fund don't properly forecast the stock and/or bond market, you might find yourself not only earning no interest on your investment but losing some of your investment as well.

Mutual funds charge administrative and/or managing fees, and many of them charge these fees at the outset of your contribution —be sure to ask.

What is a retirement annuity?

Retirement annuities are insurance policies which give you a regular income starting at a specified age after 59¹/₂, with the amount based on your contributions and the interest on these contributions. This income will continue for a fixed period of time, for your life, or for the life of you and your spouse, depending on the type of annuity you choose.

Annuities may not be a particularly good buy, however. Insurance companies must pay commissions to agents and other expenses that affect the income you receive after retirement and the cash you would receive if you terminate your retirement plan before retirement. According to Alexandra Holubowich in "Pension Plans for Artists," *American Artist,* January, 1977:

Many of these plans were designed so that you pay a very large starting or setup fee. These fees are usually deducted in the first couple of years. The fees are non-refundable. If you elect to discontinue the plan after a year because you get a job where you're included in an employer's qualified benefit plan, or you cannot keep up your payments, or you just decide you want to go into another plan, you have to pay all the fees. A New York Times investigative report revealed that with certain policies, at the end of the first year, if $1,470.60 were paid in, the amount of money in the account actually earning interest would have been $985, or $485.60 less. This $485.60 represents all the fees that were charged against the account the first year. If the owner of this account had to withdraw his money at the end of one year, he would probably lose the $485.60.

So make sure you know what these upfront costs will be before you buy an annuity.

What's an endowment policy and a retirement income policy?

This is a package insurance policy similar to the annuity policy described above. It also provides some life insurance, however, and the cost of the life insurance cannot be considered a part of your contribution to a retirement fund for tax purposes. So you must find out from the insurance company how much of your yearly premium represents a contribution to a retirement plan and how much represents the premium on a life insurance policy. You can only deduct the former from your income.

Do I have to make a contribution every year to a retirement plan?

If you buy an insurance policy, you naturally have to pay yearly premiums. Otherwise, no. In fact, you can stop investing in a retirement plan completely any time you want and then simply withdraw funds from it when you become 59½ or older. This is called freezing an account.

Can I have only one Keogh or I.R.A. plan?

No, you can have as many Keoghs or I.R.A.s as you want—but you can't have both types. You might, for example, invest part of your $7,500 (if you plan to invest the maximum amount allowable to Keoghs) in a mutual fund and part in a time deposit. There are also plans that allow you to make many different types of investments—say a time deposit, an annuity, and mutual fund shares—all under the aegis of one program. These programs are usually offered by banks. If you're interested in this service, you can find the names of these organizations in the financial pages of metropolitan newspapers where banks usually advertise their Keogh and I.R.A. programs.

How do I decide which plans are best for me?

Ask yourself a number of questions about your financial situation:

Do you expect to be contributing to your retirement plan for only a short period of time, such as under 10 years? If so, this would mitigate against insurance policies that charge large upfront fees. It might also influence you against other plans that have substantial initial costs.

If a financial emergency arises before you are 59½, is it likely that you'll have to make a withdrawal from your retirement fund? In this case, you would again probably rule out an insurance policy. You would also not want to lock yourself into a time deposit that imposes stiff penalties for withdrawals on top of the early withdrawal penalty you'll have to pay the I.R.S.

Do you need a definite amount for your retirement? If so, consider a type that assures you at least that amount. Retirement bonds and annuities can promise this. So can time deposits if you can continue to get guaranteed high interest rates. Mutual funds can't.

Do you have some flexibility in the amount you can invest? For instance, if you're not strapped for funds and you're relatively young, you'd probably want to split your funds between growth and conservative investments, i.e., a mutual fund and a high-interest time deposit.

Can I transfer funds from one account to another?

Yes. If you choose one Keogh plan and decide you want to transfer these funds into another account, you can do so as many times as you want. The only snag here is that you personally can't transfer the money. For example, you can't close out your time deposit, take the funds, and put them into another bank. This transaction must be handled by the banks. If you take possession of the money, you'll be taxed and penalized on that amount just as if you made an early withdrawal.

If you make the switch between two I.R.A. accounts, you can take possession of the money, but you must make the transfer within 60 days. Right now you can make a switch only once in three years without incurring the early termination penalty, but that may change in the future.

When can I start a retirement plan?

Any time before the year in which you reach the age of 70½. Plans must be set up before the end of a tax year in order to be deductible for that tax year, but funds don't have to be contributed until later. Contributions to I.R.A.s must be made by February 14 of the following year and contributions to Keoghs by April 15. This too may change in the future.

Can I expect other changes?

Yes. The whole concept of individuals starting their own retirement plans is relatively new, and the I.R.S. is constantly changing its regulations on them. Check out facts and figures every year.

Where do I report my contributions to a retirement fund?

On Form 1040. If you have an I.R.A., you must also file Forms 5329 and 5498. If you have a Keogh, you must file Form 5500K.

Why would I want to incorporate?

There are two basic reasons why businesses incorporate, businesses meaning any commercial activity from the art you make for sale all the way up to the operations of multimillion dollar companies. These reasons are limited liability and tax advantages. But first you must understand just what a corporation is.

What is a corporation?

A corporation is a separate legal entity owned by one or more stockholders. Although the stockholders run the corporation, it operates solely in its own name. It can sue or be sued, hold legal title to property, and otherwise perform the same business acts as an individual. Thus, the corporation—not the stockholders—

owns or rents the premises where work is performed, pays the bills out of a bank account that's in its own name, collects checks written to it, pays salaries to employees, and distributes profits to the stockholders.

To you this means that, when you incorporate, you become the sole stockholder, or at least the majority stockholder (many states require more than one stockholder), of a company in the business of producing artwork. Since you're the producer, you also become an employee of the corporation. When artwork is sold, the corporation—not you—pockets the money and pays you a salary, which, since you run the company, you determine. Then, if there are any profits left over after all business expenses, including your salary, have been deducted and taxes have been paid, you can return these profits to yourself in the form of a dividend.

What is limited liability?

Since the corporation is distinct from its stockholders, they're not liable for the debts and obligations of the corporation. However great the corporation's debts, creditors can't get at the personal assets of the stockholders because the debts of the corporation are not the debts of the stockholders. All of which adds up to what is called limited liability.

Why would I want limited liability?

There aren't too many instances that an artist would. In the course of your business, it's unlikely that you would incur very large debts. But the one example that does come to mind is if projects that might imperil others are your business.

Suppose, for example, you construct large sculptures for public places and assume all expenses until the projects are complete. No matter how unlikely it might seem, there's always the possibility that the scaffolding might topple over during creation or installation, seriously injuring bystanders. You'll be carrying business liability insurance (see Chapter 11), of course, but the corporate form of doing business would limit your liability if damages exceeded the sum you're insured for. In other words, you personally could not be sued for injury or death.

What are the tax advantages of incorporation?

A corporation is able to deduct from its taxable income the following benefits for its employees as business expenses:

1. Health and disability insurance. (Or, instead of paying insurance premiums, the corporation can elect to pay medical bills.)

2. A $50,000 term insurance policy.

3. Contributions to a retirement plan equal to 25% of the employee's salary (instead of 15%, the maximum amount that can be invested in a Keogh plan) with no dollar limits.

Because these benefits are tax deductible for the corporation, you, as an individual, get them at a lower cost than if you paid for them yourself. Furthermore, these deductions—plus a deduction for your salary—reduce corporate taxes, which may reduce the total amount of taxes you'll have to pay (see Figure 18).

These benefits assume even greater importance if family members work for the corporation. If your spouse, for example, acts as your agent and your son as your assistant, both are also eligible for insurance and a larger pension plan.

What are the disadvantages of a corporation?

Double taxation, for one. As a corporate employee, your wages are deducted from taxable corporate income, but you must pay personal income tax on your salary (and on dividends, if there are any). So you're really taxed twice, unless you form a Subchapter S corporation (see below).

And even if you do manage to make a small savings in taxes, it still may not be worth it. A small savings on taxes may not justify the extra time you'll have to devote to maintaining a corporation. And therein lies the second big disadvantage. The I.R.S. is a stickler about individuals or small groups abiding by the formalities that go along with doing business as a corporation, such as calling stockholders' meetings, recording minutes, submitting reports, and so on. Sloppy corporate minutes and other seemingly minor matters often provide the I.R.S. with an opening for a successful attack on your right to be a corporation.

What is a Subchapter S corporation?

One way to describe it would be to say it's a mini-corporation. A Subchapter S corporation, sometimes known as a small business corporation, must pay state and city corporate taxes (if there are any), but, unlike a regular corporation, it doesn't pay federal corporate income taxes. You only pay personal income tax on all taxable income that the corporation earns.

Figure 18. This table is meant to give you a rough idea of how you can compare the taxes you would owe as an individual and as a corporation. The tax rates are based on an unmarried individual who isn't the head of a household, and it doesn't take into consideration itemized deductions from Schedule A or exemptions. The small savings shown here might not be worth the amount of time and energy needed to do the recordkeeping involved in running a corporation.

A COMPARISON OF INCOME TAXES FOR AN ARTIST WHO HAS INCORPORATED AND ONE WHO HAS NOT

The Corporate Tax Return

			Individual	Corporation
1. Gross receipts			$60,000	$60,000
2. Less expenses				
A. Expenses allowed to corporations and individuals			15,000	15,000
B. Expenses allowed to corporations only	1. Your salary		-	35,000
	2. Pension plan		-	7,500
	3. Group insurance	a. Life	-	800
		b. Health	-	400
		c. Disability	-	800
3. Taxable income			45,000	500
4. Federal tax			-	100

The Individual Returns

	Individual	Corporation
5. Personal gross income	45,000	35,000
6. Less contributions to Keogh plan	6,750	-
7. Taxable income	38,250	35,000
8. Tax per individual return	13,427.50	12,790
9. Total Taxes (items 4 & 8)	13,427.50	12,890
10. Taxes saved		$537.50

Does a Subchapter S corporation offer the same limited liability as a regular corporation?

Yes, you cannot be held personally liable for death, injury, or damages from any lost lawsuit.

Does a Subchapter S corporation offer the other advantages of a regular corporation?

Yes, with the exception of the large retirement plan. In a Subchapter S corporation, the corporation can only make a tax-deductible contribution of 15% of your annual salary to a pension plan.

How much money should I be earning to consider incorporation?

As a rule of thumb, don't think about incorporating unless you've got a net income from your self-employment (income after business expenses have been deducted) of $50,000 or more. Nor should you consider a small business corporation unless you've got a net income of $25,000 or more.

If I earn that much, how should I decide to incorporate?

In the first place, get an accountant or lawyer to help you. The decision to incorporate can only be made after an in-depth analysis of your particular financial position.

Many artists, for example, already have insurance coverage and pension plans through their teaching positions or other jobs. So they would have no reason to incorporate to acquire these benefits. Other artists may not feel they can afford to put away 25% of their salary in a pension plan. On the other hand, some artists might incorporate to be eligible for the larger pension plan. If they have a large income from sources other than their self-employed art business, for example, they may want to shelter as much income as they can through a bigger tax-free pension plan.

But what it all boils down to is this: where tax advantages are marginal—unless there is some other compelling reason, such as the need for limited liability or the ability to establish a large retirement fund—incorporating, either as a regular or Subchapter S corporation isn't worth it in terms of the time and energy spent maintaining the corporation or the money to pay someone to do it for you.

How much does it cost to incorporate?

The cost of filing for incorporation varies from state to state. But most states charge a fee of around $150. You'll need a lawyer to draft the certificate of incorporation, run it through the various state offices that must approve your request, and write the bylaws of the corporation. This could cost from $150 to as much as $700, if you choose an expensive lawyer. So the whole thing—lawyer's fee plus the state's fee for incorporation—might range from $300 to $850.

16. You and Your Estate

· Estate Taxes
· Valuation
· Estate planning
· Wills
· Executors

Sometime back in 1976, Arizona artist Ted de Grazia burned 100 of his paintings atop Angel Cliff in the Superstition Mountains in a romantic protest against estate taxes. According to a newspaper account of the event, de Grazia was reported to have said, "When I sell a painting and take in money, I expect to be taxed. But I don't think there should be a tax on paintings and other works of art that aren't sold. My heirs couldn't afford to inherit my works."

What he said isn't exactly accurate, but he gets his point across. The fact is that artwork left in an estate may be taxable, increasing its value enormously, and the artist's heirs might end up with very little after estate taxes have been paid.

This is a big problem for artists. So, too, is the problem of how these taxes will be paid. Will your estate contain enough in insurance policies, savings accounts, or other assets that can easily be converted into cash to satisfy the tax bill? If so, will this mean that after taxes are paid, your family will be left with little readily available cash? Or will your executors try to pay taxes by selling artwork? If this is the case, and your artwork is dumped on to the market all at once for a quick sale, will prices go down in a buyer's market forcing more artwork to be sold than intended? And will any artwork be saved for your heirs to hold as assets? Furthermore, if artwork is sold to pay estate taxes, the income earned from the sale will be subject to income tax—resulting in double taxation.

Since de Grazia's protest, Congress changed the law regulating estate taxes so artists don't have to worry so much any more about how their heirs will fare after they die. The new law—the Tax Reform Act of 1976—increased the amount that is automatically exempt from estate taxes as well as the amount a spouse can claim as a deduction. The result of these actions, explained below in greater detail, is that the estates of some artists will never be taxed at all.

Still, many artists' estates will be, and they may be taxed for one and only one reason: when unsold artwork is included in an artist's estate, the value of the estate is increased.

Before exploring the ways in which you may be able to avoid the potentially devastating effects of the inclusion of artwork in an estate, however, let's first look at estate taxes themselves.

How are federal estate taxes calculated?

First of all, all property you owned at death is totaled to arrive at a figure called the total gross estate. Property in the total gross estate includes life insurance policies, real estate, stocks, bonds, artwork, and so on.

Second, debts—such as medical bills, mortgages, and funeral expenses—are subtracted from the total gross estate to give you the adjusted gross estate.

Third, if you leave at least half of your estate to your spouse, a marital deduction (defined below) is deducted from the adjusted gross estate. The result is called the taxable estate.

Finally, once taxes have been calculated on this amount, a tax credit (defined below) is deducted to determine the amount the estate owes the federal government.

What is a marital deduction?

If you leave at least half of your estate to your spouse, the law allows the spouse to automatically deduct up to $250,000 or half the estate, whichever is *greater,* from the adjusted gross estate. This is called a marital deduction.

What is a tax credit?

A tax credit is the amount that is automatically subtracted from estate taxes before they're paid. In 1978, the tax credit equals about $34,000, and this will increase about $4,000 a year until 1981, when the credit reaches its peak, $47,000.

Put in different terms, the tax credit is equivalent to an exemption of $131,000 from the estate in 1977, or $175,000 by 1981. Thus, if you have an adjusted gross estate of $425,000 by 1981, and you leave it all to your spouse, it will be completely tax free. Why? Because she can claim a marital deduction of $250,000 plus a tax credit, which is equal to an exemption of $175,000.

This is a tremendous increase over the marital deduction and the automatic exemption that had been in force before the 1976 Tax Reform Act. Before this law came into effect, the marital deduction was half the estate, and the automatic exemption was only $60,000.

What else did the 1976 Tax Reform Act Do?

Besides increasing the marital deduction and the automatic exemption, it changed the latter into a tax credit. Practically speaking, they amount to the same thing. Claiming a tax credit (an amount subtracted from actual taxes) of $47,000 (in 1981) is the same financially as exempting $175,000 from your taxable estate. The change was made to allow the I.R.S. to equalize estate taxes and gift taxes.

What are gift taxes?

Taxes that are paid by the giver of a gift worth over $3,000. You can give away $3,000 or less to as many people as you want to each year tax-free (or $6,000 if you give gifts jointly with your spouse). But you must file a gift tax return and pay a tax on gifts over that amount.

Before the 1976 Tax Reform Act, you could also give away another $30,000 (or $60,000 if gifts were given jointly with your spouse) during your lifetime tax-free, but the 1976 Tax Act eliminated this provision.

How are gifts taxed?

Gifts are taxed at progressive rates that rise from 18% on an accumulated total of taxable gifts of under $10,000 to 70% on taxable gifts over $5,000,000—the same as estates are taxed. Before the 1976 Tax Reform Act, gift taxes were less than estate taxes, which encouraged people to give gifts rather than make bequests.

But now the law says you can either give $131,000 away in 1977 (increasing to $175,000 by 1981) tax-free during your lifetime or leave the same amount tax-free in your estate, but not both. If you choose to give gifts during your lifetime, you must file a gift tax return and pay the tax. Then when you die, the I.R.S. adds the amounts of the gifts and the taxes back into the estate, and you're given a tax credit of $47,000 (in 1981). Marital deductions on gifts are also calculated to approximate the marital deduction allowed on an estate. The way the law reads, the first $100,000 in gifts made to a spouse is considered a marital deduction. The second $100,000 is subject to tax, and one-half of all gifts over $200,000 can be claimed as a marital deduction.

Did the 1976 Tax Reform Bill make other changes?

Yes, it changed not only the estate and gift taxes, but also the income taxes an heir must pay when he sells assets left to him in an estate. This was done in another effort to equalize the effects of giving gifts during one's life and of leaving assets to heirs in estates, so one method would not be more desirable than the other. But before explaining how the law changed, let me explain how income taxes are paid when a person sells a gift: this procedure was not changed by the law. (In this chapter, all assets given as gifts or left in an estate refer specifically to artwork.)

How are income taxes paid when someone sells artwork he received as a gift? When a person sells artwork he received as a gift, he pays income tax on the profits just as the artist would, i.e., he pays a tax on the difference between the sales price and the price of the materials that went into it—if the artist has not already deducted them. So if a person sells a painting he was given for $3,000 and the cost of the materials was deducted by the artist, the recipient of the gift would have to pay income tax on $3,000.

How are income taxes paid when someone sells artwork he received as a bequest? Before the 1976 Tax Reform Act, artwork was taxed as a capital asset. A capital asset is considered a type of long-term capital investment, and, when it is sold, the profit is taxed at a different rate than ordinary income. Furthermore, profits are calculated on the difference between sales price and its fair market value when acquired. Thus because the artwork was taxed as a capital asset, the heir paid a tax on the difference between the sales price and the fair market value of the work at the time of the artist's death. For example, if the heir sold a painting for $3,000 that was worth $2,000 when the artist died, he would pay tax only on $1,000. Furthermore, while the gift-receiver paid ordinary income tax on the profit he made ($3,000), the heir paid capital gains tax (on $1,000), a situation much to his advantage because capital gains are taxed at a lower rate than ordinary income.

But the 1976 Tax Reform Act changed all that. Now the heir must pay ordinary income tax, and, with one exception, he, too, pays tax on the difference between the sales price and the price of materials in the work. The total effect is an equalization of all taxes concerned with gifts and estates.

What's the exception to this new ruling ?

Works created before December 31, 1976, are taxed somewhat differently than works created after December 31, 1976, when the Tax Reform Act went into effect. Although ordinary income tax is imposed on the sale of these pre-1976 works, they're treated almost as if they're a semi-capital asset. In other words, the basis on which the tax is computed is sort of a combination of the bases for capital gains and ordinary income.

How would an heir compute his tax? By doing the following:

1. Determine the amount of time in days that the creator owned the work from completion to December 31, 1976.

2. Figure out the amount of time the creator owned the work from completion to his death.

3. Divide the amount arrived at in (1) by the amount determined in (2).

4. Multiply the result by the profits. So if an artist finished a painting on January 1, 1976, and died on December 31, 1977, he would have owned the painting for one year (365 days) prior to December 31, 1976, and two years (730 days) altogether.

Therefore, the heir would figure the basis for computing tax on the painting that sold for $500 by multiplying 1/2 (365/730) by $500, giving him a taxable income of $250.

When must federal estate taxes be paid?

Federal estate taxes must be paid in cash nine months after death unless at least 35% of the value of the adjusted gross estate or 50% of the taxable estate is composed of your artwork. If this is the case, your executor will be allowed to extend payments over 10 years.

If your artwork represents 65% of your adjusted gross estate, your executor can ask that the estate be allowed 15 years to pay in installments. The first payment is not due for five years under this ruling, and then the whole amount must be paid in 10 equal installments over the next 10 years. Interest of 4%, however, must be paid on these delayed tax payments.

Will there be state estate taxes?

Your estate may be subject to a state tax, usually called an inheritance tax, if your state has such a tax. In fact, your estate may even have to pay an inheritance tax in several states. If you have property in more than one state—say you have a house in one and a vacation retreat in another—each state, if it has a tax, can impose tax on the property located within its borders.

The regulations governing state inheritance taxes vary greatly from state to state, so it's impossible to generalize about them; find out what they are in your state.

How can estate taxes be reduced?

Estate taxes can be reduced in two ways. First, your executor can place a low evaluation on your work when calculating the value of your estate. Second, by estate planning, discussed a little later.

What do you mean by valuation?

Valuation is the fair market value of any property at the time of death or six months after death, whichever is less. Or, as the I.R.S. defines it, valuation is, "The price at which the property would change hands between a willing buyer and a willing seller, neither being under any compulsion to buy or sell and both having reasonable knowledge of relevant facts."

In other words, what a work would normally sell for if the buyer wasn't a close friend of yours buying work as a favor, and you or your dealer aren't cutting the price to pay the rent or some other drastic personal reason.

Does fair market value include gallery commission?

Unfortunately, yes. The market value is what the property would sell for to a purchaser, not what you would net from a sale. The same principle holds true with other property, such as real estate and stocks and bonds. They're valued in the estate at what they sell for in the marketplace, without regard to broker's fees.

Who makes the valuation?

The executor of your will, whose role is discussed at the end of the chapter.

How does the executor make the valuation?

He bases fair market value on what your work regularly sells for. If you didn't sell regularly before death, he will probably ask for a lower evaluation of your work. To justify a low valuation, he'll argue that, while your work was offered for sale over a period of time, the public didn't buy it, meaning that its value was lower than its selling price. For example, if you sold some works five years ago at $1,000 but nothing since, and you didn't reduce your prices, the executor will claim that your work wasn't worth $1,000 per piece. Instead, he might say it was worth $500 or $100, whatever he thinks is justified.

Why is a low valuation a good idea?

Because it reduces the value of your estate, and, hence, estate taxes. By now you probably think that because the tax credit and marital deduction are so large, your estate won't be taxed. And that may be so, but don't be too sure. Suppose you don't have a spouse. This means the value of your estate that exceeds $175,000 (by 1981) will be taxed. And it's not that hard to accumulate a $175,000 estate. For example, you might own a $60,000 house, a $35,000 vacation retreat, furnishings and cars worth $25,000, a $30,000 life insurance policy, and $10,000 in a savings account. Already your estate adds up to $160,000. And your artwork hasn't yet been taken into consideration.

Suppose further that you leave 50 unsold paintings, which sell regularly in galleries for $1,000. This means another $50,000 excess over $175,000. Now wouldn't it be nice if your executor could justify a valuation on your work of no more than $15,000 so your total estate would be tax-exempt?

How can an executor justify a lower valuation than fair market value?

More often than not, prices for artists' work decline, not increase, after death. Even if you're a popular artist, unless you have a solid critical reputation, chances are prices won't hold up. A well known lawyer was quoted in *American Artist* (January, 1975) as saying:

I have a friend (not a client, I might add) who gets $15,000 to $20,000 a painting and has done so for years. If I were the executor of his will, I would take the position that his paintings were worth not more than say $10,000 at death and I'd justify that amount by arguing that his prices might go down just as well as up. Fashions in art are capricious; what's in today is out tomorrow. Even if an artist has a big name during his lifetime, it may vanish quickly after death.

The lawyer told me in private the name of this friend, and he did indeed have a big name and one backed by purchases by the largest museums and by critical acclaim.

Is going for a low valuation the best course of action?

In most cases, yes, and the I.R.S. usually accepts the line of reasoning mentioned above. Some executors with very prestigious clients, however, will claim the actual valuation of a body of work, arguing that it's more important to them to protect the artist's reputation than it is to reduce his estate. In other words, in order to maintain sales prices at the level they were before the artist's death and increase them if they can, these executors won't want the word to get out that they undervalued the artwork, even though they did it only for tax purposes.

What happens if the I.R.S. doesn't accept my executor's valuation?

After your executor files the estate tax return on your estate, the I.R.S. has three years to challenge the return. If the I.R.S. challenges the valuation of works that are each valued by the executor at $20,000 or more, the works are submitted to the I.R.S. Art Advisory Panel for its valuation. This panel is made up of a rotating group of museum directors, curators, and art dealers.

For works valued under $20,000 apiece, your executor will have to try to convince the I.R.S. of the validity of his valuation by backing it up with the testimony of dealers, auction houses, or appraisers.

What is estate planning?

Estate planning is what you can do now to reduce estate taxes and provide more income for your heirs. A complete discussion of estate planning is outside the scope of this book because it's concerned only with what you decide to do with one particular kind of asset—artwork. But all your assets should be taken into consideration when planning a strategy to reduce taxes and maximize income for heirs. One way to reduce taxes, for example, is to make sure life insurance policies aren't calculated as part of the value of your estate. You can do this by signing over total rights to the policy to your spouse or child, although you continue to pay the premiums.

How do you design an estate plan?

Estate planning is a total concept—of what you can do now to maximize your estate when you die—that can only be put together after you make an assessment of your assets, your heirs' needs, and your life situation. You start by making an inventory of all your assets and calculating the taxes that must be paid on them. Then analyze the needs of your heirs by asking yourself such questions as: how much will my spouse need to run the household after I'm gone? Can she keep up the mortgage payments? Can she earn this amount herself or must I provide for it in the will? Must I provide some long-term support for an aging mother or a handicapped child?

Finally, you must take a hard look at the facts of your own life. For example, while eliminating a life insurance policy from your estate by signing all rights over to your spouse is a good way to reduce your estate, it may not be such a good idea if you have something less than the perfect marriage and divorce is a possibility.

In essence, what you're doing is examining a number of alternatives in view of your particular situation. Even the two basic objectives of estate planning—reducing taxes and maximizing income—may at times be seen as alternatives. Reducing taxes may, on certain occasions (discussed below), conflict with maximizing income. The whole point is to pick the best alternative to solve your estate problems.

Will I need professional help to do this?

Yes. A professional knows how to steer you through all the estate tax traps that might cost your heirs thousands of dollars. For example, the laws governing exemptions from state inheritance taxes vary from state to state, and the professional who knows how they work may be able to cut down the size of your state tax bill. A professional can also tell you when joint ownership of property is a good thing and when it's not. A professional can set up trusts for those whom you feel need long-term support, but aren't capable of managing assets themselves. And a professional can advise you on the type of insurance best suited for your needs, among other things.

Who will I ask to be my estate planner?

First you'll want a lawyer. He will not only help you plan your estate but also write your will for you. Then, as estate planning continues, you may want to request specific help from an accountant, an insurance agent, and officers in a bank trust department, if necessary.

And keep in mind that when you pick a lawyer, make sure that estates are his specialty. General practice lawyers do not have sufficient expertise in the field.

How does artwork enter into estate planning?

In two ways. As mentioned above, estate planning has two major objectives: to reduce taxes and to maximize income for your heirs. To achieve the first objective, you should try to reduce the value of your taxable estate by eliminating artwork. This can be accomplished by leaving art to a museum or other charitable institutions in your will so your estate can claim a charitable deduction, and by giving artwork away during your lifetime.

To accomplish the second objective you can try: (1) to enhance the value of the artwork, so, when your heirs sell it, they'll receive as much for it as they can; and (2) to insure that they'll pay as little income tax on the profit they receive from the sale of artwork as possible.

How does leaving work in my will to a museum reduce my tax?

Works given to tax-exempt cultural institutions, such as museums or schools, historical societies, and the like, are eliminated from your gross estate as charitable deductions. Therefore, if the market value of your paintings is $1,000 each and you leave 20 paintings to a museum, you'll, in effect, have reduced your estate by $20,000.

Are there any other advantages to leaving work to museums?

Yes. A museum that knows it will get a bequest from you on your death may be highly motivated to sustain interest in your work. It may give you shows during your lifetime and commitments for exhibitions after death. Such exhibitions should increase your reputation and, hence, the market value of all of your artwork— both now while you're alive and later when your heirs sell work left to them.

If I leave work to a museum, can I demand that it be exhibited?

Not really. Although leaving work to a museum is generally a good idea because the museum may feel it's in its best interest to nurture your reputation both before and after death, this isn't always the case. The largest and most prestigious museums— which are bombarded by bequests—refuse to accept any with strings attached. Others, particularly if they're financially strapped, may accept a bequest because they plan to immediately resell it. But all of this should be made clear in an agreement with the museum before you put any such bequests in your will.

What can I do to insure exhibition in a museum that I leave works to?

What you can do depends on the kind of clout you have and the kind of relationship you have with the museum (or other cultural institution). It may be possible for you and your lawyer to work out a compromise agreement with an institution that would be mutually beneficial. Take, for example, the agreement abstract painter Hans Hoffman made with the University of California. To make sure that his work was displayed, he promised the university a considerable amount of money to build a wing to house his work. You, too, might have to offer the institution you're dealing with something—perhaps the right to sell a certain number of works in return for a guarantee to exhibit what's left in the bequest—in order you get the deal you want.

What if the museum fails to fulfill its part of the contract?

What happens then depends on your executor. If you've picked someone who's unable or unwilling to fight a legal battle for you, the institution will probably get away with it.

But, aside from what an executor can do after the fact, you may be able to take some preventative action in advance. You could demand that a clause be inserted into the contract giving your heirs the right to buy back the work at a specific price if the museum no longer wishes to stand by its part of the bargain.

Is there a disadvantage to leaving work to a museum?

Yes. While the amount of taxes are deducted, the value of the estate will be decreased. In other words, your heirs may lose valuable income.

How do I decide which is best?

By making an inventory of your assets, recommended as a prerequisite to designing an estate plan, and figuring out the taxes on them. In this way, you can see what your heirs will have to live on after taxes. If your liquid assets (insurance policies, savings accounts, and other assets that can easily be converted into cash) are on the slim side, you might be more apt to bequeath a good portion of your work, thus reducing taxes. If, on the other hand, liquid assets are sufficient for your heirs and you're confident that the prices on your work will remain the same or rise, you might consider leaving all or almost all of your work to your heirs.

Is giving artwork away during my lifetime a good way to reduce the value of an estate?

Giving artwork worth $3,000 (or $6,000 if your spouse gives the gift jointly) a year is definitely a good strategy since it is tax-free. Giving away work worth more than this amount may not be because it will be taxed at the same rate as assets in your estate.

Nevertheless, it may still be a good strategy to give artwork as gifts and pay tax on them, even if they're worth more than $3,000, if you expect them to appreciate in value. If they do increase in value over the years, your estate will be just that much larger. For example, if you give three paintings away to your son worth $6,000 now and pay gift tax on them, even if their value rises to $12,000 when you die, the other $6,000 won't be taxed.

From an income tax standpoint, is it better to give work away or leave it in an estate?

With respect to income tax, it doesn't make any difference to your heirs unless the work was created before December 31, 1976. In this case, it may be more beneficial from a tax standpoint to leave that work in your will rather than to give it to your heirs during your lifetime since the tax basis is more advantageous. (See *What's the exception to this new ruling?*, above.)

Is there any legislative effort to help the artist and his problems with estate taxes?

Yes, Congressman Fred Richmond, (Democrat, New York) has introduced a bill which would subject artwork to estate taxes only on the value of the materials in it. This makes sense when you consider that the I.R.S. allows a tax deduction covering only the cost of materials when an artist donates his work to an institution. Unfortunately, the prospects of the bill being passed aren't good, particularly in the near future—but it is a start.

Why do I need a will?

Basically for three reasons: to insure that your estate goes to whomever you want; to reduce taxes and maximize income for those you want to be your heirs; and to make sure the assets in your estate are disposed of in the way you want and by whom you want.

What if I don't have a will?

In this case, all these matters will be decided by state law. For example, if you don't leave a will, the state will decide who your heirs are—and they may not be the ones you had in mind. You might have wanted your estate to go to a friend or friends, for instance, because you were never close to your blood relatives. The state, however, will undoubtedly decide that various members of your family should inherit your estate.

Can lack of a will increase taxes and reduce income to heirs?

Yes. Many people who refuse to make wills frequently think their whole estate will automatically go to their spouse. This isn't necessarily true. In New York State, for instance, if you're survived by a spouse and a child but leave no will, two-thirds of the estate is left to the child and the spouse receives only one-third. This means the spouse can't claim her full marital deduction, forcing the estate to pay more taxes and allowing her less income. Furthermore, if the child is under 18, the law imposes many restrictions on his share of the estate.

Who will dispose of my estate if I don't have a will?

The state will appoint an administrator to handle your estate. This person may be a family member, but he may also be a complete stranger. If you had a will, you would have named your own executor to do the job, and you could have provided in your will for the way you wanted to have it handled. You could have specified who was to have specific pieces—relatives, friends, cultural institutions—and how you wanted work sold, exhibited, and reproduced. Work left intestate (through an estate without a will) and disposed of by an outsider appointed by the state—who probably has no knowledge of the art world—may not fare as well.

What does an executor do?

An executor administers the estate. This means he pays all outstanding debts incurred before death as well as funeral expenses, places a valuation on your work, files a tax return, and distributes the assets according to directions in the will. If artwork is used to pay taxes or provide income for heirs, he must try to sell it for the best price. He may also have to negotiate for reproduction rights and to register copyrights. And since he's bound by strict legal standards, he must act prudently and in the best interests of the estate. For example, he may have to decide whether a lucrative offer to reproduce one piece of artwork, which would increase the heirs' income, would be detrimental to the critical reputation of a total body of work. All in all, the job of an executor of an artist's will can be a tricky one. (See the end of the chapter for whom to pick as your executor.)

Who should write a will?

You can, legally. But I can't think of a worse idea. This is not a do-it-yourself project—vague, improperly worded wills are frequently found invalid by the courts. So get yourself an estate lawyer, preferably one with an understanding of the commercial aspects of the art world.

What goes into a will?

Wills come in all sizes and shapes from the simplest to the most elaborate. If it's the latter, you might be setting up a trust for your children who aren't competent to manage their own affairs yet. In general, however, a will simply specifies what you want done with your assets. (If there are any specific bequests, such as a wish to give a particular work to a particular person, make sure the work is labeled, indicating that it's to become the property of the person named in the will.)

A will also names your executor and defines his powers. And you can spell out how you want your artwork to be sold, exhibited, reproduced, restored, and altered. Or you can put this in a letter of instructions.

What is a letter of instructions?

A letter of instructions consists of guidelines for the executor to follow at his discretion in handling the estate. It's not a legally binding document, but is extremely useful to the executor in fulfilling his duties.

How do I decide what goes into a will and what goes into a letter of instructions?

Since wills are legally binding, they should contain only those instructions about your artwork that you feel must be carried out by the executor. And, if you have properly planned your estate, you'll know precisely what these instructions should be. In other words, once you've determined what your assets are and what your heirs need, you can develop a policy on how your artwork should be disposed of. Therefore, if you have other assets sufficient to satisfy the needs of your heirs, you can afford to define strictly what the executor may or may not do with your artwork in a will.

However, where artwork must be sold to maximize income for heirs or pay taxes, you won't want to place so many restrictions on the executor that he won't be able to properly execute his duty to increase your heirs' income as much as possible. In this case you should put your words of advice to him on these matters in a letter of instructions.

What instructions should I give concerning the sale of my work?

Suppose it's not necessary to sell artwork to pay taxes or provide income, and you have great faith in your dealer and wish him to continue to represent your estate after you die. In this case, you could insert a clause in your gallery contract providing for the continuation of his representation after your death. Then, in the will, you might say, "I hereby direct the executor to sell my paintings only through XYZ Gallery."

But if artwork must be sold to pay taxes or provide income, you may not want to tie your executor to one particular dealer no matter how pleased you've always been with him. Maybe they won't get along; maybe the executor should be allowed the flexibility to change galleries to get a better deal. So you might simply advise your executor to deal with the XYZ Gallery in a letter of instructions. This gives him the option of changing galleries if he thinks it best.

What should I say about exhibitions?

Some exhibitions of your work, whether you're alive or not, don't enhance your reputation. This might be because the work is shown in an inappropriate place or alongside inferior artwork. The point is that you have to figure out what sort of exhibitions are inappropriate so you can prevent your work from being shown in them after your death. For example, Mark Rothko, the abstract expressionist, considered the placement of his paintings within the Four Seasons restaurant located in New York's Seagram Building an inappropriate atmosphere for his work despite the fact that both the restaurant and the building are among the most elegant in the country. You may not be quite so particular, but you might object to the display of your work in a commercial venture, such as a restaurant.

Since the inappropriateness of exhibitions is somewhat difficult to define precisely, the place for such instructions would probably be in a letter of instructions rather than in the will.

What about repairs and completions?

You should leave instructions on how and by whom work should be repaired or restored and how it should be completed and by whom, if you want it to be completed. Once again, the most appropriate place for these instructions would probably be a letter.

What should I say about alterations?

Instruct your executor not to allow any alterations, unless, of course, you don't care whether your work is altered. You might not think this issue will come up, but look what happened to David Smith's estate.

David Smith, one of America's most important abstract sculptors, chose art critic Clement Greenberg as one of the executors of his estate, which consisted primarily of welded steel sculptures. In 1974, word leaked out that Greenberg had altered some of the works remaining in the estate: one work was stripped of its paint and apparently varnished, another repainted, and a third permitted to rust and deteriorate. It's hard to believe that Smith, who renounced one of his own works as "60 pounds of scrap steel" after alteration by a purchaser, would have wanted his work to be treated like this. But there was nothing in his will or in a letter of instructions that prohibited alterations.

So you might want to take a strong stand on this issue and state firmly in your will that your work is not to be altered in any way.

What should I do about reproductions?

Throughout your career, you may have maintained a certain policy in regard to reproductions. For example, you may have allowed your oil paintings to be made into reproductions suitable for framing. If so, you might advise your executor to continue this policy in a letter of instructions. But don't stop there. After your death, he may be confronted with a situation that never presented itself to you. Someone may come along and offer to reproduce your work in a totally different media—jewelry, fabrics, or whatever. If the offer is lucrative, he may feel compelled to accept, or at least seriously consider it so as not to be accused by the heirs of wasting the assets of the estate. But would you want to see your work reproduced like this? Think about the possibilities involved in reproductions, far out though they may seem, and let your executor know your feelings on the subject in the letter of instructions.

Less extreme are the problems involved when executors and/or heirs reproduce sculpture.

What are the problems involved with sculpture?

These are ethical problems that arise when executors and/or heirs, without any authorization from a will or a letter of instructions casts bronzes, not from master plasters or waxes, but from bronzes made by the sculptor; enlarge the work; or translate it into new materials. The heirs of Julie Gonzales, for example, cast some of his works in bronze although he always used iron.

How can I prevent these practices from happening?

The College Art Association recommends that you leave clear and complete instructions in a letter of instructions or a will as to how you want your work reproduced or whether you want it reproduced at all. You might, like Jacques Lipschitz, reject the idea. Said Lipschitz in his will:

These terra cotta and plaster models are the prime of my inspiration, my only true original work, and are the most precious property I possess. It is my desire that no reproduction of any sort except photographs be made from said terra cotta and plaster models.

Who can I pick to be my executor?

You can pick anyone, but your choice will probably be a family member, a friend, your dealer, your lawyer, or your bank.

Are executors paid for their work?

They can be. Executors who benefit from the will themselves waive all fees as a rule. Others are allowed to charge a fee that represents a percentage of the estate. The maximum percentage is usually limited by state law, and you can count on banks to go for the highest fees, with lawyers right behind them.

Can I have more than one executor?

Yes. But this is practical only if your estate is unusually large and complex, or if you want to make sure that any conflict of interest will be detected by the other executor or executors.

What if the executor dies before my estate is settled?

You should provide for this event by naming an alternative (or alternatives) in your will.

Who should I pick as an executor?

Choose someone with the following qualifications: absolute integrity; general business acumen (this might eliminate family and friends); specific knowledge of your art business (banks will, and lawyers may, rate low on this score); and the ability to gain the trust and confidence of whoever is inheriting your estate to prevent arguments from arising between them and the executor.

Also, since settling an estate can be both a time-consuming job and one which could take years to accomplish if artwork must be sold at maximum profits, look for someone who is young enough and possesses enough energy to get the job done.

And at the same time that you're making up your mind, make sure that there's no conflict between the interest of your estate and your executor. A conflict of interest would generally occur if your executor sells other artwork besides yours and he might therefore be in a dilemma over whose work to promote more strenuously. In other words, an artist-friend or a dealer might not be an ideal choice.

Who is the ideal choice?

Providing he or she has all the qualifications mentioned above, pick the person who will inherit the bulk of the estate. In other words, someone who has his own best interests at heart as well as yours, since you think enough of him to leave him most of your worldly possessions. This way you won't have to worry whether he'll do right by the estate or the other heirs. And such a choice won't deplete the estate with a large executor's fee. Even if your heir/executor retains a lawyer to help him settle the estate, the lawyer's fee will be—or should be—less than if he were the executor.

If your estate is very large and consists of much artwork which must be disposed of, you might consider joint executors. In this case, the wisest choice might be one executor with a wide knowledge of the art world and another with business expertise. In other words, your spouse, dealer, or an artist friend, and a lawyer or bank officer. If you choose a dealer or an artist as an executor, however, think about limiting his responsibilities strictly to those connected with your art—where his expertise lies—and let the bank or lawyer do the rest.

Conclusion

From the beginning, this book has stressed the fact that if artists know what their rights are under the law, they'll be able to safeguard those rights. The laws governing contracts, copyright, and bailments offer protection to the artist and his work in almost every facet of his business dealings. The First Amendment defends him against accusations of obscenity, flag desecration, libel, and invasions of privacy.

But there is one area of the law that seems designed to hurt the artist: tax law. Tax law is unfair to the artist as follows:

First, by requiring that income equal home-studio expenses in order for them to be fully deductible. This seems an unnecessarily harsh ruling, particularly when compared to the hobby-loss problem. In general, the I.R.S.—while applying the two-profitable-years-out-of-five formula as an objective standard of one's professionalism—allows the circumstances of an artist's occupation to be judged before expenses are denied. Under the home-studio ruling, however, there are no mitigating circumstances taken into consideration.

Second, by denying fair market value deductions for the artist donating work to cultural institutions. By refusing artists deductions available to collectors, the flow of artwork from artist to museums has dried up, leaving a gap.

Third, by requiring that an artist's estate include his artwork valued at the fair market worth. This is an incredible contradiction of the law that refuses market value deductions for donations. One can only hope that Congressman Richmond or others who may introduce similar bills in the future will be successful in reducing the value of artwork included in an estate to the cost of materials. If this effort doesn't succeed, another tax reform of this measure should at least allow heirs to pay capital gains tax, instead of income tax, on the sale of artwork just as heirs of other inherited property, such as land, jewels, and stocks and bonds, do.

What are the chances of redress in these areas? As mentioned above, Congressman Richmond's bill seems doomed at least for this congressional session. A bill to increase the amount of deductions allowable for donations has been before Congress practically every year since 1969 when it went into effect and has gone down to defeat every time.

Nevertheless, more and more Congresspeople and others influential in Washington are expressing concern over the plight of the artist and seem determined to reverse some of these tax injustices. So the time may be ripe for change.

Bibliography

Chamberlain, Betty. *An Artist's Guide to His Market.* New York: Watson-Guptill Publications, 1976.

———. "Prints: Can We Legislate." *American Artist,* April, 1976.

Cochrane, Diane. "The Artist and His Estate Taxes." *American Artist,* January, 1974.

Crawford, Tad. "Hobbies, Horses and the Struggling Artist." *Art and The Law,* Summer, 1975.

———. "The Hobby-Loss Challenge." *American Artist,* February, 1976.

Feldman, Franklin, and Weil, Stephen. *Art Works: Law, Policy, Practice.* New York: Practising Law Institute, 1974.

Goodman, Calvin J. *Marketing Art: A Handbook for Artists and Art Dealers.* Los Angeles: Gee Tee Bee, 1972.

Hines, Diane Casella. "How to Approach a Museum with Your Work." *American Artist,* January, 1977.

Holubowich, Alexandra. "Pension Plans for Artists." *American Artist,* January, 1977.

"A How-to Guide to Fine Arts Insurance." *Art Letter,* June 1976. (Published by *Art in America.*)

Merryman, John, and Sandison, Hamish. "The California Royalty Bill." *American Artist,* February, 1977.

Rogovin, Mark, et al. *Mural Manual.* Boston: Beacon Press, 1973.

Sandison, Hamish ed. *The Visual Arts and the Law.* San Francisco: Bay Area Lawyers for the Arts, 1975.

Shapiro, Cecile and Mason, Lauris. *Fine Prints: Collecting, Buying and Selling.* New York: Harper & Row, 1976.

Zigrosser, Carl and Gaehde, Christina. *A Guide to the Collecting and Care of Original Prints.* New York: Crown Publishers, 1965.

Appendix:
Volunteer Lawyers
for the Arts

These volunteer organizations were founded to deal with arts-related legal problems and to help artists who lack the financial ability to retain their own lawyers.

CALIFORNIA

Hamish Sandison, Esq.
Bay Area Lawyers for the Arts
25 Taylor Street
Berkeley, California 94102
(415) 775-7200

Audrey Greenberg
Advocates for the Arts
Law School, Room 2467C
University of California
Los Angeles, California 90024
(213) 825-3309 or (213) 825-4841

CONNECTICUT

Ms. Rand Foreman
Connecticut Commission on the Arts
340 Capital Avenue
Hartford, Connecticut 06106

DISTRICT OF COLUMBIA

Charles B. Rutenberg, Esq.
Arent, Fox, Kintner, Plotkin & Kahn
Federal Bar Building
1815 H Street, N.W.
Washington, D.C. 20006

GEORGIA

Robert C. Lower, Esq.
Georgia Volunteer Lawyers for the Arts, Inc.
c/o Alston, Miller & Gaines
1200 C & S National Bank Building
Atlanta, Georgia 30303
(404) 588-0300

ILLINOIS

Tom Leavens, Esq.
Lawyers for the Creative Arts
111 North Wabash Avenue
Chicago, Illinois 60602
(312) 263-6989

MASSACHUSETTS

Linda McKinney
Lawyers for the Arts
Massachusetts Council for the Arts and Humanities
14 Beacon Street
Boston, Massachusetts 02108
(617) 723-3851

MINNESOTA (UPPER MIDWEST)

Michael Skindrud, Esq.
Affiliated Arts Agencies
Butler Square Number 349
100 North Sixth Street
Minneapolis, Minnesota 55403
(612) 338-1158

NEW JERSEY

Harry Devlin, Esq.
Cultural Law Committee
New Jersey State Bar Association
172 West State Street
Trenton, New Jersey 08608
(201) 232-2323

NEW YORK

James J. Fishman, Esq.
Volunteer Lawyers for the Arts
36 West 44 Street
New York, New York 10036
(212) 575-1150

Mrs. Carol Bullard
Albany League of the Arts, Inc.
135 Washington Avenue
Albany, New York 12210
(518) 449-5380

Maxine Brandenburg
Arts Development Services
237 Main Street
Buffalo, New York 14203
(716) 856-7520

*The Arts Development Services of Buffalo has
also established a Volunteer Accountants for the
Arts program in a joint venture with the local
chapter of the National Association of Accountants. The accountants will make their professional services available to artists unable to buy
them.*

Robert J. Kafin, Esq.
115 Maple Street
Glens Falls, New York 12801
(518) 793-6631

Mrs. Elizabeth F. Howard
Huntington Area Arts Council, Inc.
12 New Street
Huntington, New York 11743
(516) 271-8423

Upper Catskill Community Council of the
Arts, Inc.
101 Old Milne Library
State University College
Oneonta, New York 13820
(607) 432-2070

John Berg
Dutchess County Arts Council
Cunneen-Hackett Cultural Center
9 Vassar Street
Poughkeepsie, New York 12601
(914) 454-3222

Valerie Sapf
Arts Council of Rochester, Inc.
930 East Avenue
Rochester, New York 14607
(716) 442-0570

OHIO

Volunteer Lawyers for the Arts
c/o Cleveland Area Arts Council
140 The Arcade
Cleveland, Ohio 44114
(216) 781-0045

OREGON

Leonard DuBoff
Assistant Professor at Law
Lewis and Clark College
    Northwestern School of Law
Portland, Oregon 97219
(503) 244-1181

PENNSYLVANIA

Ned Donohue, Esq.
Lawyers for the Arts Committee
3400 Central Square West
1500 Market Street
Philadelphia, Pennsylvania 19102
(215) 972-3539

TEXAS

Jay M. Vogelson, Esq.
Steinberg, Generes, Luerssen & Vogelson
2200 Fidelity Union Tower
Dallas, Texas 75201
(214) 748-9312

WASHINGTON

Barbara Hoffman, Esq.
Washington Volunteer Lawyers for the
    Arts
University of Puget Sound Law School
55 Tacoma Way
Tacoma, Washington
(206) 756-3327

Index

Edited by Ellen Zeifer
Designed by Jay Anning
Set in 11/12 Baskerville